The William Carlos Williams Reader

For Florence Williams

By William Carlos Williams

The Autobiography
The Build-Up
Collected Earlier Poems
Collected Later Poems
The Embodiment of Knowledge
The Farmers' Daughters
I Wanted to Write a Poem
Imaginations
Interviews with W. C. Williams
In the American Grain
In the Money
Kora in Hell: Improvisations†
Many Loves and Other Plays
Paterson, Books 1-5
Pictures from Brueghel and Other Poems
The Selected Essays
Selected Poems
A Voyage to Pagany
White Mule
The William Carlos Williams Reader
Yes, Mrs. Williams

† *City Lights Books*

The William Carlos Williams Reader

edited with an introduction by

M. L. Rosenthal

A NEW DIRECTIONS BOOK

Published simultaneously in Canada by George J. McLeod, Ltd., Toronto
The selections from *Kora in Hell* are reprinted by
courtesy of City Lights Books, San Francisco.

Parts of the introduction, in somewhat different form, appeared in
The New York Times Book Review.

Library of Congress catalog card number: 66–17817

ISBN: 0-8112-0239-9

Manufactured in the United States of America.
New Directions books are published for James Laughlin
by New Directions Publishing Corporation, 80 Eighth
Avenue, New York 10011

SEVENTH PRINTING

Contents*

INTRODUCTION   ix

I. POEMS

* Dates following titles refer to first publication in book form. See Textual Note (pp. 410-412) for explanation.

II. "IMPROVISATIONS"

III. FICTION

IV. DRAMA

V. AUTOBIOGRAPHY

VI. OTHER PROSE

Introduction

William Carlos Williams:
More Than Meets the Eye

1.

The death of William Carlos Williams on March 4, 1963, at the age of seventy-nine, ended his unusual career, at once so brilliant and so humble, in the most literal sense only. Two days later, the news broke that finally a British publisher was going to bring out his poems—a special irony because he had waged bitter war against the English influence on American poetry and because the English had been largely deaf to his voice in the past. In May he received posthumously both the Pulitzer Prize and the Gold Medal for Poetry of the National Institute of Arts and Letters. In the same year the expanded edition of *The Collected Later Poems* and the paperback edition of the complete *Paterson* sequence appeared. The present volume is a response to the widening and deepening interest in Williams. It is a selection from the whole range of his writings: poetry, drama, fiction, and other prose.

Prolific as he was in various genres, Dr. Williams was clearly a poet first of all, as the whole emphasis of his career and of his development as a craftsman proves. The rest of his work, therefore, is from a critical standpoint important primarily for its relationship to his poetry. Yet it is misleading to put the matter so, for much of that work is absorbing in its own right even if the reader has no great interest in poetry. Williams's short stories are often vital evocations of ordinary American reality—its toughness, squalor, pathos, intensities. Many have to do with his relation as a doctor to poor folk and their children in the industrialized section of New Jersey in which he lived and had his practice. (Medicine not only enabled him to support his family. It gave him emotional ballast and was itself the source of some of his most impressive writing.) His method in these stories approaches that of Anderson and Hemingway, but when he becomes white hot in his excitement over the characters, as in "Jean Beicke" or "A Face of Stone," the work is essential Williams and nobody else.

So also in the Stecher trilogy, in which the author seeks to repossess the childhood of his wife: her babyhood, her parents' characters, her relation to her older sister, the total quality of this immigrant family on the rise in the years before the first World War. The novels of this trilogy, which appeared at distant intervals (1937, 1940, 1952), are uneven and sometimes sketchy and derivative. Again, though, the most striking chapters are informed by Williams's experience as pediatrician and obstetrician, a fact that may well account for the superiority of the earlier volumes, *White Mule* and *In the Money*, to the last one, *The Build-Up*. The interpretations of a baby's awareness (in pleasure, illness, fears), the accurate pictures of the mentality and anxieties of mothers, the understanding of what we might call the imperturbability of physiological fact—all with its Rabelaisian aspects as well as its anguish— are unique, and uniquely interesting, in our literature. The driving, insensitive ambition of the mother and the contrastingly introverted individualism of the highly intelligent father are set against one another with unforgettable authority. Sometimes, as in the story of Joe Stecher's triumph over crookedness and bribery in his fight to get a government printing contract, Williams gives sharp glimpses of a world of business and power outside the one of women and babies and the local ecology of family life. The scene in which Joe Stecher and Teddy Roosevelt face each other in a momentary tangency of their so different orbits, the public man speaking of "my policy" and the ironic creative man whose whole sense of value centers on concrete techniques, is based on an actual incident in the life of Williams's father-in-law.

Behind the Stecher trilogy we can see some overriding preoccupations relevant to all of Williams's work. His special interest in women—what they are really like, how they grow into their maturity, their sources of strength and weakness, their real relationship to the oversimplified visions of male sexuality—is certainly implied in this extensive imaginative exploration of his wife's early life and ambience. *The Autobiography*, short stories, and poems give further emphasis, explicitly, to this preoccupation. It is at once a matter of the normal erotic range of interest and curiosity and of something else, a romantic sense of mystery pursued through the unorthodox methods of the realist. (See, for instance, the short story "The Burden of Loveliness" and the poem "The Raper from Passenack.") It sometimes appears that the more gross or brutal the details, the more the mystery is heightened for Williams, and the more he is in love with the female principle in all its bewildering variations. Compassion is an important ingredient, but also there is a curious bafflement at once challenging and discouraging, and perhaps a sense of the entrapment of the demonic male in a kind of maze of domesticities characteristic of the whole modern relationship between men and women. More than a hint of his bafflement is given in the scene printed in the present collection from the play *A Dream of Love*, and his essay "Jacataqua" locates its source as specifically American. But this is only the negative side of Williams's romantic preoccupation with certain mysteries. *The Autobiography* gives us the other side, in a passage concerning the meaning to him of his medical career:

> And my "medicine" was the thing that gained me entrance to . . . [the] secret gardens of the self. It lay there, another world, in the self. I was permitted by my medical badge to follow the poor, defeated body into those gulfs and grottos. And the astonishing thing is that at such times and in such places—foul as they may be with the stinking ischio-rectal abscesses of our comings and goings—just there, the thing, in all its greatest beauty, may for a moment be freed to fly for a moment guiltily about the room. In illness, in the permission I as a physician have had to be present at deaths and births, at the tormented battles between daughter and diabolic mother, shattered by a gone brain—just there—for a split second—from one side or the other, it has fluttered before me for a moment . . .
>
> (*The Autobiography*, pp. 288-289)

Another preoccupation of Williams's thought and art reflected in the Stecher novels is the meaning of the American
relationship to Europe. The well-known native ambivalence
on this subject is not lacking in Williams, himself a second-
generation American. The familiar contradictory pulls of
attraction to the culture of Europe, determination to make
a new start in terms as indigenous to the United States as
possible, and a sense of the distorting and demeaning effect
on personality of the American absorption in power, wealth,
and abstract process are important in the novels. An insistent longing to restore or at least rediscover lost continuities
without surrendering to them asserts itself in different ways
in all the important characters. In an earlier autobiographical
novel, *A Voyage to Pagany* (1928), and then in *The Autobiography* (1951), the poet pursues the meaning for himself of these warring feelings and attitudes. German medicine, the artistic and intellectual vitality of Paris, the self-
acceptance of European women are placed, in *A Voyage
to Pagany*, in direct confrontation with the hero's sense
of his "hard, barren life" at home, "where I am 'alone' and
unmolested (work as I do in the thick of it) though in constant danger lest some slip send me to perdition but which,
being covetous not at all, I enjoy for the seclusion and
primitive air of it."

Both this book and *The Autobiography* show how important European study and experience were to Williams
as a boy and again as a grown man with a certain reputation in avant-garde circles, the literary associate of Ezra
Pound, Robert McAlmon, and other Americans of some
recognition in Paris and London. Equally, they show how
impossible for him the life of the expatriate artist would
have been. As he goes on to explain in the passage just
quoted, America possessed for him, despite his isolation
there and despite its "primitive" character, "an attraction in
all the inanimate associations of my youth, shapes, foliage,
trees to which I am used—and a love of place and the characteristics of place—good or bad, rich or poor." (Inciden-
tally, the chapter in which these remarks are made was
omitted from the printed version of the novel because the

publisher considered the book too long, though Williams considered it "the best chapter." It was later published as a short story, "The Venus," and is therefore included separately under that title in the present collection.)

Williams was not precocious, though he was constantly and intimately in touch with precocious people. He was in his early thirties when he began to find himself as a poet, and in his later thirties when he did really find himself. His development was a slow one for an artist of such spontaneous and passionate energies. This fact, together with his feeling for place and the effects of having had a medical rather than a literary education, accounts for his resistance to the expatriate life of so many of his friends.

It also, quite obviously, helps account for his interest in making his work idiosyncratically American, but in a cosmopolitan rather than merely a provincial sense. He well understood the advantages of European culture and manners but taught himself to redirect those values in the American context. One might note with surprise the way in which his "early" prose poems in *Kora in Hell* and his prose-poetic chapters in *The Great American Novel* parallel French models and are nevertheless American in much of their substance and attitude—their humor, for instance, and their frank homeliness: *"A man watches his wife clean house. He is filled with knowledge by his wife's exertions. This is incomprehensible to her. Knowing she will never understand his excitement he consoles himself with the thought of art."* (*Kora in Hell*, p. 67). But then one should remind oneself that he was thirty-seven when the former book was published and forty—just the age of the hero of *A Voyage to Pagany*—when the latter book appeared.

The "Prologue" to *Kora in Hell** is too lengthy and diffuse, despite its importance for students of poetry, to be published in this volume. But it is significant for the light it throws on Williams's literary position at a critical point in his development. It is partly an account and evaluation of various fellow poets, partly a defense and proliferation of

* Reprinted in *Selected Essays*, pp. 3–29.

the "improvisations" in his book, and partly a presentation and consideration of criticisms by other poets of his work so far. Thus, he quotes from a letter of Pound's attacking his pretensions to being especially American in his poetry:

> . . . What the h–l do you a blooming foreigner know about the place. Your *père* only penetrated the edge, and you've never been west of Upper Darby, or the Maunchunk switchback.
> Would H. [Harriet Monroe] with the swirl of the prairie wind in her underwear, or the Virile Sandburg recognize you, an effete Easterner as a REAL American? INCONCEIVABLE! ! ! ! !
> My dear boy you have never felt the woop of the PEEraries. . . .
> The thing that saves your work is opacity, and don't forget it. Opacity is NOT an American quality. Fizz, swish, gabble, and verbiage, these are *echt american-isch*. . . .

Williams replies indirectly, but what he says is especially interesting in that he implies that there is some truth to what Pound is saying but suggests that he is getting at a nativist poetry in a new way. He will use European methods but at the same time will turn his back on Europe and allow the methods to find their American expression:

> I like to think of the Greeks as setting out for the colonies in Sicily and the Italian peninsula. The Greek temperament lent itself to a certain symmetrical sculptural phase and to a fat poetical balance of line that produced important work but I like better the Greeks setting their backs to Athens. The ferment was always richer in Rome, the dispersive explosion was always nearer, the influence carried further and remained hot longer. . . .

Again, he considers a criticism by Hilda Doolittle of one of his poems. H. D. had written:

> I trust you will not hate me for wanting to delete from your poem all the flippancies. The reason I want to do this is that the beautiful lines are so very beautiful . . . and real beauty is a rare and sacred thing in this generation. . . . I don't know what you think but I consider this business of writing a very sacred thing! . . . I feel in the hey-ding-ding touch running through your poem a deriva-

tive tendency which, to me, is not *you*—not your very self.
It is as if you were ashamed of your Spirit, ashamed of
your inspiration!—as if you mocked at your own song!
It's very well to mock at yourself—it is a spiritual sin to
mock at your inspiration.

Williams defends his buffoonery because it helps him liberate imaginative energy and counteract the too confining
expectations of formal perfectionism:

> . . . There is nothing sacred about literature, it is damned
> from one end to the other. There is nothing in literature
> but change and change is mockery. I'll write whatever I
> damn please, whenever I damn please and it'll be good if
> the authentic spirit of change is on it.
> But in any case H. D. misses the entire intent of what
> I am doing no matter how just her remarks concerning that
> particular poem happen to have been. The hey-ding-ding
> touch *was* derivative, but it filled a gap that I did not
> know how better to fill at the time. It might be said that
> that touch is the prototype of the improvisations.
> It is to the inventive imagination we look for deliverance
> from every other misfortune as from the desolation of a
> flat Hellenic perfection of style. . . . If the inventive
> imagination must look, as I think, to the field of art for
> its richest discoveries today it will best make its way by
> compass and follow no path.
> But before any material progress can be accomplished
> there must be someone to draw a discriminating line be-
> tween true and false values.
> The true value is that particularity which gives an
> object a character by itself. The associational or senti-
> mental value is the false. Its imposition is due to lack of
> imagination, to an easy lateral sliding. The attention has
> been held too rigid on the one plane instead of following
> a more flexible, jagged resort. It is to loosen the attention,
> my attention since I occupy part of the field, that I write
> these improvisations.

The defense against H. D.'s strictures turned without
warning into a reply to objections by Wallace Stevens in
still another letter. Stevens had complained about the "casual
character" of Williams's poems. His letter, containing the
famous observation that "a book of poems is a damned serious affair," argued for a consistency of method and viewpoint such as one does find, indeed, in Stevens's own poetry:

> . . . My idea is that in order to carry a thing to the
> extreme necessity to convey it one has to stick to it; . . .
> Given a fixed point of view, realistic, imagistic, or what
> you will, everything adjusts itself to that point of view;
> the process of adjustment is a world in flux, as it should
> be for a poet. But to fidget with points of view leads al-
> ways to new beginnings and incessant new beginnings
> lead to sterility. . . .

Williams felt that his reply to H. D. was a reply to
Stevens as well. It is easy, he wrote, to fall under the spell
of Stevens's mode of work, but the real problem is that of
"lifting to the imagination those things which lie under the
direct scrutiny of the senses, close to the nose. It is this difficulty that sets a value upon all works of art and makes
them a necessity."

In all these instances, Williams makes allowance for the
validity of his friends' *descriptions* of his work, but he also
readjusts the perspective, as it were. What they consider
weaknesses he views as veerings in a new direction. Taken
together, the letters and his responses give us the context
and kernel of his attitudes as a practicing poet.

I have grouped *The Great American Novel* with *Kora in
Hell* because the term "improvisations" applies to it equally
well. In both these experimental forays Williams reworks
the prose poem in such a way as to allow for free narrative
movement and association, for outbursts of exuberant buffoonery, for the introduction of critical assertions and of
historical data and theory, and for autobiographical and
confessional details. But *The Great American Novel* is far
less "literary" and precious than *Kora in Hell*, though I do
not mean, obviously, to disparage the germinal inventive-
ness of the latter book. In a short time, Williams had advanced toward the sure voice of a poetic master, taking the
best qualities of *Kora in Hell* and widening their usefulness.
He was now able to involve his immediate experiences as a
doctor and his personal knowledge of the sexual and marital
problems of a mature adult in his poems, and to bring
sharply to bear, for instance, the role of the automobile in
all its ludicrous, ironic, and deadly serious and deeply American importance. The gaiety and melancholy that result, and

the total relevance, far surpass those of *Kora in Hell.* It is easy to see *Paterson* and the other work of the older Williams emphatically foreshadowed here.

Williams, then, had over a period of time given himself room and time to study his own possibilities and to formulate them. Not unlike Yeats, he "remade" himself and opted for new beginnings, brutal and abrupt if necessary, using himself as the embodiment of an American self-awareness free of that kind of innocence which is actually ignorance. His prose matrix for the poems of *Spring and All,* dropped after the first publication of 1923,* was already the work of a mature thinker with a good idea of what he was doing. So was his recapitulation of what Horace Gregory called America's "mythical history": *In the American Grain* (1925). An explosive, freshly improvisatory intelligence, able to think imagistically and to see thoughts as new, sensuously felt insights, was being put to the service of a long-pondered program.

2.

I have already noted that Williams was of course a poet first of all, and it is in the poetry that his deep contemplation of his principles as a writer counts the most finally. We have no other poet so intriguing, and so misleading, to a reader who takes up his work for the first time. How vulnerable to imitation, how simple and spontaneous he seems!

> The sea that encloses her young body
> ula lu la lu
> is the sea of many arms—

But have a care! Even this fragment, the beginning stanza of "The Sea," has more than spontaneity and immediacy alone—though these are in themselves a great deal. It has

* The poems were later printed in sequence without the prose, and still later given individual titles instead of being merely numbered, though they are still grouped in *The Collected Later Poems* as "Spring and All." I have included a selection from the original prose in this book, and kept the original whimsical numbering in the portions here reprinted, though the simple typographical foolery of shuffling the order of numbers, printing upside-down, and shifting from Arabic to Roman numerals cannot be fully represented in our shortened text.

the accurate pitch, the sure music, of "When that Aprille with his shoures soote" or "Shall I compare thee to a summer's day." Williams's disingenuousness of technique reveals itself in the counterpointing of front and back vowels, in the "light" rhymes and repetitions ("sea," "body," "many"), and in the intruded lullabying break that prepares us for similar refrain effects later in the poem. With this stanza as a start the poet goes into a varied contemplation of the multiple symbolism of woman and sea, maintaining a penumbra of mystery through varied shiftings of intensity and shadings of thought:

> In the sea the young flesh playing
> floats with the cries of far off men
> who rise in the sea . . .

Beneath the impromptu surface many associations are made to converge in a single vision of all-embracing sexuality; the sea has been psychologically—that is, humanly—re-embodied.

Quite as deceptive, many of Williams's shorter poems seem at first glance mere impressionistic notes or figures caught shimmering in a momentary visual frame. Among the best known of these pieces is "The Red Wheelbarrow":

> so much depends
> upon
>
> a red wheel
> barrow
>
> glazed with rain
> water
>
> beside the white
> chickens.

The sense of being alive, this poem and many others imply, depends on our viewing the familiar world with a fresh eye. The standpoint from which we view that world and its intensities determines the scope of life's meaning for us. The humblest objects of perception are also elements in a symbolic design with a transcendent aesthetic function. To see them thus is to liberate ourselves and them from the rut and squalor in which the mass of men lead their "lives of

quiet desperation." It is to bring to bear upon any momentary observation or set of circumstances the whole of imagination and sensibility, and to gain courage from the application.

> . . . the thing that stands eternally in the way of really good writing is always one: the virtual impossibility of lifting to the imagination those things which lie under the direct scrutiny of the senses, close to the nose. It is this difficulty that sets a value upon all works of art and makes them a necessity. The senses witnessing what is immediately before them in detail see a finality which they cling to in despair, not knowing which way to turn. Thus the so-called natural or scientific array becomes fixed, the walking devil of modern life. He who even nicks the solidity of this apparition does a piece of work superior to that of Hercules when he cleaned the Augean stables.
>
> ("Prologue," *Kora in Hell*)

To Williams it seemed a natural corollary of this emphasis to remain close to native American sources. Moreover, this program seemed the way to get out from under the derivativeness that saddled his peers and rivals:

> But our prize poems [he wrote in 1920] are especially to be damned not because of superficial bad workmanship, but because they are rehash, repetition—just as Eliot's more exquisite work is rehash, repetition in another way of Verlaine, Baudelaire, Maeterlinck—conscious or unconscious—just as there were Pound's early paraphrases from Yeats and his constant later cribbing from the Renaissance, Provence and the modern French: Men content with the connotations of their masters.
> . . . Eliot is a subtle conformist. . . .
>
> ("Prologue," *Kora in Hell*)

No wonder Pound (always a close friend) was irritated into replying:

> There is a blood poison in America; you can idealize the place (easier now that Europe is so damn shaky) all you like, but you haven't a drop of the cursed blood in you, and you don't need to fight the disease day and night; you never have had to. Eliot has it worse than I—poor devil.
> You have the advantage of arriving in the milieu with a fresh flood of Europe in your veins, Spanish, French, Eng-

lish, Danish. You had not the thin milk of New York and
New England from the pap; and you can therefore keep
the environment outside you, and decently objective.*

But one has only to read "To Elsie"—

> The pure products of America
> go crazy—

to realize that Williams had a sense as bitter as Pound's of
the "poison" in the native blood. In fact, he *stayed* in
America just as angrily and vigorously as Pound *left* America. Each of them is in a curious way an alternative possibility of the other. Simply to contemplate this fact is to see
something of Williams's role and location in contemporary
poetry.

The two poets met at the University of Pennsylvania,
shortly after the turn of the century. Pound exerted a tremendous influence from the start, though in part this influence generated a movement in poetry directly opposed to
his own conceptions. The first thing Williams's preface to
the *Selected Essays* tells us, for instance, is how he came to
know Pound. And if we glance, however idly, through the
pages of that collection of essays and reviews, we can hardly
help noting the many reminders of Pound and his passions.
Thus, we find a defense of Antheil's music, a scattering of
enthusiastic comments on *The Cantos*, a deep though cagey
and sometimes determinedly hostile interest in "the tradition," and sympathetic interpretations of Joyce, Gertrude
Stein, and Marianne Moore. Pound, Joyce, and Stein are
held up to younger writers as models. *The Cantos* are crit-
icized frankly in some respects, yet an essential admiration
and rapport is the dominant note: "We have, examining the
work, successes—great ones—the first molds—clear cut, never
turgid, not following the heated trivial—staying cold, 'classical' but swift with a movement of thought." ("Excerpts
from a Critical Sketch")

In both writers, too, an attack on the main direction of
American society goes together with a radical rejection of

---

* *The Letters of Ezra Pound: 1907–1941*, ed. by D. D. Paige (N.Y.:
Harcourt, Brace, 1950), p. 158.

modern economic practices and a call for the violent break-
through of human creativity. Williams's insertion of a
Social-Credit propaganda leaflet in the poem *Paterson* and
his portrait of Poe striving desperately to originate a truly
American poetry amid the corruption and imitativeness of
the national drift are two obvious examples among many
of this identity or at least overlap of attitude. Certainly
Williams and Pound are at one in a driving conviction,
evangelical in nature, that man's best possibilities, brutally
subverted and driven underground, must be brought to the
surface through a freeing of pagan impulses—a "revelation"
which is also a moral and cultural revolution: "to get at the
actual values that concern man where they frequently lie
buried in his mind." ("Revelation," *Selected Essays*, p. 271)
Here is their kinship with Blake, Whitman, and the Romantic spirit. The Romantic aim of actualizing the ideal becomes
that of reactivating natural men's motives through art.
Thinking in his *Autobiography* of Pound's "mission," Williams says:

> The poem is a capsule where we wrap up our punish-
> able secrets. And as they confine in themselves the only
> "life," the ability to sprout at a more favorable time, to
> come true in their secret structure to the very minutest
> details of our thoughts, so they get their specific virtue.
> (*The Autobiography*, p. 343)

But Williams was his own man, and one of his most striking characteristics is the fashion in which he worked his
shared interests toward unique, idiosyncratic ends. For
instance, he tells us that he began to be interested in La-
forgue, an important figure for Pound and Eliot, only when
he read an article by Kenneth Burke demonstrating how the
French poet "has taken what he finds most suitable to his
own wants, what at least he has, and made it *the* thing" by
"building upon the basis of what is observed, what is proved,
and what is of value to the man in the welter as he found it."
By a similar shift of emphasis, Williams's essay on Poe finds
that the nineteenth-century poet was struggling with precisely the problems of technique and of the meaning of an
American art that Williams struggled with. This essay,

therefore, becomes one of our clearest expositions of Williams's own poetic rationale. Similarly, he praises a Matisse painting not because of its relation either to tradition or to "modernism," but because it is so easily and rightly of its own place, as American art should be of *its* place:

> No man in my country has seen a woman naked and painted her as if he knew anything except that she was naked. No woman in my country is naked except at night.
> In the french sun, on the french grass in a room on Fifth Ave., a french girl lies and smiles at the sun without seeing us.
>
> ("A Matisse," *Selected Essays*, p. 31)

The work of Ford Madox Ford is valued for the same reason: "His British are British in a way the American, Henry James, never grasped. They fairly smell of it." In the poem "To Ford Madox Ford in Heaven," a further implication of this conception of the values inherent in place is brought into the open. The novelist is beatified as the apostle of the sensual and earthy:

> A heavenly man you seem to me now, never
>   having been for me a saintly one.
> It lived about you, a certain grossness that
>   was not like the world.
> The world is cleanly, polished and well
>   made but heavenly man
> is filthy with his flesh and corrupt that
>   loves to eat and drink and whore . . .

Williams's enthusiasm for local values, then, carries readily with it a sense of the paradoxical "heavenliness" of the physical and the ordinary. America, impatient to loose its own still unexplored meanings, is the more open to the new because of the past suppression of American sensibility in favor of European and English standards. Hence, it was natural, as Williams points out in his devastating defense of Joyce against Rebecca West's strictures, for Americans to respond more quickly to Joyce than the British could:

> Joyce is breaking with a culture older than England's when he goes into his greatest work. It is the spirit liberated to run through everything, that makes him insist on

unexpurgated lines and will not brook the limitations
which good taste would enforce. It is to break the limitations, not to conform to the taste that his spirit runs.
("A Point for American Criticism," *Selected Essays*, p. 88)

These are recurring motifs in Williams's criticism. What he
says about Joyce is very much like what he says about
Whitman, and seeing the quotations side by side may help
dispel any notion that his nativism is at all parochial:

> Whitman. . . . For God's sake! He broke through the
> deadness of copied forms which keep shouting above
> everything that wants to get said today drowning out one
> man with the accumulated weight of a thousand voices
> in the past—re-establishing the tyrannies of the past . . .
> The structure of the old is active, it says no! to every-
> thing in propaganda and poetry that wants to say yes.
> Whitman broke through that.
> ("Against the Weather," *Selected Essays*, p. 218)

All these considerations carry with them the danger that
we may forget we are talking about a poet, and one whose
chief talent, at that, lies in the writing of "simple, sensuous,
and passionate" rather than ratiocinative verse. "All I do,"
Pound quotes Williams as saying, "is to try to understand
something in its natural colours and shapes"; and Pound ob-
serves: "There could be no better effort underlying any
literary process, or used as preparative for literary process."*
The claim Williams makes for himself may be too modest,
but his amazingly vivid sense of the life around him is certainly the foundation of everything he writes. Randall Jarrell's characterization is arch but to the point.

> Williams' poetry is more remarkable for its empathy,
> sympathy, its muscular and emotional identification with
> its subject, than any other contemporary poetry except
> Rilke's. When you have read *Paterson* you know for the
> rest of your life what it is like to be a waterfall; and what
> other poet has turned so many of his readers into trees?
> Occasionally one realizes that this latest tree of Williams'
> is considerably more active than anyone else's grizzly

* *The Literary Essays of Ezra Pound* (N.Y.: New Directions, 1954),
p. 390.

bear; but usually the identification is so natural, the feel and rhythm of the poem so hypnotic, that the problem of belief never arises.*

This extraordinary empathic responsiveness, to trees and flowers especially, recalls D. H. Lawrence, with whom Williams has other affinities also. By the time he was nine or ten, the poet tells us in his *Autobiography*, he had learned

> the way moss climbed about a tree's roots, what growing dogwood and iron wood looked like; the way rotten leaves will mat down in a hole—and their smell when turned over —every patch among those trees had its character, moist or dry. . . .
>
> It is a pleasure for me now to think of these things, but especially of the flowers I got to know. . . . The slender neck of the anemone particularly haunts me for some reason and the various sorts of violets. . . . My curiosity in these things was unbounded—secret certainly. There is a long history in each of us that comes as not only a re-awakening but a repossession when confronted by this world. . . .
>
> (*The Autobiography*, p. 19)

In the poems this repossession is visceral, complete. We see a young tree rising

> bodily
> into the air with
> one undulant
> thrust half its height. . . .
> ("Young Sycamore")

Other trees, seen on a winter night, present a grotesque Tam O'Shanter dance vision:

> Limb to limb, mouth to mouth
> with the bleached grass
> silver mist lies upon the back yards
> among the outhouses.
>   The dwarf trees
> pirouette awkwardly to it—
> whirling round on one toe;
> the big tree smiles and glances
>   upward!
> ("Winter Quiet")

* "Introduction" to Williams's *Selected Poems* (N.Y.: New Directions, 1949), p. xii.

Williams never wanted to wear his mind on his sleeve, but it is hard to attribute his reputation as a completely unintellectual poet, in fact an anti-intellectual one, to any cause but unsympathetic reading. "Almost everything in Dr. Williams's poetry," says R. P. Blackmur,

> almost everything, . . . including the rendering, is unexpanded notation. He isolates and calls attention to what we are already presently in possession of. Observation of which any good novelist must be constantly capable, here makes a solo appearance: the advantage is the strength of isolation as an attention-caller to the terrible persistence of the obvious, the unrelenting significance of the banal. Dr. Williams perhaps tries to write as the average man—that man who even less than the normal man hardly exists but is immanent. The conviction which attaches to such fine poems as . . . "Spring and All" perhaps has its source, its rationale, in our instinctive willingness to find ourselves immanently average; just as, perhaps, the conviction attaching to tragic poetry is connected with our fascinated dread of seeing ourselves as normal. Dr. Williams has no perception of the normal; no perspective, no finality—for these involve, for imaginative expression, both the intellect which he distrusts and the imposed form which he cannot understand. What he does provide is a constant freshness and purity of language which infects with its own qualities an otherwise gratuitous exhibition of the sense and sentiment of humanity run-down—averaged—without a trace of significance or a vestige of fate in the fresh familiar face.*

Mr. Blackmur is, of course, a critic from whose "expanded notations"—to alter his phrase—many of us have learned a good deal. Misled by Williams's anti-academic stance, however, he made the mistake of seeing the poem's surface as the whole work. In February 1922, when all the world was new, Kenneth Burke had written that in Williams's poetry "the process is simply this: There is the eye, and there is the thing upon which the eye alights; while the relationship existing between the two is a poem." But Burke's mind would take for granted the whole process between germination and completion, and would hardly choose—either then or seventeen years later, when Black-

* R. P. Blackmur, *Language As Gesture* (N.Y.: Harcourt, Brace, 1952), pp. 349–350.

mur's comment was first published—to beat the poet over the head with his talent. Other critics, following such judgments too literally and overstressing by Williams's early imagism and objectivism, have discounted his "perspective," "finality," and "formal power" (Blackmur's criteria) despite the many clear evidences, several of which we have noted, to the contrary in Williams's poetry and prose.* Doubtless this development was unavoidable, since any continued attempt to absorb the exact inner "feel" of things outside oneself would inevitably lead to an initial effect of glancing impressionism, however successful or unsuccessful the full effort might turn out to be.

Actually, Williams worked out of a sophisticated and developed tradition, in whose principles he slowly educated himself throughout his career. Implicit in it is the avowal of the assumptions of the religion of art by which the symbolists and their successors have lived. (René Taupin, indeed, sought to locate Williams as a direct heir, though not a slavish imitator, of Rimbaud and the French symbolists.) The fundamental premise is that the meanest of experiential data have their transcendent aesthetic potentiality, and hence that experience is the key to realization. Characteristically, the formal structure of a Williams poem involves a closing in on the realization involving several shifts of attention or focus along the way. It is not that nothing has significance, but that everything has it; not that eye and object alone make the poem, but that these, together with ear and intellect and formal movement, shape a poem through their convergence. Conception, empathy, compassion, and technique become functions of the same thing in many of the pieces; that is, they become inseparable functions of poetic process. Hence Williams's irritation with Wallace Stevens's praise of his use of the "anti-poetic."

---

* Two notable exceptions to this kind of critical discounting were René Taupin, L'Influence du symbolisme français sur la poésie américaine (Paris: H. Champion, 1929) and Yvor Winters, Primitivism and Decadence (N.Y.: Arrow Editions, 1937).

Poor Stevens had only wished to find an elegantly paradoxical way to appreciate the process.

Here again, it is useful to recall the resemblance between
Williams's sensibility and that of D. H. Lawrence. Think of
the close-ups which strengthen our knowledge of the individual flame behind the common mask of anonymity. Or
think of Lawrence's anguished description of the carnage
winter wreaks on the birds, or of his sense of the blazing
life of flowers. In "To a Dog Injured in the Street," Williams recalls further instances of suffering innocence summoned up by sight of the screaming dog. Remembering
these moments of cruelty and pain, he cries out his kinship
with still another poet, René Char, whose theme has like his
own been the imaginative or aesthetic resolution of the
violence man's condition subjects him to.

> René Char
>   you are a poet who believes
>   in the power of beauty
>   to right all wrongs.
>   I believe it also.

Though Williams parts company with Lawrence in his
unfaltering confidence in art's redeeming and healing
powers, the difference between them on this score can
easily be exaggerated. For example, the motifs of symbolic
death and rebirth are important in both poets, and in parallel forms. (See, for instance, Lawrence's "New Heaven and
Earth," a poem which might almost serve as a credo, in all
its aspects, for Williams quite as much as for Lawrence.)
But the salvation implied in the localist program of Williams, and in his many poems informed primarily by compassion, is finally aesthetic rather than purely religious,
mystical, or social. In an early poem, "The Wanderer,"
whose motifs are later absorbed into the *Paterson* sequence,
the poet shows himself attempting to awaken the people to
their own rich possibility. Finally, though, it is he himself
who is awakened and purified, by taking into himself the
whole degradation of modern industrial life bereft of all

traditional graces. The waters of the "filthy Passaic" enter his heart and soul and transform him. But it is a transformation like that in Yeats's "Byzantium" or "The Circus Animals' Desertion"—from the "foul rag-and-bone shop of the heart" to the "masterful images" of the "pure mind." As he says to René Char, it is "beauty" that will "right all wrongs."

So there's more to Williams, putting the matter very gently, than meets the eye. Even the sharp, objective snapshots which Blackmur calls "obvious"—"what we are already in possession of"—have the "more" buried in them, and not really so very deeply. The *Paterson* sequence is the outgrowth of Williams's need to bring the inner meanings out into the open and to pursue them more explicitly:

> The first idea centering upon the poem, *Paterson*, came alive early: to find an image large enough to embody the whole knowable world about me. The longer I lived in my place, among the details of my life, I realized that these isolated observations and experiences needed pulling together to gain "profundity." I already had the river . . . I wanted, if I was to write in a larger way than of the birds and flowers, to write about the people close about me: to know in detail, minutely what I was talking about—to the whites of their eyes, to their very smells.
>
> That is the poet's business. Not to talk in vague categories but to write particularly, as a physician works, upon a patient, upon the thing before him, in the particular to discover the universal. . . .
>
> (*The Autobiography*, p. 391)

If we follow the main currents of *Paterson* through its several books we find that the effort to create "an image large enough to embody the whole knowable world" of the poet is also an effort to deal with the bleakness of that world. There is first of all its imperviousness to meaning, projected at the very start in the personification of the city as a sleeping stone-giant:

> Eternally asleep,
> his dreams walk about the city where he persists
> incognito. Butterflies settle on his stone ear.
> Immortal he neither moves nor rouses and is seldom
> seen, though he breathes and the subtleties of his
> machinations . . .

animate a thousand automatons. Who because they
neither know their sources nor the sills of their
disappointments walk outside their bodies aimlessly . . .
locked and forgot in their desires—unroused.

The whole problem is failure of communication. The people
"walk incommunicado"—

> The language is missing them
> they die also
> incommunicado.

Against this failure is set the primary symbolism of primitive or peasant cultures. A picture in the *National Geo-
graphic* is described:

> . . . the 9 women
> of some African chief semi-naked
> astraddle a log. . . .

In a "descending scale of freshness" from the proud, young-
est queen, "conscious of her power"—with "uppointed
breasts" that are "charged with pressures unrelieved"—to
the oldest, with

> . . . careworn eyes
> serious, menacing—but unabashed; breasts
> sagging from hard use

we see the organic relationship of natural and social orders;
there is communication and wholeness here. But our modern
theme is divorce: "the sign of knowledge in our time." Nature offers the same resources to us as it does to other cultures—the swirling, roaring river, the greenness of spring,
or "half-grown girls hailing hallowed Easter." But in perspective nothing comes into realization. Williams reaches
into local history to find the backgrounds of a world lacking in the language of personal awakening, and finds em-
blems of destructive violence in the origins of the Jackson's
Whites community north of Paterson, in the story of Sam
Patch and his daring leaps, in the account of the death by
falling of Mrs. Cummings. In the second section of Part I
the poet closes in on a more personal theme: the failure of
communication in love and friendship. And in the third sec-

tion he faces his own hard artistic task within the limits he has set himself, recalling Pound's old taunt: "Your interest is in the bloody loam but what I am interested in is the finished product." Williams wants both, but seems unconvinced he can get them.

The quarrel with Pound continues into Part II, which explores and on the whole rejects the usefulness of libraries and traditional resources for Williams's present purposes. On Sunday in the park, we pass with him among the people, locating what he calls "the modern replicas" of the motifs already delineated in Paterson's past. What he sees still attracts and repels him in the same fashion as in "The Wanderer":

> .   .   the ugly legs of the young girls,
> pistons too powerful for delicacy!   .
> the men's arms, red, used to heat and cold,
> to toss quartered beeves and   .
>
> > > > Yah! Yah! Yah! Yah!
>
> -over-riding
>
> > > the risks:
>
> > > > pouring down!
>
> For the flower of a day!

Pound's "Canto 45" had blamed the loss of standards and perspectives on *Usura*, the triumph of the principle of usury in the banking system:

> with usura the line grows thick
> with usura is no clear demarcation

Williams, without denying the charge, shifts the emphasis entirely in a passage that appears to be a reply to Pound:

> Without invention nothing is well spaced,
> unless the mind change, unless
> the stars are new measured, according
> to their relative positions, the
> line will not change. . . .

The call is for new constructs, new poetic measures, taking the risk of loss and immersion in the amorphous, pleasure-seeking, undirected mass of energies that is our American scene.

Everywhere, though, there is interference. The second section of Part II begins with the word "blocked." "An orchestral dullness overlays their world." The "massive church," the mulcters of cash, the political interests all interfere with creative invention: "I see they—the Senate, is trying to block Lilienthal and deliver 'the bomb' over to a few industrialists." The closest we seem to come to beauty is the kind of free-wheeling evangelism heard from a vigorous speaker in the park—an irresponsibly sharpshooting, half-deadly-accurate, half-charlatanish operator. The pessimistic prayer, growing out of the poet's bitter love for America, with which this section ends, and the almost unrelieved negations of the next section make Part II the most intense and concentrated writing of the book.

There is a "prose correlative" running through the poem —in the form of letters, news items, and other documentary passages, interesting in themselves but as it were providing a continual "outside" commentary as well as the raw material out of which the high poetic moments seem to arise. One voice in particular makes itself felt in the prose correlative, that of a woman writer whose utter loneliness and inability to come to terms with herself or to develop her poetic talents are seen as a function of the national indifference to the ideals of civilization. Her reproaches to the poet—the cry of failure reaching up to him, irrevocable and tragic, from the sea of desolation (that sea pictured so brilliantly and painfully in "The Yachts")—are part of the burden of the creative spirit in America. The block to communication between man and man, man and woman, man and his land is the result of centuries of violation of the human need for *concern*—the rape of the land pictured in *In the American Grain*, betrayal of the Indian, power monomania, brutalizing of the frontier woman, terror, and civil war. *Paterson* recalls this background at scattered moments, adds the figures of the Jackson's Whites, and presents the complaint of the woman writer as a sort of chorus, climactically effective at the end of Part II. As D. H. Lawrence's review of *In the American Grain* puts it, "The author sees the genius of the continent as a woman with exquisite, super-subtle tenderness and recoiling cruelty," who will "demand of men sensitive awareness, sensuous delicacy, infinitely tempered resistance."*

In *Paterson* as a whole, the poet is seen exploring the resources of the modern city, using its history, its population, its institutions as a "second body for the human mind" (Santayana's phrase, quoted as epigraph to Part III). He is seeking to close the sexual circuit, to re-establish the contact between the male and female components of life. Unfortunately, like Lincoln as portrayed in *In the American Grain*, the poet is faced with the characteristic American confusion of the functions of the sexes. The library, symbolizing the accumulated civilization of the past, cannot help him face the "roar of the present," and there are no rules of law or love that will guide him. The poem as originally planned ends, in Part IV, with a group of tentative approaches to the meaning of love and of the future; Williams was bravely following Lawrence's challenge in the review just noted: "*Touch* America as she is; dare to touch her!" A series of brief "pastoral" dialogues involving the poet himself, a younger woman called "Phyllis," and an older woman (a Lesbian who calls herself "Corydon" and employs Phyllis as a masseuse) brings us to the heart of the sexual confusion, and to the entire cultural confusion around it.† Pound's ideas on economics and art, and his Odyssean theme in *Mauberley* and *The Cantos*, are brought to bear on the situation, but in such a way that Part IV ends modestly and familiarly—as it began—in the midst of things, finding something like an inner calm despite the turmoil and scramble of events and things.

Then, in the unexpectedly added fifth book, Williams refocused the issues. The transforming and saving power of the aesthetic imagination plays like a brilliant light over the

* D. H. Lawrence, *Phoenix* (N.Y.: Viking, 1936), p. 335.

† Some of the passages in these dialogues, "casual" or "slight" in their first impact, are among the most original in *Paterson* and have perhaps touched off new tendencies in verse.

old oppositions of sexuality and chastity, and of reality and the ideal. The Virgin and the Whore, the hunted-down Unicorn pictured (in a famous tapestry) in the midst of nature —images such as these do the refocusing. The poet's own perspectives have been put into sharper relation to the confused perspectives of the culture at large.

Is *Paterson* a success structurally? On the whole we should say yes, with these qualifications: *Paterson* is an *open* sequence, like *The Cantos*. As many critics have noted, the first two parts hold together as a single aesthetic compartment more beautifully and convincingly than does the whole poem finally. However, the scheme of the poem is based on a search, on a continuity, rather than on the containment of a watertight finality. It is the flow of a *river* Williams is after. "From the beginning," he wrote, "I decided there would be four books following the course of the river whose life seemed more and more to resemble my own life . . . : above the Falls, the catastrophe of the Falls itself, . . . below the Falls, and the entrance at the end into the great sea." It would have been easier to end with Part II ("catastrophe"), but twice Williams chose to reopen the poem, to stick with his own understanding of the nature of things, pragmatically and stubbornly in the midst of tragedy and confusion: "Say it, no ideas but in things." So long as the poet does not accept the "failure of speech" in modern civilization as final, so long (as Williams wrote in a comment on *Paterson*) does he "hold the key to . . . final rescue" among his still undiscovered resources. For himself, certainly, *this* poet won a decisive release through his completion of *Paterson*.

The fact lies outside the strict domain of criticism, perhaps, but it is instructive to read "Asphodel, That Greeny Flower," in the light of the search of *Paterson*. It is the work of a man who did in some fashion "come through." In it, simply, naturally, he was able to bring together the motifs of the meaning of old age and death, the nature of love, the function of poetry—all as aspects of his awareness of his relation to his wife. Even the three-unit, stanzaic broken line employed in "Asphodel" represents a coming-through.

It is the line Williams always looked for—free-flowing and
organic yet tightly disciplined, a beautifully patterned
musical involvement of form and feeling within one another,
the earned prize of Williams's poetic development:

> So let us love
> confident as is the light
> in its struggle with darkness
> that there is as much to say
> and more
> for the one side
> and that not the darker . . .

3.

I came to know William Carlos Williams only a couple of
years after the last war, when he had already begun to suffer
those strokes that cruelly, and often, marked in his last years.
It was characteristic of the man that, death being on his
mind, he began to speak to me of it without preliminaries—
"I think constantly of death." Of all the distinguished elder-
ly writers I have met, he was certainly the one who stood
least on ceremony. Perhaps in earlier years he had been less
accessible, and vulnerable, to others. Some of his letters at
the beginning of his career show that he could be short with
people, and even difficult. But as he grew older he came to
be bathed in the affection of many younger writers, and because he was unfailingly courteous and had the great gift of
enthusiasm for the work of other poets, whether known or
unknown, his influence grew. Some of the younger people
who admired him never realized, I believe, the rigorous self-
perfecting implied in his achievements. They never saw
that what he called beauty and what his arch-"enemy"
Eliot called beauty had many points in common despite
their differences.

The two had other attitudes in common as well, including
that unfortunate tendency to make racial generalizations
often found in people educated before the first World War.
Some of the comments on Jews and "niggers" one finds in
Williams seem to belie his finest virtues, but they do not

recur in his writing after the beginning of World War II. The issues of that war, in which his own sons served, and his revulsion against the ideas of Ezra Pound concerning it, probably brought him up to date with a jolt, although as early as "Impromptu: The Suckers," his 1927 poem on Sacco and Vanzetti, he had given evidence that he was very far indeed from anything that could be reduced to stereotype. Looking for the colorfully energetic and the interesting grotesque, writers of his generation stumbled over a psychic landscape the full danger of which had not been revealed to them in time.

I remember Williams best as a serious, wonderfully articulate, and good man talking about ordinary life and about poetry with an absolute immediacy of involvement. His thoughts, like his published criticism, were not always consistent and were certainly not uniformly original or impressive. But they were the product of long contemplation of a few principles brought to bear on the accidental issues of the moment. He admired the young and the unknown too much perhaps, and was always saying that he had learned something from any kind of passing manuscript. This made for a "soft" criticism, some people said, but he strengthened the hand of many a young man and woman by his generous, unsqueamish praise—such names as Allen Ginsberg's and Charles Olson's are only the ones that have come to some public attention, and he was equally able to praise more conventionally perfectionist poets like Lowell and Shapiro if he felt the kick of life and commitment in them. I know several young people, unpublished save in student magazines, who possess long appreciations by Williams of poems they sent him in the mail. A personal relationship, even with a stranger in this way, held sacred meaning for Williams,* as did any vivid experience. Not long before his death, he and Mrs. Williams came to see us on the dirty old Erie Railroad, a frail-looking couple whose anonymous presence nevertheless awoke delicate instincts of courtesy in everyone involved with the railroad all the way from

* "He bore with me sixty years," wrote Pound in his message of condolence to Mrs. Williams. "I shall never find another friend like him."

Rutherford, New Jersey, to Suffern, New York. The later memory of Dr. Williams on a living-room sofa, explaining to a sixteen-year-old boy who wished to be a poet the meaning of the "variable foot"—starting his sentences, losing track of them, but keeping the inward thought fully in view all the while—is of the order of things too rich and too sad to describe. But it is of the essence of so much that made his art the moving force that it is.

I have not reproduced any of Dr. Williams's letters in this collection. Despite their interesting and illuminating passages, very few of them stand up from beginning to end as examples of his best writing. I do, however, want to quote from one letter that somehow is of a piece with the incident just described and perhaps, in its very quiet way, the best brief comment the poet could give us on the relationship between his writing and his personality. He wrote this letter to Marianne Moore on May 2, 1934, when his health and work were in full, vigorous career. She had spoken, in a review, of the "inner security" of his poems.

> The inner security . . . is something which occurred once when I was about twenty, a sudden resignation to existence, a despair—if you wish to call it that, but a despair which made everything a unit and at the same time a part of myself. I suppose it might be called a sort of nameless religious experience. I resigned, I gave up. I decided there was nothing else in life for me but to work. It is the explanation for the calumny that is heaped on my head by women and men alike once they know me long enough. I won't follow causes. I can't. The reason is that it seems so much more important to me that I *am*. Where shall one go? What shall one do? Things have no names for me and places have no significance. As a reward for this anonymity I feel as much a part of things as trees and stones. Heaven seems frankly impossible. I am damned as I succeed. I have no particular hope save to repair, to rescue, to complete. . . .*

Suffern, N.Y.   M.L.R.
August, 1964

* *The Selected Letters of William Carlos Williams*, edited by John C. Thirlwall (N.Y.: McDowell, Obolensky, 1957), p. 147.

I
Poems

Danse Russe

If when my wife is sleeping
and the baby and Kathleen
are sleeping
and the sun is a flame-white disc
in silken mists
above shining trees,—
if I in my north room
dance naked, grotesquely
before my mirror
waving my shirt round my head
and singing softly to myself:
"I am lonely, lonely.
I was born to be lonely,
I am best so!"
If I admire my arms, my face,
my shoulders, flanks, buttocks
against the yellow drawn shades,—

Who shall say I am not
the happy genius of my household?

Tract

I will teach you my townspeople
how to perform a funeral
for you have it over a troop
of artists—
unless one should scour the world—
you have the ground sense necessary.

3

See! the hearse leads.
I begin with a design for a hearse.
For Christ's sake not black—
nor white either—and not polished!
Let it be weathered—like a farm wagon—
with gilt wheels (this could be
applied fresh at small expense)
or no wheels at all:
a rough dray to drag over the ground.

Knock the glass out!
My God—glass, my townspeople!
For what purpose? Is it for the dead
to look out or for us to see
how well he is housed or to see
the flowers or the lack of them—
or what?
To keep the rain and snow from him?
He will have a heavier rain soon:
pebbles and dirt and what not.
Let there be no glass—
and no upholstery, phew!
and no little brass rollers
and small easy wheels on the bottom—
my townspeople what are you thinking of?

A rough plain hearse then
with gilt wheels and no top at all.
On this the coffin lies
by its own weight.

                No wreaths please—
especially no hot house flowers.
Some common memento is better,
something he prized and is known by:

his old clothes—a few books perhaps—
God knows what! You realize
how we are about these things
my townspeople—
something will be found—anything
even flowers if he had come to that.
So much for the hearse.

For heaven's sake though see to the driver!
Take off the silk hat! In fact
that's no place at all for him—
up there unceremoniously
dragging our friend out to his own dignity!
Bring him down—bring him down!
Low and inconspicuous! I'd not have him ride
on the wagon at all—damn him—
the undertaker's understrapper!
Let him hold the reins
and walk at the side
and inconspicuously too!

Then briefly as to yourselves:
Walk behind—as they do in France,
seventh class, or if you ride
Hell take curtains! Go with some show
of inconvenience; sit openly—
to the weather as to grief.
Or do you think you can shut grief in?
What—from us? We who have perhaps
nothing to lose? Share with us
share with us—it will be money
in your pockets.
                              Go now
I think you are ready.

El Hombre

It's a strange courage
you give me ancient star:

Shine alone in the sunrise
toward which you lend no part!

Sympathetic Portrait of a Child

The murderer's little daughter
who is barely ten years old
jerks her shoulders
right and left
so as to catch a glimpse of me
without turning round.

Her skinny little arms
wrap themselves
this way then that
reversely about her body!
Nervously
she crushes her straw hat
about her eyes
and tilts her head
to deepen the shadow—
smiling excitedly!

As best she can
she hides herself
in the full sunlight
her cordy legs writhing

beneath the little flowered dress
that leaves them bare
from mid-thigh to ankle—

Why has she chosen me
for the knife
that darts along her smile?

Winter Quiet

Limb to limb, mouth to mouth
with the bleached grass
silver mist lies upon the back yards
among the outhouses.
                    The dwarf trees
pirouette awkwardly to it—
whirling round on one toe;
the big tree smiles and glances
                           upward!
Tense with suppressed excitement
the fences watch where the ground
has humped an aching shoulder for
                     the ecstasy.

January Morning

SUITE:

I

I have discovered that most of
the beauties of travel are due to
the strange hours we keep to see them:

the domes of the Church of
the Paulist Fathers in Weehawken
against a smoky dawn—the heart stirred—
are beautiful as Saint Peters
approached after years of anticipation.

II

Though the operation was postponed
I saw the tall probationers
in their tan uniforms
                              hurrying to breakfast!

III

—and from basement entries
neatly coiffed, middle aged gentlemen
with orderly moustaches and
well-brushed coats

IV

—and the sun, dipping into the avenues
streaking the tops of
the irregular red houselets,
                                        and
the gay shadows dropping and dropping.

V

—and a young horse with a green bed-quilt
on his withers shaking his head:
bared teeth and nozzle high in the air!

VI

—and a semicircle of dirt-colored men
about a fire bursting from an old
ash can,

VII

                    —and the worn,
blue car rails (like the sky!)
gleaming among the cobbles!

VIII

—and the rickety ferry-boat "Arden"!
What an object to be called "Arden"
among the great piers,—on the
ever new river!
                    "Put me a Touchstone
at the wheel, white gulls, and we'll
follow the ghost of the *Half Moon*
to the North West Passage—and through!
(at Albany!) for all that!"

IX

Exquisite brown waves—long
circlets of silver moving over you!
enough with crumbling ice crusts among you!
The sky has come down to you,
lighter than tiny bubbles, face to
face with you!
                    His spirit is
a white gull with delicate pink feet
and a snowy breast for you to
hold to your lips delicately!

9

X

The young doctor is dancing with happiness
in the sparkling wind, alone
at the prow of the ferry! He notices
the curdy barnacles and broken ice crusts
left at the slip's base by the low tide
and thinks of summer and green
shell-crusted ledges among
                    the emerald eel-grass!

XI

Who knows the Palisades as I do
knows the river breaks east from them
above the city—but they continue south
—under the sky—to bear a crest of
little peering houses that brighten
with dawn behind the moody
water-loving giants of Manhattan.

XII

Long yellow rushes bending
above the white snow patches;
purple and gold ribbon
of the distant wood:
                    what an angle
you make with each other as
you lie there in contemplation.

XIII

Work hard all your young days
and they'll find you too, some morning
staring up under
your chiffonier at its warped
bass-wood bottom and your soul—
out!
—among the little sparrows
behind the shutter.

XIV

—and the flapping flags are at
half mast for the dead admiral.

XV

All this—
        was for you, old woman.
I wanted to write a poem
that you would understand.
For what good is it to me
if you can't understand it?
                But you got to try hard—
But—
    Well, you know how
the young girls run giggling
on Park Avenue after dark
when they ought to be home in bed?
Well,
that's the way it is with me somehow.

11

Waiting

When I am alone I am happy.
The air is cool. The sky is
flecked and splashed and wound
with color. The crimson phalloi
of the sassafras leaves
hang crowded before me
in shoals on the heavy branches.
When I reach my doorstep
I am greeted by
the happy shrieks of my children
and my heart sinks.
I am crushed.

Are not my children as dear to me
as falling leaves or
must one become stupid
to grow older?
It seems much as if Sorrow
had tripped up my heels.
Let us see, let us see!
What did I plan to say to her
when it should happen to me
as it has happened now?

Spouts

In this world of
as fine a pair of breasts
as ever I saw
the fountain in

Madison Square
spouts up of water
a white tree
that dies and lives
as the rocking water
in the basin
turns from the stonerim
back upon the jet
and rising there
reflectively drops down again.

The Widow's Lament in Springtime

Sorrow is my own yard
where the new grass
flames as it has flamed
often before but not
with the cold fire
that closes round me this year.
Thirtyfive years
I lived with my husband.
The plumtree is white today
with masses of flowers.
Masses of flowers
load the cherry branches
and color some bushes
yellow and some red
but the grief in my heart
is stronger than they
for though they were my joy
formerly, today I notice them
and turned away forgetting.
Today my son told me

13

that in the meadows,
at the edge of the heavy woods
in the distance, he saw
trees of white flowers.
I feel that I would like
to go there
and fall into those flowers
and sink into the marsh near them.

The Lonely Street

School is over. It is too hot
to walk at ease. At ease
in light frocks they walk the streets
to while the time away.
They have grown tall. They hold
pink flames in their right hands.
In white from head to foot,
with sidelong, idle look—
in yellow, floating stuff,
black sash and stockings—
touching their avid mouths
with pink sugar on a stick—
like a carnation each holds in her hand—
they mount the lonely street.

from *Spring and All*

Spring and All

By the road to the contagious hospital
under the surge of the blue
mottled clouds driven from the
northeast—a cold wind. Beyond, the
waste of broad, muddy fields
brown with dried weeds, standing and fallen

patches of standing water
the scattering of tall trees

All along the road the reddish
purplish, forked, upstanding, twiggy
stuff of bushes and small trees
with dead, brown leaves under them
leafless vines—

Lifeless in appearance, sluggish
dazed spring approaches—

They enter the new world naked,
cold, uncertain of all
save that they enter. All about them
the cold, familiar wind—

Now the grass, tomorrow
the stiff curl of wildcarrot leaf
One by one objects are defined—
It quickens: clarity, outline of leaf

But now the stark dignity of
entrance—Still, the profound change
has come upon them: rooted, they
grip down and begin to awaken

The Rose

The rose is obsolete
but each petal ends in
an edge, the double facet
cementing the grooved
columns of air—The edge
cuts without cutting
meets—nothing—renews
itself in metal or porcelain—

whither? It ends—

But if it ends
the start is begun
so that to engage roses
becomes a geometry—

Sharper, neater, more cutting
figured in majolica—
the broken plate
glazed with a rose

Somewhere the sense
makes copper roses
steel roses—

16

The rose carried weight of love
but love is at an end—of roses
It is at the edge of the
petal that love waits

Crisp, worked to defeat
laboredness—fragile
plucked, moist, half-raised
cold, precise, touching

What

The place between the petal's
edge and the

From the petal's edge a line starts
that being of steel
infinitely fine, infinitely
rigid penetrates
the Milky Way
without contact—lifting
from it—neither hanging
nor pushing—

The fragility of the flower
unbruised
penetrates space.

To Elsie

The pure products of America
go crazy—
mountain folk from Kentucky

or the ribbed north end of
Jersey
with its isolate lakes and

valleys, its deaf-mutes, thieves
old names
and promiscuity between

devil-may-care men who have taken
to railroading
out of sheer lust of adventure—

and young slatterns, bathed
in filth
from Monday to Saturday

to be tricked out that night
with gauds
from imaginations which have no

peasant traditions to give them
character
but flutter and flaunt

sheer rags—succumbing without
emotion
save numbed terror

under some hedge of choke-cherry
or viburnum—
which they cannot express—

Unless it be that marriage
perhaps
with a dash of Indian blood

will throw up a girl so desolate
so hemmed round
with disease or murder

that she'll be rescued by an
agent—
reared by the state and

sent out at fifteen to work in
some hard-pressed
house in the suburbs—

some doctor's family, some Elsie—
voluptuous water
expressing with broken

brain the truth about us—
her great
ungainly hips and flopping breasts

addressed to cheap
jewelry
and rich young men with fine eyes

as if the earth under our feet
were
an excrement of some sky

and we degraded prisoners
destined
to hunger until we eat filth

while the imagination strains
after deer
going by fields of goldenrod in

the stifling heat of September
Somehow
it seems to destroy us

It is only in isolate flecks that
something
is given off

No one
to witness
and adjust, no one to drive the car

The Sea

The sea that encloses her young body
ula lu la lu
is the sea of many arms—

The blazing secrecy of noon is undone
and and and
the broken sand is the sound of love—

The flesh is firm that turns in the sea
O la la
the sea that is cold with dead men's tears—

Deeply the wooing that penetrated
to the edge of the sea
returns in the plash of the waves—

a wink over the shoulder
large as the ocean—
with wave following wave to the edge

coom barroom—

It is the cold of the sea
broken upon the sand by the force
of the moon—

In the sea the young flesh playing
floats with the cries of far off men
who rise in the sea

with green arms
to homage again the fields over there
where the night is deep—

la lu la lu
but lips too few
assume the new—marruu

Underneath the sea where it is dark
there is no edge
so two—

The Red Wheelbarrow

        so much depends
        upon

        a red wheel
        barrow

        glazed with rain
        water

        beside the white
        chickens.

At the Ball Game

The crowd at the ball game
is moved uniformly

by a spirit of uselessness
which delights them—

all the exciting detail
of the chase

and the escape, the error
the flash of genius—

all to no end save beauty
the eternal—

So in detail they, the crowd,
are beautiful

for this
to be warned against

saluted and defied—
It is alive, venomous

it smiles grimly
its words cut—

The flashy female with her
mother, gets it—

The Jew gets it straight—it
is deadly, terrifying—

It is the Inquisition, the
Revolution

It is beauty itself
that lives

day by day in them
idly—

This is
the power of their faces

It is summer, it is the solstice
the crowd is

cheering, the crowd is laughing
in detail

permanently, seriously
without thought

. . . . . .

Portrait of a Lady

Your thighs are appletrees
whose blossoms touch the sky.
Which sky? The sky
where Watteau hung a lady's
slipper. Your knees
are a southern breeze—or
a gust of snow. Agh! what
sort of man was Fragonard?
—as if that answered

anything. Ah, yes—below
the knees, since the tune
drops that way, it is
one of those white summer days,
the tall grass of your ankles
flickers upon the shore—
Which shore?—
the sand clings to my lips—
Which shore?
Agh, petals maybe. How
should I know?
Which shore? Which shore?
I said petals from an appletree.

The Trees

The trees—being trees
thrash and scream
guffaw and curse—
wholly abandoned
damning the race of men—

Christ, the bastards
haven't even sense enough
to stay out of the rain—

Wha ha ha ha

Wheeeeee
Clacka tacka tacka
tacka tacka
wha ha ha ha ha
ha ha ha

knocking knees, buds
bursting from each pore
even the trunk's self
putting out leafheads—

Loose desire!
we naked cry to you—
"Do what you please."

You cannot!

—ghosts
sapped of strength

wailing at the gate
heartbreak at the bridgehead—
desire
dead in the heart

haw haw haw haw
—and memory broken

wheeeeee

There were never satyrs
never maenads
never eagle-headed gods—
These were men
from whose hands sprung
love
bursting the wood—

Trees their companions
—a cold wind winterlong
in the hollows of our flesh
icy with pleasure—

no part of us untouched

The Sea-Elephant

Trundled from
the strangeness of the sea—
a kind of
heaven—

Ladies and Gentlemen!
the greatest
sea-monster ever exhibited
alive

the gigantic
sea-elephant! O wallow
of flesh were
are

there fish enough for
that
appetite stupidity
cannot lessen?

Sick
of April's smallness
the little
leaves—

Flesh has lief of you
enormous sea—
Speak!
Blouaugh! (feed

me) my
flesh is riven—

fish after fish into his maw
unswallowing

to let them glide down
gulching back
half spittle half
brine

the
troubled eyes—torn
from the sea.
(In

a practical voice) They
ought
to put it back where
it came from.

Gape.
Strange head—
told by old sailors—
rising

bearded
to the surface—and
the only
sense out of them

is that woman's
Yes
it's wonderful but they
ought to

put it
back into the sea where

it came from.
Blouaugh!

Swing—ride
walk
on wires—toss balls
stoop and

contort yourselves—
But I
am love. I am
from the sea—

Blouaugh!
there is no crime save
the too-heavy
body

the sea
held playfully—comes
to the surface
the water

boiling
about the head the cows
scattering
fish dripping from

the bounty
of . . . . and spring
they say
Spring is icummen in—

Death

He's dead
the dog won't have to
sleep on his potatoes
any more to keep them
from freezing

he's dead
the old bastard—
He's a bastard because

there's nothing
legitimate in him any
more
      he's dead
He's sick-dead

              he's
a godforsaken curio
without
any breath in it

He's nothing at all
      he's dead
shrunken up to skin

      Put his head on
one chair and his
feet on another and
he'll lie there
like an acrobat—

Love's beaten. He
beat it. That's why
he's insufferable—

        because
he's here needing a
shave and making love
an inside howl
of anguish and defeat—

He's come out of the man
and he's let
the man go—
            the liar

Dead
        his eyes
rolled up out of
the light—a mockery

                        which
love cannot touch—

just bury it
and hide its face
for shame.

The Botticellian Trees

        The alphabet of
        the trees

        is fading in the
        song of the leaves

        the crossing
        bars of the thin

letters that spelled
winter

and the cold
have been illumined

with
pointed green

by the rain and sun—
The strict simple

principles of
straight branches

are being modified
by pinched-out

ifs of color, devout
conditions

the smiles of love—
. . . . . .

until the stript
sentences

move as a woman's
limbs under cloth

and praise from secrecy
quick with desire

love's ascendancy
in summer—

In summer the song
sings itself

above the muffled words—

from *The Descent of Winter*

The justice of poverty
    its shame its dirt
are one with the meanness
    of love

its organ its tarpaulin
    the green birds
the fat sleepy horse
    the old men

the grinder sourfaced
    hat over eyes
the beggar smiling all open
    the lantern out

and the popular tunes—
    sold to the least bidder
for a nickel
    two cents or

nothing at all or even
    against the desire
forced on us

This Is Just To Say

I have eaten
the plums
that were in
the icebox

and which
you were probably
saving
for breakfast

Forgive me
they were delicious
so sweet
and so cold

Flowers by the Sea

When over the flowery, sharp pasture's
edge, unseen, the salt ocean

lifts its form—chicory and daisies
tied, released, seem hardly flowers alone

but color and the movement—or the shape
perhaps—of restlessness, whereas

the sea is circled and sways
peacefully upon its plantlike stem

To a Poor Old Woman

munching a plum on
the street a paper bag
of them in her hand

They taste good to her
They taste good
to her. They taste
good to her

You can see it by
the way she gives herself
to the one half
sucked out in her hand

Comforted
a solace of ripe plums
seeming to fill the air
They taste good to her

Proletarian Portrait

A big young bareheaded woman
in an apron

Her hair slicked back standing
on the street

One stockinged foot toeing
the sidewalk

Her shoe in her hand. Looking
intently into it

She pulls out the paper insole
to find the nail

That has been hurting her

The Raper from Passenack

was very kind. When she regained
her wits, he said, It's all right, kid,
I took care of you.

What a mess she was in. Then he added,
You'll never forget me now.
And drove her home.

Only a man who is sick, she said
would do a thing like that.
It must be so.

No one who is not diseased could be
so insanely cruel. He wants to give it
to someone else—

to justify himself. But if I get a
venereal infection out of this
I won't be treated.

I refuse. You'll find me dead in bed
first. Why not? That's
the way she spoke,

I wish I could shoot him. How would
you like to know a murderer?
I may do it.

I'll know by the end of this week.
I wouldn't scream. I bit him
several times

but he was too strong for me.
I can't yet understand it. I don't
faint so easily.

When I came to myself and realized
what had happened all I could do
was to curse

and call him every vile name I could
think of. I was so glad
to be taken home.

I suppose it's my mind—the fear of
infection. I'd rather a million times
have been got pregnant.

But it's the foulness of it can't
be cured. And hatred, hatred of all men
—and disgust.

The Yachts

contend in a sea which the land partly encloses
shielding them from the too-heavy blows
of an ungoverned ocean which when it chooses

tortures the biggest hulls, the best man knows
to pit against its beatings, and sinks them pitilessly.
Mothlike in mists, scintillant in the minute

brilliance of cloudless days, with broad bellying sails
they glide to the wind tossing green water
from their sharp prows while over them the crew crawls

ant-like, solicitously grooming them, releasing,
making fast as they turn, lean far over and having
caught the wind again, side by side, head for the mark.

In a well guarded arena of open water surrounded by
lesser and greater craft which, sycophant, lumbering
and flittering follow them, they appear youthful, rare

as the light of a happy eye, live with the grace
of all that in the mind is fleckless, free and
naturally to be desired. Now the sea which holds them

is moody, lapping their glossy sides, as if feeling
for some slightest flaw but fails completely.
Today no race. Then the wind comes again. The yachts

move, jockeying for a start, the signal is set and they
are off. Now the waves strike at them but they are too
well made, they slip through, though they take in canvas.

Arms with hands grasping seek to clutch at the prows.
Bodies thrown recklessly in the way are cut aside.
It is a sea of faces about them in agony, in despair

until the horror of the race dawns staggering the mind,
the whole sea become an entanglement of watery bodies
lost to the world bearing what they cannot hold. Broken,

beaten, desolate, reaching from the dead to be taken up
they cry out, failing, failing! their cries rising
in waves still as the skillful yachts pass over.

The Catholic Bells

Tho' I'm no Catholic
I listen hard when the bells
in the yellow-brick tower
of their new church

ring down the leaves
ring in the frost upon them
and the death of the flowers
ring out the grackle

toward the south, the sky
darkened by them, ring in
the new baby of Mr. and Mrs.
Krantz which cannot

for the fat of its cheeks
open well its eyes, ring out
the parrot under its hood
jealous of the child

ring in Sunday morning
and old age which adds as it
takes away. Let them ring
only ring! over the oil

painting of a young priest
on the church wall advertising
last week's Novena to St.
Anthony, ring for the lame

young man in black with
gaunt cheeks and wearing a
Derby hat, who is hurrying
to 11 o'clock Mass (the

grapes still hanging to
the vine along the nearby
Concordia Halle like broken
teeth in the head of an

old man) Let them ring
for the eyes and ring for
the hands and ring for
the children of my friend

who no longer hears
them ring but with a smile
and in a low voice speaks
of the decisions of her

daughter and the proposals
and betrayals of her
husband's friends. O bells
ring for the ringing!

the beginning and the end
of the ringing! Ring ring
ring ring ring ring ring!
Catholic bells—!

St. Francis Einstein of the Daffodils

*On the first visit of Professor Einstein to
the United States in the spring of 1921.*

"Sweet land"
at last!
out of the sea—

the Venusremembering wavelets
rippling with laughter—
freedom
for the daffodils!
—in a tearing wind
that shakes
the tufted orchards—
Einstein, tall as a violet
in the lattice-arbor corner
is tall as
a blossomy peartree

A Samos, Samos
dead and buried. Lesbia
a black cat in the freshturned
garden. All dead.
All flesh they sung
is rotten
Sing of it no longer—

Side by side young and old
take the sun together—
maples, green and red
yellowbells
and the vermilion quinceflower
together—

The peartree
with fœtid blossoms
sways its high topbranches
with contrary motions
and there are both pinkflowered
and coralflowered peachtrees
in the bare chickenyard
of the old negro

with white hair who hides
poisoned fish-heads
here and there
where stray cats find them—
find them

Spring days
swift and mutable
winds blowing four ways
hot and cold
shaking the flowers—

Now the northeast wind
moving in fogs leaves the grass
cold and dripping. The night
is dark. But in the night
the southeast wind approaches.
The owner of the orchard
lies in bed
with open windows
and throws off his covers
one by one

The Term

A rumpled sheet
of brown paper
about the length

and apparent bulk
of a man was
rolling with the

wind slowly over
and over in
the street as

a car drove down
upon it and
crushed it to

the ground. Unlike
a man it rose
again rolling

with the wind over
and over to be as
it was before.

Paterson: Episode 17

Beat hell out of it
    Beautiful Thing
    spotless cap
and crossed white straps
over the dark rippled cloth—
    Lift the stick
above that easy head
where you sit by the ivied
church, one arm
    buttressing you
long fingers spread out
among the clear grass prongs—
    and drive it down
    Beautiful Thing

that your caressing body kiss
   and kiss again
that holy lawn—

And again: obliquely—
legs curled under you as a
   deer's leaping—
pose of supreme indifference
   sacrament
to a summer's day
   Beautiful Thing
in the unearned suburbs
   then pause
   the arm fallen—
what memories
of what forgotten face
brooding upon that lily stem?

   The incredible
nose straight from the brow
   the empurpled lips
and dazzled half-sleepy eyes
   Beautiful Thing
of some trusting animal
   makes a temple
of its place of savage slaughter
   revealing
the damaged will incites still
   to violence
consummately beautiful thing
and falls about your resting
   shoulders—

Gently! Gently!
as in all things an opposite
   that awakes

the fury, conceiving
   knowledge
by way of despair that has
   no place
to lay its glossy head—
Save only—Not alone!
   Never, if possible
alone! to escape the accepted
   chopping block
and a square hat!—

And as reverie gains and
   your joints loosen
   the trick's done!
Day is covered and we see you—
   but not alone!
drunk and bedraggled to release
the strictness of beauty
under a sky full of stars
   Beautiful Thing
and a slow moon—

               The car
   had stopped long since
   when the others
came and dragged those out
   who had you there
   indifferent
to whatever the anesthetic
   Beautiful Thing
might slum away the bars—
Reek of it!
   What does it matter?
   could set free
only the one thing—
But you!
—in your white lace dress
   "the dying swan"

and high heeled slippers—tall
as you already were—
   till your head
through fruitful exaggeration
was reaching the sky and the
prickles of its ecstasy
   Beautiful Thing!

And the guys from Paterson
   beat up
the guys from Newark and told
them to stay the hell out
of their territory and then
socked you one
   across the nose
   Beautiful Thing
for good luck and emphasis
   cracking it
till I must believe that all
desired women have had each
   in the end
   a busted nose
and live afterward marked up
   Beautiful Thing
   for memory's sake
to be credible in their deeds

Then back to the party!
   and they maled
and femaled you jealously
   Beautiful Thing
as if to discover when and
   by what miracle
there should escape what?
still to be possessed
out of what part
   Beautiful Thing

should it look?
   or be extinguished—
Three days in the same dress
   up and down—
   It would take
a Dominie to be patient
   Beautiful Thing
with you—

The stroke begins again—
   regularly
automatic
   contrapuntal to
the flogging
like the beat of famous lines
in the few excellent poems
woven to make you
gracious
and on frequent occasions
   foul drunk
   Beautiful Thing
pulse of release
   to the attentive
and obedient mind.

A Sort of a Song

Let the snake wait under
his weed
and the writing
be of words, slow and quick, sharp
to strike, quiet to wait,
sleepless.

—through metaphor to reconcile
the people and the stones.
Compose. (No ideas
but in things) Invent!
Saxifrage is my flower that splits
the rocks.

The Dance

In Brueghel's great picture, The Kermess,
the dancers go round, they go round and
around, the squeal and the blare and the
tweedle of bagpipes, a bugle and fiddles
tipping their bellies (round as the thick-
sided glasses whose wash they impound)
their hips and their bellies off balance
to turn them. Kicking and rolling about
the Fair Grounds, swinging their butts, those
shanks must be sound to bear up under such
rollicking measures, prance as they dance
in Brueghel's great picture, The Kermess.

Sometimes It Turns Dry and the Leaves Fall before They Are Beautiful

This crystal sphere
upon whose edge I drive
turns brilliantly—
The level river shines!

47

My love! My love!
how sadly do we thrive:
thistle-caps and
sumac or a tree whose

sharpened leaves
perfect as they are
look no farther than—
into the grass.

The Night Rider

Scoured like a conch
or the moon's shell
I ride from my love
through the damp night.

there are lights
through the trees,
falling leaves,
the air and the blood

an even mood
warm with summer dwindling,
relic of heat:
Ruin dearly bought

smoothed to a round
carved by the sand
the pulse a remembered pulse
of full-tide gone

To Ford Madox Ford in Heaven

Is it any better in Heaven, my friend Ford,
     than you found it in Provence?

I don't think so for you made Provence a
     heaven by your praise of it
to give a foretaste of what might be
     your joy in the present circumstances.
It was Heaven you were describing there
     transubstantiated from its narrowness
to resemble the paths and gardens of a
     greater world where you now reside.
But, dear man, you have taken a major
     part of it from us.
          Provence that you
praised so well will never be the same
     Provence to us
          now you are gone.

A heavenly man you seem to me now, never
     having been for me a saintly one.
It lived about you, a certain grossness that
     was not like the world.
The world is cleanly, polished and well
     made but heavenly man
is filthy with his flesh and corrupt that
     loves to eat and drink and whore—
to laugh at himself and not be afraid of
     himself knowing well he has
no possessions and opinions that are worth
     caring a broker's word about
and that all he is, but one thing, he feeds
     as one will feed a pet dog.

So roust and love and dredge the belly full
in Heaven's name!
I laugh to think of you wheezing in Heaven.
Where is Heaven? But why
do I ask that, since you showed the way?
I don't care a damn for it
other than for that better part lives beside
me here so long as I
live and remember you. Thank God you
were not delicate, you let the world in
and lied! damn it you lied grossly
sometimes. But it was all, I
see now, a carelessness, the part of a man
that is homeless here on earth.

Provence, the fat assed Ford will never
again strain the chairs of your cafés
pull and pare for his dish your sacred garlic,
grunt and sweat and lick
his lips. Gross as the world he has left to
us he has become
a part of that of which you were the known
part, Provence, he loved so well.

The Thing

Each time it rings
I think it is for
me but it is
not for me nor for

anyone it merely
rings and we
serve it bitterly
together, they and I

When Structure Fails
Rhyme Attempts to Come to the Rescue

The old horse dies slow.
By gradual degrees
the fervor of his veins
matches the leaves'

stretch, day by day. But
the pace that his
mind keeps is the pace
of his dreams. He

does what he can, with
unabated phlegm,
ahem! but the pace that
his flesh keeps—

leaning, leaning upon
the bars—beggars
by far all pace and every
refuge of his dreams.

The Horse Show

Constantly near you, I never in my entire
sixty-four years knew you so well as yesterday
or half so well. We talked. You were never
so lucid, so disengaged from all exigencies
of place and time. We talked of ourselves,
intimately, a thing never heard of between us.
How long have we waited? almost a hundred years.

You said, Unless there is some spark, some
spirit we keep within ourselves, life, a
continuing life's impossible—and it is all
we have. There is no other life, only the one.
The world of the spirits that comes afterward
is the same as our own, just like you sitting
there they come and talk to me, just the same.

They come to bother us. Why? I said. I don't
know. Perhaps to find out what we are doing.
Jealous, do you think? I don't know. I
don't know why they should want to come back.
I was reading about some men who had been
buried under a mountain, I said to her, and
one of them came back after two months,

digging himself out. It was in Switzerland,
you remember? Of course I remember. The
villagers tho't it was a ghost coming down
to complain. They were frightened. They
do come, she said, what you call
my "visions." I talk to them just as I
am talking to you. I see them plainly.

Oh if I could only read! You don't know
what adjustments I have made. All
I can do is to try to live over again
what I knew when your brother and you
were children—but I can't always succeed.
Tell me about the horse show. I have
been waiting all week to hear about it.

Mother darling, I wasn't able to get away.
Oh that's too bad. It was just a show;

they make the horses walk up and down
to judge them by their form. Oh is that
all? I tho't it was something else. Oh
they jump and run too. I wish you had been
there, I was so interested to hear about it.

And Who Do You Think "They" Are?

The day when the under-cover writings
of the Russians are in, that day
we'll have an anthology, all around,
to knock their heads off.

War will grow sick, puke its guts
and if, dog-like, it wants to lick up
that, let it (after we have
put poison in it) for good and all.

The Centenarian

I don't think we shall
any of us live as long as
has she, we haven't the
steady mind and strong heart—

Wush a deen a daddy O
There's whisky in the jar!

I wish you could have seen
her yesterday
with her red cheeks and
snow-white hair
so cheerful and contented—
she was a picture—

We sang hymns for her.

She couldn't join us but
when we had done she raised
her hands and clapped them
softly together.

Then when I brought her
her whisky and water I said
to her as we always do—

*Wush a deen a daddy O
There's whisky in the jar!*

She couldn't say the first
part but she managed to
repeat at the end—

There's whisky in the jar!

April Is the Saddest Month

There they were
stuck
dog and bitch
halving the compass

Then when
with his yip

they parted
oh how frolicsome

she grew before him
playful
dancing and
how disconsolate

he retreated
hang-dog
she following
through the shrubbery

A Note

When the cataract dries up, my dear
all minds attend it.
There is nothing left. Neither sticks
nor stones can build it up again
nor old women with their rites of green twigs

Bending over the remains, a body
struck through the breast bone
with a sharp spear—they have borne him
to an ingle at the wood's edge
from which all maidenhood is shent

—though he roared
once the cataract is dried up and done.
What rites can do to keep alive
the memory of that flood they will do
then bury it, old women that they are,
secretly where all male flesh is buried.

The Sound of Waves

A quatrain? Is that
the end I envision?
Rather the pace
which travel chooses.

Female? Rather the end
of giving and receiving
—of love: love surmounted
is the incentive.

Hardly. The incentive
is nothing surmounted,
the challenge lying
                    elsewhere.

No end but among words
looking to the past,
plaintive and unschooled,
wanting a discipline

But wanting
more than discipline
a rock to blow upon
as a mist blows

or rain is driven
against some
headland jutting into
a sea—with small boats

perhaps riding under it
while the men fish
there, words blowing in
taking the shape of stone

                        .   .   .   .   .

Past that, past the image:
a voice!
out of the mist
above the waves and

the sound of waves, a
voice   .   speaking!

Impromptu: The Suckers

Take it out in vile whisky, take it out
in lifting your skirts to show your silken
crotches; it is this that is intended.
You are it. Your pleas will always be denied.
You too will always go up with the two guys,
scapegoats to save the Republic and
especially the State of Massachusetts. The
Governor says so and you ain't supposed
to ask for details—

Your case has been reviewed by high-minded
and unprejudiced observers (like hell
they were!) the president of a great
university, the president of a noteworthy
technical school and a judge too old to sit
on the bench, men already rewarded for
their services to pedagogy and the enforcement
of arbitrary statutes. In other words
pimps to tradition—

Why in hell didn't they choose some other
kind of "unprejudiced adviser" for their
death council? instead of sticking to that

57

autocratic strain of Boston backwash, except
that the council was far from unprejudiced
but the product of a rejected, discredited
class long since outgrown except for use in
courts and school, and that they
wanted it so—

Why didn't they choose at least one decent
Jew or some fair-minded Negro or anybody
but such a triumvirate of inversion, the
New England aristocracy, bent on working off
a grudge against you, Americans, you
are the suckers, you are the ones who will
be going up on the eleventh to get the current
shot into you, for the glory of the state
and the perpetuation of abstract justice—

And all this in the face of the facts: that
the man who swore, and deceived the jury
wilfully by so doing, that the bullets found
in the bodies of the deceased could be
identified as having been fired from the pistol
of one of the accused—later
acknowledged that he could not so identify
them; that the jurors now seven years after
the crime do not remember the details and
have wanted to forget them; that the
prosecution has never succeeded in
apprehending the accomplices nor in connecting
the prisoners with any of the loot stolen—

The case is perfect against you, all the
documents say so—in spite of the fact that
it is reasonably certain that you were not
at the scene of the crime, shown, quite as
convincingly as the accusing facts in the

court evidence, by better reasoning to have
been committed by someone else with whom
the loot can be connected and among whom the
accomplices can be found—

It's no use, you are Americans, just the dregs.
It's all you deserve. You've got the cash,
what the hell do you care? You've got
nothing to lose. You are inheritors of a great
tradition. My country right or wrong!
You do what you're told to do. You don't
answer back the way Tommy Jeff did or Ben
Frank or Georgie Washing. I'll say you
don't. You're civilized. You let your
betters tell you where you get off. Go
ahead—

But after all, the thing that swung heaviest
against you was that you were scared when
they copped you. Explain that you
nature's nobleman! For you know that every
American is innocent and at peace in his
own heart. He hasn't a damned thing to be
afraid of. He knows the government is for
him. Why, when a cop steps up and grabs
you at night you just laugh and think it's
a hell of a good joke—

This is what was intended from the first.
So take it out in your rotten whisky and
silk underwear. That's what you get out of
it. But put it down in your memory that this
is the kind of stuff that they can't get away
with. It is there and it's loaded. No one
can understand what makes the present age
what it is. They are mystified by certain
insistences.

The Last Words of My English Grandmother

1920

There were some dirty plates
and a glass of milk
beside her on a small table
near the rank, disheveled bed—

Wrinkled and nearly blind
she lay and snored
rousing with anger in her tones
to cry for food,

Gimme something to eat—
They're starving me—
I'm all right I won't go
to the hospital. No, no, no

Give me something to eat
Let me take you
to the hospital, I said
and after you are well

you can do as you please.
She smiled, Yes
you do what you please first
then I can do what I please—

Oh, oh, oh! she cried
as the ambulance men lifted
her to the stretcher—
Is this what you call

making me comfortable?
By now her mind was clear—
Oh you think you're smart
you young people,

she said, but I'll tell you
you don't know anything.
Then we started.
On the way

we passed a long row
of elms. She looked at them
awhile out of
the ambulance window and said,

What are all those
fuzzy-looking things out there?
Trees? Well, I'm tired
of them and rolled her head away.

To a Dog Injured in the Street

It is myself,
            not the poor beast lying there
                        yelping with pain
that brings me to myself with a start—
            as at the explosion
                        of a bomb, a bomb that has laid
all the world waste.
            I can do nothing
                        but sing about it
and so I am assuaged
            from my pain.

A drowsy numbness drowns my sense
        as if of hemlock
                I had drunk. I think
of the poetry
        of René Char
                and all he must have seen
and suffered
        that has brought him
                to speak only of
sedgy rivers,
        of daffodils and tulips
                whose roots they water,
even to the free-flowing river
        that laves the rootlets
                of those sweet-scented flowers
that people the
        milky
                way   .

I remember Norma
        our English setter of my childhood
                her silky ears
and expressive eyes.
        She had a litter
                of pups one night
in our pantry and I kicked
        one of them
                thinking, in my alarm,
that they
        were biting her breasts
                to destroy her.

I remember also
        a dead rabbit
                lying harmlessly

on the outspread palm
           of a hunter's hand.
                      As I stood by
watching
           he took a hunting knife
                      and with a laugh
thrust it
           up into the animal's private parts.
                      I almost fainted.

Why should I think of that now?
           The cries of a dying dog
                      are to be blotted out
as best I can.
           René Char
                      you are a poet who believes
in the power of beauty
           to right all wrongs.
                      I believe it also.
With invention and courage
           we shall surpass
                      the pitiful dumb beasts,
let all men believe it,
           as you have taught me also
                      to believe it.

Suzy

I

women your age have decided
wars and the beat
of poems your grandfather

is a poet and loves you
pay attention
to your lessons an inkling

of what beauty means to
a girl your age
may dawn soon upon you

II

life is a flower when it
opens you will
look trembling into it unsure

of what the traditional
mirror may reveal
between hope and despair while

a timorous old man
doubtfully half
turns away his foolish head

III

a bunch of violets clutched
in your idle
hand gives him a place

beside you which he cherishes
his back turned
from you casually appearing

not to look he yearns after
you protectively
hopelessly wanting nothing

Asphodel, That Greeny Flower

BOOK I

Of asphodel, that greeny flower,
        like a buttercup
                upon its branching stem—
save that it's green and wooden—
        I come, my sweet,
                to sing to you.
We lived long together
        a life filled,
                if you will,
with flowers. So that
        I was cheered
                when I came first to know
that there were flowers also
        in hell.
                Today
I'm filled with the fading memory of those flowers
        that we both loved,
                even to this poor
colorless thing—
        I saw it
                when I was a child—
little prized among the living
        but the dead see,
                asking among themselves:
What do I remember
        that was shaped
                as this thing is shaped?
while our eyes fill
        with tears.
                Of love, abiding love
it will be telling

                    though too weak a wash of crimson
                              colors it
to make it wholly credible.
                    There is something
                              something urgent
I have to say to you
                    and you alone
                              but it must wait
while I drink in
                    the joy of your approach,
                              perhaps for the last time.
And so
                    with fear in my heart
                              I drag it out
and keep on talking
                    for I dare not stop.
                              Listen while I talk on
against time.
                    It will not be
                              for long.
I have forgot
                    and yet I see clearly enough
                              something
central to the sky
                    which ranges round it.
                              An odor
springs from it!
                    A sweetest odor!
                              Honeysuckle! And now
there comes the buzzing of a bee!
                    and a whole flood
                              of sister memories!
Only give me time,
                    time to recall them
                              before I shall speak out.
Give me time,
                    time.

When I was a boy
                I kept a book
                                to which, from time
to time,
                I added pressed flowers
                                until, after a time,
I had a good collection.
                The asphodel,
                                forebodingly,
among them.
                I bring you,
                                reawakened,
a memory of those flowers.
                They were sweet
                                when I pressed them
and retained
                something of their sweetness
                                a long time.
It is a curious odor,
                a moral odor,
                                that brings me
near to you.
                The color
                                was the first to go.
There had come to me
                a challenge,
                                your dear self,
mortal as I was,
                the lily's thoat
                                to the hummingbird!
Endless wealth,
                I thought,
                                held out its arms to me.
A thousand topics
                in an apple blossom.
                                The generous earth itself

gave us lief.
                    The whole world
                              became my garden!
But the sea
              which no one tends
                          is also a garden
when the sun strikes it
              and the waves
                          are wakened.
I have seen it
              and so have you
                          when it puts all flowers
to shame.
                    Too, there are the starfish
                              stiffened by the sun
and other sea wrack
              and weeds. We knew that
                          along with the rest of it
for we were born by the sea,
              knew its rose hedges
                          to the very water's brink.
There the pink mallow grows
              and in their season
                          strawberries
and there, later,
              we.went to gather
                          the wild plum.
I cannot say
              that I have gone to hell
                          for your love
but often
              found myself there
                          in your pursuit.
I do not like it
              and wanted to be
                          in heaven. Hear me out.

Do not turn away.

I have learned much in my life
              from books
                        and out of them
about love.
              Death
                        is not the end of it.
There is a hierarchy
              which can be attained,
                        I think,
in its service.
              Its guerdon
                        is a fairy flower;
a cat of twenty lives.
              If no one came to try it
                        the world
would be the loser.
              It has been
                        for you and me
as one who watches a storm
              come in over the water.
                        We have stood
from year to year
              before the spectacle of our lives
                        with joined hands.
The storm unfolds.
              Lightning
                        plays about the edges of the clouds.
The sky to the north
              is placid,
                        blue in the afterglow
as the storm piles up.
              It is a flower
                        that will soon reach
the apex of its bloom.
              We danced,

                              in our minds,
        and read a book together.
                    You remember?
                              It was a serious book.
        And so books
                    entered our lives.

        The sea! The sea!
                    Always
                              when I think of the sea
        there comes to mind
                    the *Iliad*
                              and Helen's public fault
        that bred it.
                    Were it not for that
                              there would have been
        no poem but the world
                    if we had remembered,
                              those crimson petals
        spilled among the stones,
                    would have called it simply
                              murder.
        The sexual orchid that bloomed then
                    sending so many
                              disinterested
        men to their graves
                    has left its memory
                              to a race of fools
        or heroes
                    if silence is a virtue.
                              The sea alone
        with its multiplicity
                    holds any hope.
                              The storm
        has proven abortive
                    but we remain
                              after the thoughts it roused

to
          re-cement our lives.
                It is the mind
the mind
          that must be cured
                short of death's
intervention,
          and the will becomes again
                a garden. The poem
is complex and the place made
          in our lives
                for the poem.
Silence can be complex too,
          but you do not get far
                with silence.
Begin again.
          It is like Homer's
                catalogue of ships:
it fills up the time.
          I speak in figures,
                well enough, the dresses
you wear are figures also,
          we could not meet
                otherwise. When I speak
of flowers
          it is to recall
                that at one time
we were young.
          All women are not Helen,
              I know that,
but have Helen in their hearts.
          My sweet,
                you have it also, therefore
I love you
          and could not love you otherwise.
                Imagine you saw

a field made up of women
                    all silver-white.
                              What should you do
but love them?
                    The storm bursts
                              or fades! it is not
the end of the world.
                    Love is something else,
                              or so I thought it,
a garden which expands,
                    though I knew you as a woman
                              and never thought otherwise,
until the whole sea
                    has been taken up
                              and all its gardens.
It was the love of love,
                    the love that swallows up all else,
                              a grateful love,
a love of nature, of people,
                    animals,
                              a love engendering
gentleness and goodness
                    that moved me
                              and *that* I saw in you.
I should have known
                    though I did not,
                              that the lily-of-the-valley
is a flower makes many ill
                    who whiff it.
                              We had our children,
rivals in the general onslaught.
                    I put them aside
                              though I cared for them
as well as any man
                    could care for his children
                              according to my lights.

You understand
        I had to meet you
                after the event
and have still to meet you.
        Love
                to which you too shall bow
along with me—
        a flower
                a weakest flower
shall be our trust
        and not because
                we are too feeble
to do otherwise
        but because
                at the height of my power
I risked what I had to do,
        therefore to prove
                that we love each other
while my very bones sweated
        that I could not cry to you
                in the act.
Of asphodel, that greeny flower,
        I come, my sweet,
                to sing to you!
My heart rouses
        thinking to bring you news
                of something
that concerns you
        and concerns many men. Look at
                what passes for the new.
You will not find it there but in
        despised poems.
                It is difficult
to get the news from poems
        yet men die miserably every day
                for lack

of what is found there.
>   Hear me out
                    for I too am concerned
and every man
          who wants to die at peace in his bed
                    besides.

from **Paterson**

from *Book II*

Sunday in the Park

I.

Outside

                    outside myself

                              there is a world,
he rumbled, subject to my incursions
—a world

            (to me) at rest,

                        which I approach
concretely—

            The scene's the Park
            upon the rock,
            female to the city

—upon whose body Paterson instructs his thoughts
(concretely)

                        —late spring,
            a Sunday afternoon!

—and goes by the footpath to the cliff (counting:
the proof)

75

　　　　　　　himself among the others,
—treads there the same stones
on which their feet slip as they climb,
paced by their dogs!

laughing, calling to each other—

　　　　　　　　　　Wait for me!

.　　.　the ugly legs of the young girls,
pistons too powerful for delicacy!
the men's arms, red, used to heat and cold,
to toss quartered beeves and　　　.

　　　　　　　　　Yah!　Yah!　Yah!　Yah!

—over-riding
　　　　　　　　　the risks:
　　　　　　　　　　　　pouring down!
For the flower of a day!

Arrived breathless, after a hard climb he,
looks back (beautiful but expensive!) to
the pearl-grey towers! Re-turns
and starts, possessive, through the trees,

　　　　　　　　　　—　that love,
that is not, is not in those terms
to which I'm still the positive
in spite of all;
the ground dry, — passive-possessive

Walking　—

　　　　Thickets gather about groups of squat sand-pine,
　　　　all but from bare rock　　.　　.

—a scattering of man-high cedars (sharp cones),
antlered sumac   ,

—roots, for the most part, writhing
upon the surface
                    (so close are we to ruin every
day!)
          searching the punk-dry rot

Walking —

The body is tilted slightly forward from the basic standing
position and the weight thrown on the ball of the foot,
while the other thigh is lifted and the leg and opposite
arm are swung forward (fig. 6B). Various muscles, aided .

Despite my having said that I'd never write to you again, I do so
now because I find, with the passing of time, that the outcome of
my failure with you has been the complete damming up of all my
creative capacities in a particularly disastrous manner such as I
have never before experienced.

For a great many weeks now (whenever I've tried to write poetry) every thought I've had, even every feeling, has been struck
off some surface crust of myself which began gathering when I
first sensed that you were ignoring the real contents of my last
letters to you, and which finally congealed into some impene-
trable substance when you asked me to quit corresponding with
you altogether without even an explanation.

That kind of blockage, exiling one's self from one's self—have
you ever experienced it? I dare say you have, at moments; and if
so, you can well understand what a serious psychological injury
it amounts to when turned into a permanent day-to-day condition.

How do I love you? These!

(He hears! Voices . indeterminate! Sees them
moving, in groups, by twos and fours — filtering
off by way of the many bypaths.)

77

I asked him, What do you do?

*He smiled patiently, The typical American question.
In Europe they would ask, What are you doing? Or,
What are you doing now?*

*What do I do? I listen, to the water falling. (No
sound of it here but with the wind!) This is my entire
occupation.*

No fairer day ever dawned anywhere than May 2, 1880, when
the German Singing Societies of Paterson met on Garret Mountain, as they did many years before on the first Sunday in May.

However the meeting of 1880 proved a fatal day, when William Dalzell, who owned a piece of property near the scene of
the festivities, shot John Joseph Van Houten. Dalzell claimed that
the visitors had in previous years walked over his garden and
was determined that this year he would stop them from crossing
any part of his grounds.

Immediately after the shot the quiet group of singers was
turned into an infuriated mob who would take Dalzell into their
own hands. The mob then proceeded to burn the barn into which
Dalzell had retreated from the angry group.

Dalzell fired at the approaching mob from a window in the
barn and one of the bullets struck a little girl in the cheek . . .
Some of the Paterson Police rushed Dalzell out of the barn [to]
the house of John Ferguson some half furlong away.

The crowd now numbered some ten thousand,

"a great beast!"

for many had come from the city to join the
conflict. The case looked serious, for the Police were greatly
outnumbered. The crowd then tried to burn the Ferguson house
and Dalzell went to the house of John McGuckin. While in this
house it was that Sergeant John McBride suggested that it might
be well to send for William McNulty, Dean of Saint Joseph's
Catholic Church.

In a moment the Dean set on a plan. He proceeded to the
scene in a hack. Taking Dalzell by the arm, in full view of the
infuriated mob, he led the man to the hack and seating himself
by his side, ordered the driver to proceed. The crowd hesitated,
bewildered between the bravery of the Dean and

Signs everywhere of birds nesting, while
in the air, slow, a crow zigzags
with heavy wings before the wasp-thrusts
of smaller birds circling about him
that dive from above stabbing for his eyes

Walking —

       he leaves the path, finds hard going
across-field, stubble and matted brambles
seeming a pasture—but no pasture
—old furrows, to say labor sweated or
had sweated here   .
                                a flame,
spent.

            The file-sharp grass   .

When! from before his feet, half tripping,
picking a way, there starts
                a flight of empurpled wings!
—invisibly created (their
jackets dust-grey) from the dust kindled
to sudden ardor!

             They fly away, churring! until
their strength spent they plunge
to the coarse cover again and disappear
—but leave, livening the mind, a flashing
of wings and a churring song   .

AND a grasshopper of red basalt, boot-long,
tumbles from the core of his mind,
a rubble-bank disintegrating beneath a
tropic downpour

Chapultepec! grasshopper hill!

—a matt stone solicitously instructed
to bear away some rumor
of the living presence that has preceded
it, out-precedented its breath   .

These wings do not unfold for flight—
no need!
the weight (to the hand) finding
a counter-weight or counter buoyancy
by the mind's wings   .

He is afraid! What then?

Before his feet, at each step, the flight
is renewed. A burst of wings, a quick
churring sound   :

       couriers to the ceremonial of love!

—aflame in flight!
      —aflame only in flight!

           No flesh but the caress!

He is led forward by their announcing wings.

If that situation with you (your ignoring those particular letters
and then your final note) had belonged to the inevitable lacrimae
rerum (as did, for instance, my experience with Z.) its result
could not have been (as it *has* been) to destroy the validity for
me myself *of* myself, because in that case nothing to do with my
sense of personal identity would have been maimed—the cause of
one's frustrations in such instances being not *in* one's self nor in
the other person but merely in the sorry scheme of things. But
since your ignoring those letters was not "natural" in that sense
(or rather since to regard it as unnatural I am forced, psychologically, to feel that what I wrote you about, was sufficiently trivial
and unimportant and absurd to merit your evasion) it could not
but follow that that whole side of life connected with those let-

ters should in consequence take on for my own self that same
kind of unreality and inaccessibility which the inner lives of
other people often have for us.

> —his mind a red stone carved to be
> endless flight   .
> Love that is a stone endlessly in flight,
> so long as stone shall last bearing
> the chisel's stroke   .

> .   .   and is lost and covered
> with ash, falls from an undermined bank
> and — begins churring!
> AND DOES, the stone after the life!

> The stone lives, the flesh dies
> —we know nothing of death.

> —boot long
> window-eyes that front the whole head,
>   Red stone! as if
> a light still clung in them   .

> Love

> >   combating sleep
> >   ─────────────
> >   the sleep

> piecemeal

  Shortly after midnight, August 20, 1878, special officer Goodridge, when, in front of the Franklin House, heard a strange
squealing noise down towards Ellison Street. Running to see
what was the matter, he found a cat at bay under the water table
at Clark's hardware store on the corner, confronting a strange
black animal too small to be a cat and entirely too large for a
rat. The officer ran up to the spot and the animal got in under
the grating of the cellar window, from which it frequently poked
its head with a lightning rapidity. Mr. Goodridge made several
strikes at it with his club but was unable to hit it. Then officer
Keyes came along and as soon as he saw it, he said it was a mink,

which confirmed the theory that Mr. Goodridge had already formed. Both tried for a while to hit it with their clubs but were unable to do so, when finally officer Goodridge drew his pistol and fired a shot at the animal. The shot evidently missed its mark, but the noise and powder so frightened the little joker that it jumped out into the street, and made down into Ellison Street at a wonderful gait, closely followed by the two officers. The mink finally disappeared down a cellar window under the grocery store below Spangermacher's lager beer saloon, and that was the last seen of it. The cellar was examined again in the morning, but nothing further could be discovered of the little critter that had caused so much fun.

>   Without invention nothing is well spaced,
>   unless the mind change, unless
>   the stars are new measured, according
>   to their relative positions, the
>   line will not change, the necessity
>   will not matriculate: unless there is
>   a new mind there cannot be a new
>   line, the old will go on
>   repeating itself with recurring
>   deadliness: without invention
>   nothing lies under the witch-hazel
>   bush, the alder does not grow from among
>   the hummocks margining the all
>   but spent channel of the old swale,
>   the small foot-prints
>   of the mice under the overhanging
>   tufts of the bunch-grass will not
>   appear: without invention the line
>   will never again take on its ancient
>   divisions when the word, a supple word,
>   lived in it, crumbled now to chalk.

>   Under the bush they lie protected
>   from the offending sun—
>   11 o'clock
>   They seem to talk

—a park, devoted to pleasure : devoted to . grasshoppers!

        3 colored girls, of age! stroll by
        —their color flagrant,
                their voices vagrant
        their laughter wild, flagillant, dissociated
        from the fixed scene .

        But the white girl, her head
        upon an arm, a butt between her fingers
        lies under the bush . .

        Semi-naked, facing her, a sunshade
        over his eyes,
        he talks with her

        —the jalopy half hid
        behind them in the trees—
        I bought a new bathing suit, just

        pants and a brassier :
        the breasts and
        the pudenda covered—beneath

        the sun in frank vulgarity.
        Minds beaten thin
        by waste—among

        the working classes SOME sort
        of breakdown
        has occurred. Semi-roused

        they lie upon their blanket
        face to face,
        mottled by the shadows of the leaves

        upon them, unannoyed,
        at least here unchallenged.
        Not undignified . .

talking, flagrant beyond all talk
in perfect domesticity—
And having bathed

and having eaten (a few
sandwiches)
their pitiful thoughts do meet

in the flesh—surrounded
by churring loves! Gay wings
to bear them (in sleep)

—their thoughts alight,
away
.   .   among the grass

Walking   —

across the old swale—a dry wave in the ground
tho' marked still by the line of Indian alders

.   .   they (the Indians) would weave
in and out, unseen, among them along the stream

.   come out whooping between the log
house and men working the field, cut them
off! they having left their arms in the block-
house, and—without defense—carry them away
into captivity. One old man   .

Forget it! for God's sake, Cut
out that stuff   .

Walking   —

he rejoins the path and sees, on a treeless
knoll—the red path choking it—
a stone wall, a sort of circular

redoubt against the sky, barren and
unoccupied. Mount. Why not?

                                        A chipmunk,
with tail erect, scampers among the stones.

(Thus the mind grows, up flinty pinnacles)

                but as he leans, in his stride,
        at sight of a flint arrow-head
                                (it is not)
                                        —there
        in the distance, to the north, appear
        to him the chronic hills   .

                                Well, so they are.

                                He stops short:
        Who's here?

                To a stone bench, to which she's leashed,
within the wall a man in tweeds—a pipe hooked in his jaw—is
combing out a new-washed Collie bitch. The deliberate comb-
strokes part the long hair—even her face he combs though her
legs tremble slightly—until it lies, as he designs, like ripples
in white sand giving off its clean-dog odor. The floor, stone
slabs, she stands patiently before his caresses in that bare "sea
chamber"

                to the right
        from this vantage, the observation tower
        in the middle distance stands up prominently
        from its pubic grove

DEAR B. Please excuse me for not having told you this when I
was over to your house. I had no courage to answer your questions so I'll write it. Your dog *is* going to have puppies although
I prayed she would be okey. It wasn't that she was left alone as
she never was but I used to let her out at dinner time while I

hung up my clothes. At the time, it was on a Thursday, my
mother-in-law had some sheets and table cloths out on the end
of the line. I figured the dogs wouldn't come as long as I was
there and none came thru my yard or near the apartment. He
must have come between your hedge and the house. *Every few*
seconds I would run to the end of the line or peek under the
sheets to see if Musty was alright. She was until I looked a minute
too late. I took sticks and stones after the dog but he wouldn't
beat it. George gave me plenty of hell and I started praying that
I had frightened the other dog so much that nothing had happened. I know you'll be cursing like a son-of-a-gun and probably
won't ever speak to me again for not having told you. Don't
think I haven't been worrying about Musty. She's occupied my
mind every day since that awful event. You won't think so
highly of me now and feel like protecting me. Instead I'll bet
you could kill . . .

> And still the picnickers come on, now
> early afternoon, and scatter through the
> trees over the fenced-in acres   .

>   Voices!
> multiple and inarticulate   .   voices
> clattering loudly to the sun, to
> the clouds. Voices!
> assaulting the air gaily from all sides.

> —among which the ear strains to catch
> the movement of one voice among the rest
> —a reed-like voice
>   of peculiar accent

> Thus she finds what peace there is, reclines,
> before his approach, stroked
> by their clambering feet—for pleasure

>   It is all for

> pleasure   .   their feet   .   aimlessly
>   wandering

86

The "great beast" come to sun himself
                                    as he may
                    their dreams mingling
aloof

Let us be reasonable!

                        Sunday in the park,
limited by the escarpment, eastward; to
the west abutting on the old road: recreation
with a view! the binoculars chained
to anchored stanchions along the east wall—
            beyond which, a hawk
                                soars!

—a trumpet sounds fitfully.

Stand at the rampart (use a metronome
if your ear is deficient, one made in Hungary
if you prefer)
and look away north by east where the church
spires still spend their wits against
the sky   .   to the ball-park
in the hollow with its minute figures running
—beyond the gap where the river
plunges into the narrow gorge, unseen

—and the imagination soars, as a voice
beckons, a thundrous voice, endless
—as sleep: the voice
that has ineluctably called them—
                        that unmoving roar!
churches and factories
                        (at a price)
together, summoned them from the pit   .

—his voice, one among many (unheard)
moving under all.

                              The mountain quivers.
Time! Count! Sever and mark time!

So during the early afternoon, from place
to place he moves,
his voice mingling with other voices
—the voice in his voice
opening his old throat, blowing out his lips,
kindling his mind (more
than his mind will kindle)

                    —following the hikers.

At last he comes to the idlers' favorite
haunts, the picturesque summit, where
the blue-stone (rust-red where exposed)
has been faulted at various levels
                    (ferns rife among the stones)
into rough terraces and partly closed in
dens of sweet grass, the ground gently sloping.

Loiterers in groups straggle
over the bare rock-table—scratched by their
boot-nails more than the glacier scratched
them—walking indifferent through
each other's privacy   .

                    —in any case,
the center of movement, the core of gaiety.

Here a young man, perhaps sixteen,
is sitting with his back to the rock among
some ferns playing a guitar, dead pan

The rest are eating and drinking.

                          The big guy
in the black hat is too full to move   .

                              but Mary
is up!
          Come on! Wassa ma'? You got
broken leg?

                    It is this air!
                              the air of the Midi
and the old cultures intoxicates them:
present!

          —lifts one arm holding the cymbals
of her thoughts, cocks her old head
and dances! raising her skirts:

                    La la la la!

What a bunch of bums! Afraid somebody see
you?
          Blah!
                    Excrementi!
                              —she spits.
Look a' me, Grandma, Everybody too damn
lazy.

This is the old, the very old, old upon old,
the undying: even to the minute gestures,
the hand holding the cup, the wine
spilling, the arm stained by it:

                              Remember
          the peon in the lost
          Eisenstein film drinking

          from a wine-skin with the abandon
          of a horse drinking

          so that it slopped down his chin?
          down his neck, dribbling

                                        89

over his shirt-front and down
onto his pants—laughing, toothless?

                      Heavenly man!

—the leg raised, verisimilitude
even to the coarse contours of the leg, the
bovine touch! The leer, the cave of it,
the female of it facing the male, the satyr—
      (Priapus!)
with that lonely implication, goatherd
and goat, fertility, the attack, drunk,
cleansed

                  Rejected. Even the film
suppressed   :   but   persistent

The picnickers laugh on the rocks celebrating
the varied Sunday of their loves with
its declining light—

Walking   —

look down (from a ledge) into this grassy
den
            (somewhat removed from the traffic)
                              above whose brows
a moon! where she lies sweating at his side:

                  She stirs, distraught,
against him—wounded (drunk), moves
against him (a lump) desiring,
against him, bored

flagrantly bored and sleeping, a
beer bottle still grasped spear-like
in his hand

while the small, sleepless boys, who
have climbed the columnar rocks
overhanging the pair (where they lie
overt upon the grass, besieged—

careless in their narrow cell under
the crowd's feet) stare down,

from history!

at them, puzzled and in the sexless
light (of childhood) bored equally,
go charging off   .

There where
the movement throbs openly
and you can hear the Evangelist shouting!

—moving nearer
she—lean as a goat—leans
her lean belly to the man's backside
toying with the clips of his
suspenders   .

—to which he adds his useless voice:
until there moves in his sleep
a music that is whole, unequivocal (in
his sleep, sweating in his sleep—laboring
against sleep, agasp!)

—and does not waken.

Sees, alive (asleep)
—the fall's roar entering
his sleep (to be fulfilled)

reborn
in his sleep—scattered over the mountain
severally   .

—by which he woos her, severally.

And the amnesic crowd (the scattered),
called about   —   strains
to catch the movement of one voice   .

                                                        hears,
                        Pleasure! Pleasure!

                                                    —feels,
half dismayed, the afternoon of complex
voices its own—
                        and is relieved
                                            (relived)

        A cop is directing traffic
        across the main road up
        a little wooded slope toward
        the conveniences:

                                oaks, choke-cherry,
dogwoods, white and green, iron-wood   :
humped roots matted into the shallow soil
—mostly gone: rock out-croppings
polished by the feet of the picnickers:
sweetbarked sassafras   .

leaning from the rancid grease:
                                            deformity—

—to be deciphered (a horn, a trumpet!)
an elucidation by multiplicity,
a corrosion, a parasitic curd, a clarion
for belief, to be good dogs   :

NO DOGS ALLOWED AT LARGE IN THIS PARK

from *Book V*

II.

"   .   I am no authority on Sappho and do not read her poetry particularly well. She wrote for a clear gentle tinkling voice.
She avoided all roughness. 'The silence that is in the starry sky,'
gives something of her tone,   .   "

A. P.

Peer of the gods is that man, who
face to face, sits listening
to your sweet speech and lovely
      laughter.

It is this that rouses a tumult
in my breast. At mere sight of you
my voice falters, my tongue
      is broken.

Straightway, a delicate fire runs in
my limbs; my eyes
are blinded and my ears
      thunder.

Sweat pours out: a trembling hunts
me down. I grow paler
than dry grass and lack little
      of dying.

13 Nv/   Oke Hay   my BilBill   The Bul Bull, ameer

Is there anything in Ac Bul 2/ vide enc that seems cloudy to you,
or INComprehensible/
                    or that having comprehended you disagree with?

The hardest thing to discover is WHY someone else, apparently
not an ape or a Roosevelt cannot understand something as simple
as 2 plus 2 makes four.

McNair Wilson has just writ me, that Soddy got interested and
started to study "economics" and found out what they offered him
wasn't econ/ but banditry.

Wars are made to make debt, and the late one started by the
ambulating dunghill FDR . . . has been amply successful.

                              and the stink that elevated
him still emits a smell.

Also the ten vols/ treasury reports sent me to Rapallo show that in
the years from departure of Wiggin till the mail stopped you
suckers had paid ten billion for gold that cd/ have been bought for
SIX billion.

              Is this clear or do you want DEEtails?

That sovereignty inheres in the POWER to issue money, whether
you have the right to do it or not.

                        don't let me crowd you.

If there is anything here that is OBskewer , say so.

don't worry re   .   .   .

He didn't say you told him to send me his book, merely that he
had metChu. let the young   educ   the young.

Only naive remark I found in Voltaire wuz when he found two
good books on econ/ and wrote : "Now people will understand it." end quote.

But IF the buzzards on yr(and Del M's) list had been CLEAR
I wdn't have spent so much time clarifying their indistinctnesses.

You agree that the offering da shittad aaabull instead of history is
              undesirable   ??????

94

There is a woman in our town
walks rapidly, flat bellied
in worn slacks upon the street
where I saw her.
                              neither short
nor tall, nor old nor young
her
     face would attract no

adolescent. Grey eyes looked
straight before her.
                          Her
                              hair
was gathered simply behind the
ears under a shapeless hat.

Her
     hips were narrow, her
                              legs
thin and straight. She stopped

me in my tracks — until I saw
her
     disappear in the crowd.

An inconspicuous decoration
made of sombre cloth, meant
I think to be a flower, was
pinned flat to her
                              right

breast — any woman might have
done the same to
say she was a woman and warn
us of her mood. Otherwise

she was dressed in male attire,

as much as to say to hell
with you. Her
                        expression was
serious, her
                    feet were small.

And she was gone!

    .   if ever I see you again
as I have sought you
daily without success

I'll speak to you, alas
too late! ask,
What are you doing on the

streets of Paterson? a
thousand questions:
Are you married? Have you any

children? And, most important,
your NAME! which
of course she may not

give me — though
I cannot conceive it
in such a lonely and

intelligent woman

    .   have you read anything that I have written?
It is all for you

                    or the birds   .
or Mezz Mezzrow

                who wrote   .

Knocking around with Rapp and the Rhythm Kings put the
finishing touches on me and straightened me out. To be with
those guys made me know that any white man if he thought
straight and studied hard, could sing and dance and play with the

Negro. You didn't have to take the finest and most original and honest music in America and mess it up because you were a white man; you could dig the colored man's real message and get in there with him, like Rapp. I felt good all over after a session with the Rhythm Kings, and I began to miss that tenor sax.

Man, I was gone with it — inspiration's mammy was with me. And to top it all, I walked down Madison Street one day and what I heard made me think my ears were lying. Bessie Smith was shouting the *Downhearted Blues* from a record in a music shop. I flew in and bought up every record they had by the mother of the blues — *Cemetery Blues, Bleedin' Hearted*, and *Midnight Blues* — then I ran home and listened to them for hours on the victrola. I was put in a trance by Bessie's moanful stories and the patterns of true harmony in the piano background, full of little runs that crawled up and down my spine like mice. Every note that woman wailed vibrated on the tight strings of my nervous system: every word she sang answered a question I was asking. You couldn't drag me away from that victrola, not even to eat.

.   .   or the Satyrs, a
          pre-tragic play,
                    a satyric play!
                              All plays
were satyric when they were most devout.
                    Ribald as a Satyr!

Satyrs dance!
                    all the deformities take wing
                              Centaurs
leading to the rout of the vocables
                    in the writings
of Gertrude
          Stein — but
                              you cannot be
an artist
          by mere ineptitude
The dream
          is in pursuit!
The neat figures of
          Paul Klee
                    fill the canvas
but that

is not the work
of a child
the cure began, perhaps
with the abstraction
of Arabic art
Dürer
with his *Melancholy*
was aware of it —
the shattered masonry. Leonardo
saw it,
the obsession,
and ridiculed it
in *La Gioconda*.
Bosch's
congeries of tortured souls and devils
who prey on them
fish
swallowing
their own entrails
Freud
Picasso
Juan Gris.
a letter from a friend
saying:
For the last
three nights
I have slept like a baby
without
liquor or dope of any sort!
we know
that a stasis
from a chrysalis
has stretched its wings
like a bull
or a Minotaur
or Beethoven
in the scherzo
from the Fifth Symphony
stomped

                        his heavy feet
I saw love
                    mounted naked on a horse
                        on a swan
    the tail of a fish
                    the bloodthirsty conger eel
                        and laughed
    recalling the Jew
                in the pit
                        among his fellows
    when the indifferent chap
                with the machine gun
                        was spraying the heap
    he had not yet been hit
                but smiled
    comforting his companions
                comforting
                        his companions
    Dreams possess me
                and the dance
                            of my thoughts
    involving animals
                the blameless beasts

(Q. Mr. Williams, can you tell me, simply, what poetry is?

A. Well   .   .   .   I would say that poetry is language
   charged with emotion. It's words, rhythmically organized
   .   .   .   A poem is a complete little universe. It exists
   separately. Any poem that has worth expresses the whole
   life of the poet. It gives a view of what the poet is.

Q. All right, look at this part of a poem by E. E. Cummings,
   another great American poet:

                (im) c-a-t (mo)
                b,i;l:e

                FallleA
                ps!fl
                OattumblI

                sh?dr
                IftwhirlF

(U1) (1Y)
&&&

Is this poetry?

A. I would reject it as a poem. It may be, to him, a poem. But I would reject it. I can't understand it. He's a serious man. So I struggle very hard with it — and I get no meaning at all.

Q. You get no meaning? But here's part of a poem you your-self have written: . . . "2 partridges/ 2 mallard ducks/ a Dungeness crab/ 24 hours out/ of the Pacific/ and 2 live-frozen/ trout/ from Denmark . . ." Now, that sounds just like a fashionable grocery list!

A. It is a fashionable grocery list.

Q. Well — is it poetry?

A. We poets have to talk in a language which is not English. It is the American idiom. Rhythmically it's organized as a sample of the American idiom. It has as much originality as jazz. If you say "2 partridges, 2 mallard ducks, a Dunge-ness Crab" — if you treat that rhythmically, ignoring the practical sense, it forms a jagged pattern. It is, to my mind poetry.

Q. But if you don't "ignore the practical sense" . . . you agree that it is a fashionable grocery list.

A. Yes. Anything is good material for poetry. Anything. I've said it time and time again.

Q. Aren't we supposed to understand it?

A. There is a difference of poetry and the sense. Sometimes modern poets ignore sense completely. That's what makes some of the difficulty . . . The audience is con-fused by the shape of the words.

Q. But shouldn't a word mean something when you see it?

A. In prose, an English word means what it says. In poetry, you're listening to two things . . . you're listening to the sense, the common sense of what it says. But it says more. That is the difficulty.

.   .   .   .   )

100

II

"Improvisations"

from *Kora in Hell: Improvisations**

I have placed the following *Improvisations* in groups, somewhat after the A. B. A. formula, that one may support the other, clarifying or enforcing perhaps the other's intention.

The arrangement of the notes, each following its poem and separated from it by a ruled line, is borrowed from a small volume of Metastasio, *Varie Poesie Dell'Abate Pietro Metastasio*, Venice, 1795.

September 1, 1918

I

1

FOOLS have big wombs. For the rest?—here is pennyroyal if one knows to use it. But time is only another liar, so go along the wall a little further : if blackberries prove bitter there'll be mushrooms, fairy-ring mushrooms, in the grass, sweetest of all fungi.

2

For what it's worth : Jacob Louslinger, white haired, stinking, dirty bearded, cross eyed, stammer tongued, broken voiced, bent backed, ball kneed, cave bellied, mucous faced—deathling,—found lying in the weeds "up

* The two introductory sentences appeared originally at the very end of the "Prologue" to *Kora in Hell*. See introduction, pp. xiii ff., above, for discussion of the "Prologue."

there by the cemetery". "Looks to me as if he'd been bumming around the meadows for a couple of weeks". Shoes twisted into incredible lilies : out at the toes, heels, tops, sides, soles. Meadows flower ! ha, mallow ! at last I have you. (Rot dead marigolds—an acre at a time ! Gold, are you?) Ha, clouds will touch world's edge and the great pink mallow stand singly in the wet, topping reeds and—a closet full of clothes and good shoes and my-thirty-year's-master's-daughter's two cows for me to care for and a winter room with a fire in it—. I would rather feed pigs in Moonachie and chew calamus root and break crab's claws at an open fire : age's lust loose!

3

Talk as you will, say : "No woman wants to bother with children in this country" ;—speak of your Amsterdam and the whitest aprons and brightest doorknobs in Christendom. And I'll answer you : "Gleaming doorknobs and scrubbed entries have heard the songs of the housemaids at sun-up and—housemaids are wishes. Whose? Ha ! the dark canals are whistling, whistling for who will cross to the other side. If I remain with hands in pocket leaning upon my lamppost—why—I bring curses to a hag's lips and her daughter on her arm knows better than I can tell you—best to blush and out with it than back beaten after.

———————

In Holland at daybreak, of a fine spring morning, one sees the housemaids beating rugs before the small houses of such a city as Amsterdam, sweeping, scrubbing the low entry steps and polishing doorbells and doorknobs. By night perhaps there will be an old woman with a girl on her arm, histing and whistling across a deserted canal to some late loiterer trudging aimlessly on beneath the gas lamps.

V

1

Beautiful white corpse of night actually ! So the north-
west winds of death are mountain sweet after all ! All the
troubled stars are put to bed now : three bullets from wife's
hand none kindlier : in the crown, in the nape and one
lower : three starlike holes among a million pocky pores and
the moon of your mouth : Venus, Jupiter, Mars, and all
stars melted forthwith into this one good white light over
the inquest table,—the traditional moth beating its wings
against it—except there are two here. But sweetest are the
caresses of the county physician, a little clumsy perhaps—
mais— ! and the Prosecuting Attorney, Peter Valuzzi and
the others, waving green arms of maples to the tinkling of
the earliest ragpicker's bells. Otherwise— : kindly stupid
hands, kindly coarse voices, infinitely soothing, infinitely
detached, infinitely beside the question, restfully babbling
of how, where, why and night is done and the green edge
of yesterday has said all it could.

---

*Remorse is a virtue in that it is a stirrer up of the emo-
tions but it is a folly to accept it as a criticism of conduct.
So to accept it is to attempt to fit the emotions of a certain
state to a preceding state to which they are in no way
related. Imagination though it cannot wipe out the sting of
remorse can instruct the mind in its proper uses.*

XIX

3

It is not fair to be old, to put on a brown sweater. It is
not just to walk out of a November evening bare headed
and with white hair in the wind. Oh the cheeks are ruddy

enough and the grin broad enough,   it's not that. Worse is
to ride a wheel, a glittering machine that runs without
knowing to move. It is no part of the eternal truth to wear
white canvas shoes and a pink coat. It is a damnable lie to
be fourteen. The curse of God is on her head ! Who can
speak of justice when young men wear round hate and
carry bundles wrapped in paper. It is a case for the supreme
court to button a coat in the wind, no matter how icy.
Lewd to touch an arm at a crossing ; the shame of it screams
to the man in a window. The horrible misery brought on
by the use of black shoes is more than the wind will ever
swallow. To move at all is worse than murder, worse than
Jack the Ripper. It lies, walking, spitting, breathing, coughing lies that bloom, shine sun, shine moon. Unfair to see or
be seen, snatch-purses work. Eat hands full of ashes, angels
have lived on it, time without end. Are you better than an
angel? Let judges giggle to each other over their benches
and use dirty towels in the ante-room. Gnaw, gnaw, gnaw!
at the heads of felons . . . There was a baroness lived in
Hungary bathed twice monthly in virgins' blood.

---

*A mother will love her children most grotesquely. I do
not mean by that more than the term "perversely" perhaps
more accurately describes. Oh I mean the most commonplace of mothers. She will be most willing toward that
daughter who thwarts her most and not toward the little
kitchen helper. So where one is mother to any great number of people she will love best perhaps some child whose
black and peculiar hair is an exact replica of that of the
figure in Velasques' Infanta Maria Theresa or some Italian
matron whose largeness of manner takes in the whole
street. These things relate to inner perfections which it
would be profitless to explain.*

XXI

1

There's the bathtub. Look at it, caustically rejecting its smug proposal. Ponder removedly the herculean task of a bath. There's much cameraderie in filth but it's no' that. And change is lightsome but it's not that either. Fresh linen with a dab here, there of the wet paw serves me better. Take a stripling stroking chin-fuzz, match his heart against that of grandpa watching his silver wane. When these two are compatible I'll plunge in. But where's the edge lifted between sunlight and moonlight. Where does lamplight cease to nick it? Here's hot water.

———————

It is the mark of our civilization that all houses today include a room for the relief and washing of the body, a room ingeniously appointed with water-vessels of many and curious sorts. There is nothing in antiquity to equal this.

2

Neatness and finish; the dust out of every corner! You swish from room to room and find all perfect. The house may now be carefully wrapped in brown paper and sent to a publisher. It is a work of art. You look rather askance at me. Do not believe I cannot guess your mind, yet I have my studies. You see, when the wheel's just at the up turn it glimpses horizon, zenith, all in a burst, the pull of the earth shaken off, a scatter of fragments, significance in a burst of water striking up from the base of a fountain. Then at the sickening turn toward death the pieces are joined into a pretty thing, a bouquet frozen in an ice-cake. *This* is art, *mon cher*, a thing to carry up with you on the next turn; a very small thing, inconceivably feathery.

Live as they will together a husband and wife give each other many a sidelong glance at unlikely moments. Each watches the other out of the tail of his eye. Always it seems some drunkenness is waiting to unite them. First one then the other empties some carafe of spirits forgetting that two lumps of earth are neither wiser nor sadder . . . A man watches his wife clean house. He is filled with knowledge by his wife's exertions. This is incomprehensible to her. Knowing she will never understand his excitement he consoles himself with the thought of art.

3

The pretension of these doors to broach or to conclude our pursuits, our meetings,—of these papered walls to separate our thoughts of impossible tomorrows and these ceilings—that are a jest at shelter . . . It is laughter gone mad —of a holiday—that has frozen into this—what shall I say? Call it, this house of ours, the crystal itself of laughter, thus peaked and faceted.

It is a popular superstition that a house is somehow the possession of the man who lives in it. But a house has no relation whatever to anything but itself. The architect feels the rhythm of the house drawing his mind into opaque partitions in which doors appear, then windows and so on until out of the vague or clearcut mind of the architect the ill-built or deftly-built house has been empowered to draw stone and timbers into a foreappointed focus. If one shut the door of a house he is to that extent a carpenter.

Coda

Outside, the north wind, coming and passing, swelling and dying, lifts the frozen sand   drives it arattle against the lidless windows and we my dear sit stroking the cat stroking the cat and smiling sleepily, prrrr.

A house is sometimes wine. It is more than a skin. The young pair listen attentively to the roar of the weather. The blustering cold takes on the shape of a destructive presence. They loosen their imaginations. The house seems protecting them. They relax gradually as though in the keep of a benevolent protector. Thus the house becomes a wine which has drugged them out of their senses.

XXVII

1

The particular thing, whether it be four pinches of four divers white powders cleverly compounded to cure surely, safely, pleasantly a painful twitching of the eyelids or say a pencil sharpened at one end, dwarfs the imagination, makes logic a butterfly, offers a finality that sends us spinning through space, a fixity the mind could climb forever, a revolving mountain, a complexity with a surface of glass ; the gist of poetry. *D. C. al fin.*

2

There is no thing that with a twist of the imagination cannot be something else. Porpoises risen in a green sea, the wind at nightfall bending the rose-red grasses and you—in your apron running to catch—say it seems to you to be your son. How ridiculous ! You will pass up into a cloud

and look back at me, not count the scribbling foolish that
put wings to your heels, at your knees.

3

Sooner or later as with the leaves forgotten the swinging
branch long since and summer : they scurry before a wind
on the frost-baked ground—have no place to rest—somehow invoke a burst of warm days   not of the past   nothing
decayed : crisp summer !—neither a copse for resurrected
frost eaters   but a summer removed undestroyed   a summer
of dried leaves scurrying with a screech, to and fro in the
half dark—twittering, chattering, scarping. Hagh!

———————

*Seeing the leaves dropping from the high and low
branches the thought rises : this day of all others is the one
chosen, all other days fall away from it on either side and
only itself remains in perfect fullness. It is its own summer,
of its leaves as they scrape on the smooth ground it must
build its perfection. The gross summer of the year is only
a halting counterpart of those fiery days of secret triumph
which in reality themselves paint the year as if upon a
parchment, giving each season a mockery of the warmth or
frozenness which is within ourselves. The true seasons
blossom or wilt not in fixed order but so that many of them
may pass in a few weeks or hours whereas sometimes a
whole life passes and the season remains of a piece from
one end to the other.*

THE END

from **The Great American Novel**

CHAPTER I. THE FOG

IF THERE is progress then there is a novel. Without progress there is nothing. Everything exists from the beginning. I existed in the beginning. I was a slobbering infant. Today I saw nameless grasses—I tapped the earth with my knuckle. It sounded hollow. It was dry as rubber. Eons of drought. No rain for fifteen days. No rain. It has never rained. It will never rain. Heat and no wind all day long better say hot September. The year has progressed. Up one street down another. It is still September. Down one street, up another. Still September. Yesterday was the twenty second. Today is the twenty first. Impossible. Not if it was last year. But then it wouldn't be yesterday. A year is not as yesterday in his eyes. Besides last year it rained in the early part of the month. That makes a difference. It rained on the white goldenrod. Today being misplaced as against last year makes it seem better to have white—Such is progress. Yet if there is to be a novel one must begin somewhere.

Words are not permanent unless the graphite be scraped up and put in a tube or the ink lifted. Words progress into the ground. One must begin with words if one is to write. But what then of smell? What then of the hair on the trees or the golden brown cherries under the black cliffs. What of the weakness of smiles that leaves dimples as much as to say: forgive me—I am slipping, slipping, slipping into nothing at all. Now I am not what I was when the word was forming to say what I am. I sit so on my bicycle and look at you greyly, dimpling because it is September and I am older than I was. I have nothing to say this minute. I shall never have anything to do unless there is progress, unless you write a novel. But if you take me in your arms—why the bicycle will fall and it will not be what it is now to smile greyly and a dimple is so deep—you might fall in and never, never remember to write a word to say good-bye to your cherries. For it is September. Begin with September.

To progress from word to word is to suck a nipple. Imagine saying: My dear, I am thirsty, will you let me have a little milk—This to love at first sight. But who do you think I am, says white goldenrod? Of course there is progress. Of course there are words. But I am thirsty, one might add. Yes but I love you and besides I have no milk. Oh yes, that is right. I forgot that we were speaking of words. Yet you cannot deny that to have a novel one must have milk. Not at the beginning. Granted, but at the end at least. Yes, yes, at the end. Progress from the mere form to the substance. Yes, yes, in other words: milk. Milk is the answer.

But how have milk out of white goldenrod? Why, that was what the Indians said. The bosom of the earth sprays up a girl balancing, balancing on a bicycle. Rapidly she passes through the first—the second eight years. Progress, you note. But September was rainy last year and how can it ever be dry again unless one go back to the year before that. There are no words. It cannot be any otherwise than as this is built the bosom of the earth shrinks back; phosphates. Yet to have a novel—Oh catch up a dozen good smelly names and find some reason for murder, it will do. But can you not see, can you not taste, can you not smell, can you not hear, can you not touch—words? It is words that must progress. Words, white goldenrod, it is words you are made out of—THAT is why you want what you haven't got.

Progress is to get. But how can words get.—Let them get drunk. Bah. Words are words. Fog of words. The car runs through it. The words take up the smell of the car. Petrol.

Face powder, arm pits, food-grease in the hair, foul breath, clean musk. Words. Words cannot progress. There cannot be a novel. Break the words. Words are indivisible crystals. One cannot break them—Awu tsst grang splith gra pragh og bm—Yes, one can break them. One can make words. Progress? If I make a word I make myself into a word. Such is progress. I shall make myself into a word. One big word. One big union. Such is progress. It is a novel. I begin small and make myself into a big splurging word: I take life and make it into one big blurb. I begin at my childhood. I begin at the beginning and make one big—Bah.

What difference is it whether I make the words or take the words. It makes no difference whatever.

There cannot be a novel. There can only be pyramids, pyramids of words, tombs. Their warm breasts heave up and down calling for a head to progress toward them, to fly onward, upon a word that was a pumpkin, now a fairy chariot, and all the time the thing was rolling backward to the time when one believed. Hans Andersen didn't believe. He had to pretend to believe. It is a conspiracy against childhood. It runs backward. Words are the reverse motion. Words are the flesh of yesterday. Words roll, spin, flare up, rumble, trickle, foam—Slowly they lose momentum. Slowly they cease to stir. At last they break up into their letters—Out of them jumps the worm that was—His hairy feet tremble upon them.

Leaving the meeting room where the Mosquito Extermination Commission had been holding an important fall conference they walked out on to the portico of the County Court House Annex where for a moment they remained in the shadow cast by the moon. A fog had arisen in which the egg-shaped white moon was fixed—so it seemed. They walked around the side of the old-fashioned wooden building—constructed in the style of the fine residences of sixty years ago and coming to the car he said: Go around that side as I will have to get in here by the wheel. The seat was wet with dew and cold—after the exceptionally hot day. They sat on it nevertheless. The windshield was opaque with the water in minute droplets on it—through which the moon shone with its inadequate light. That is, our eyes being used to the sun the moon's light is inadequate for us to see by. But certain bats and owls find it even too strong, preferring the starlight. The stars also were out.

Turning into the exit of the parking space he stopped the car and began to wipe the wind-shield with his hand. Take this rag said the other, with one hand already in his trowser pocket. So the glass was wiped on both sides, the top and the bottom pane and the cloth—which looked a good deal like a handkerchief—was returned to the owner—who put it back where it came from not seeming to mind that it was wet and dirty. But of course the man is a mechanic in a certain sense and doesn't care.

On the highway they began to encounter fog. It seemed in the rush of the car to come and meet them. It came suddenly, with a rush and in a moment nothing could be seen but the white billows of water crossed in front by the flares of the headlights. And so it went all the way home, sometimes clearer, sometimes so thick he had to stop, nearly—ending in his own bed-room with his wife's head on the pillow in the perfectly clear electric light. The light shone brightest on the corner of her right eye, which was nearest it, also on the prominences of her face.

Her right arm was under her head. She had been reading. The magazine Vanity Fair, which he had bought thinking of her, lay open on the coverlet. He looked at her and she at him. He smiled and she, from long practice, began to read to him, progressing rapidly until she said: You can't fool me.

He became very angry but understood at once that she had penetrated his mystery, that she saw he was stealing in order to write words. She smiled again knowingly. He became furious.

CHAPTER II.

I'M NEW, said she, I don't think you'll find my card here.
You're new; how interesting. Can you read the letters on
that chart? Open your mouth. Breathe. Do you have head-
aches? No. Ah, yes, you are new. I'm new, said the oval
moon at the bottom of the mist funnel, brightening and
paling. I don't think you'll find my card there. Open your
mouth—Breathe—A crater big enough to hold the land
from New York to Philadelphia. New! I'm new, said the
quartz crystal on the parlor table—like glass—Mr. Tiffany
bought a car load of them. Like water or white rock candy
—I'm new, said the mist rising from the duck pond, rising,
curling, turning under the moon—Unknown grasses asleep
in the level mists, pieces of the fog. Last night it was an
ocean. Tonight trees. Already it is yesterday. Turned into
the wrong street seeking to pass the power house from
which the hum, hmmmmmmmmmmmmm—sprang. Electricity has been discovered for ever. I'm new, says the great
dynamo. I am progress. I make a word. Listen! UMMMMM-
MMMMMMM—

Ummmmmmmmmmm—Turned into the wrong street at
three A.M. lost in the fog, listening, searching—Waaaa! said
the baby. I'm new. A boy! A what? Boy. Shit, said the
father of two other sons. Listen here. This is no place to
talk that way. What a word to use. I'm new, said the sudden word.

The fog lay in deep masses on the roads at three A.M.
Into the wrong street turned the car seeking the high
pitched singing tone of the dynamos endlessly spinning in
the high banquet hall, filling the house and the room where
the bed of pain stood with progress. Ow, Ow! Oh help me
somebody! said she. UMMMMMM sang the dynamo in the
next street, UMMMM. With a terrible scream she drowned
out its sound. He went to the window to see if his car was
still there, pulled the curtain aside, green—Yes it was still

there under the light where it would not be so likely to be struck by other cars coming in the fog. There it was as still as if it were asleep. Still as could be. Not a wheel moved. No sound came from the engine. It stood there under the purple arc-light, partly hidden by a pole which cast a shadow toward him in the masses of floating vapor. He could see the redtaillight still burning brightly with the electricity that came from the battery under the floor boards. No one had stolen the spare tire. It was very late.—Well, said he, dropping the shade and thinking that maybe when he was busy someone might easily come up from the meadows and take the spare tire—Well, I suppose I had better see how things have progressed.

And so he backed out into the main street and turned up another block. And there he saw. The great doors were open to full view of the world. A great amphitheatre of mist lighted from the interior of the power house. In rows sat the great black machines saying vrummmmmmmmmmm-mmm. Stately in the great hall they sat and generated electricity to light the cellar stairs with. To warm the pad on Mrs. Voorman's belly. To cook supper by and iron Abie's pyjamas. Here was democracy. Here is progress—here is the substance of words—UMMMMM: that is to say meat or linen or belly ache.—Three A.M. To be exact twenty-eight minutes past three.

And all this was yesterday—Yesterday and there at her window I saw her, the lady of my dreams her long and sallow face, held heavily near the glass, overlooking the street where the decayed-meat wagon passes and the ice-cream cart rumbles with its great power and the complicated affairs of the town twitter toward the open sewer in the meadows by the Button Factory. Orange peel, tomato peel floating in a whitish, soapy flow—Her face without expression, the lady I am dying for, her right shoulder as high as her ear, the line of the shoulder sloping down acutely to the neck, her left shoulder also raised so that her head seemed to lie loose in a kind of saddle.

Supreme in stupidity and a fog of waste, profit in what is left. Oh what delectable morsel is left. Blessed hunchback, scum of loves weekly praying in all churches—which by the way take up the very best sites in the town. There she sat, her body low down below the window frame, only her face showing, and looked at me dully, looked because I looked—and my heart leaped up to her in passionate appeal that she should be my queen and run with me over the foggy land—Forward—Onward and upward forever.

So saying the day had progressed toward the afternoon and under the poplars the dried leaves had begun to collect. It had been unbearably hot. September is a hot month. The leaves had fallen one by one. No wind. One by one pushed off by the buds which swollen by the heat had thought that winter was over. Off with you. You stand in the way of progress, say the young leaves. Sitting on his chair he seemed like any other man but to get to the bed he suddenly descended to the floor. On his long arms—he Apollo, and using the stumps of his legs, apelike on all fours and talking quietly he swung himself up over the edge of the bed and lay down.

Over the field—for the fog had left the grasses in the early morning when the sun came up with majestic progression, haughtily leaving the dropping city under him—over the field—for it was late in the afternoon and the sunlight shone in with his poor broken legs, crippled as he was—the sun shone in from the west. The car had turned into the wrong street and he had gone into the store where the paralysed Scotchman whom he had never seen before put him on the way—climbing into his bed sent his rays almost level over a patch of red grass hot and blinding. Over the field the heat rose and in it even from a distance due to the blur of light on their wings a great swarm of gnats could be seen turning, twisting in the air, rising falling—over the grass, fringed with the progressing sun.

But with great sweeps and sudden turns a dozen dragon flies seeming twice as large as they really were, from the sun blurring their transparent wings, darted back and forth over the field catching and eating the gnats. Swiftly the gnats progressed into the dragon flies, swiftly coalescing— and from time to time a droplet of stuff fell from the vent of a feeding dragon fly,—and the little sound of this stuff striking the earth could not be heard with its true poetic force. Lost. Lost in a complicated world. Except in the eyes of God. But a word, a word rang true. Shit, said the father. With this name I thee christen: he added under his breath.

And yet—one must begin somewhere.

Deeply religious, he walked into the back yard and watching lest the children see him and want what they shouldn't have he approached the grape vines. Selecting a bunch of Delawares he picked it with some difficulty spilling a few of the fruit. Then he walked to the other side and found some blue ones. These too he ate. Then some white which he ate also one by one swallowing the pulp and the seeds and spitting out the skins. He continued to eat but no word came to satisfy.

Somehow a word must be found. He felt rather a weight in his belly from eating so many grapes. He, himself that must die someday, he the deeply religious friend of great men and women in incipience, he couldn't find a word. Only words and words. He ate another bunch of the grapes. More words. And never THE word.

A novel must progress toward a word. Any word that— Any word. There is an idea.

His brother was ill. He must go home. The sun will soon be on the Pacific coast. To bed, to bed—take off the clothes beginning on the outside and working in. How would it be to take off the underwear first, then the shirt—

Progress is dam foolishness—It is a game. Either I have or—a thieves' game. Hold me close, closer, close as you can. I can't hold you any closer. I have been stealing. I should never touch anything. I should never think of anything but you. I love another. It is a word. I have left you alone to

run wild with a girl. I would be tame. Lies flicker in the
sun. Visions beset noonday. Through the back window of
the shoe-shine parlor a mass of golden glow flashes in the
heat. Come into my heart while I am running—jumping
from airplane to plane in midair. I cannot stop: the word I
am seeking is in your mouth—I cannot stop. Hold me
against—

You are wrong, wrong Alva N. Turner. It is deeper than
you imagine. I perceive that it may be permissible for a
poet to write about a poetic sweetheart but never about a
wife—should have said possible. It is not possible. All men
do the same. Dante be damned. Knew nothing at all. Lied
to himself all his life. Profited by his luck and never said
thanks. God pulled the lady up by the roots. Never even
said thank you. Quite wrong. Look what he produced. Page
after page. Helped the world to bread. Have another slice
of bread Mr. Helseth. No thank you—Not hungry tonight?
Something on his mind.

The word. Who.

Liberate the words. You tie them. Poetic sweet-heart.
Ugh. Poetic sweet-heart. My dear Miss Word let me hold
your W. I love you. Of all the girls in school you alone are
the one—

Dramatise myself make it sing together as if the world
were a bird who married to the same mate five years understood in the end transmigration of souls.

Nonsense. I am a writer and will never be anything else.
In which case it is impossible to find the word. But to have
a novel one must progress with the words. The words must
become real, they must take the place of wife and sweet-
heart. They must be church—Wife. It must be your wife.
It must be a thing adamant with the texture of wind. Wife.

Am I a word? Words, words, words—

And approaching the end of the novel in his mind as he
sat there with his wife sleeping alone in the next room he
could feel that something unusual had happened. Some-

thing had grown up in his life dearer than—It, as the end. The words from long practice had come to be leaves, trees, the corners of his house—such was the end. He had progressed leaving the others far behind him. Alone in that air with the words of his brain he had breathed again the pure mountain air of joy—there night after night in his poor room. And now he must leave her. She the—He had written the last word and getting up he understood the fog as it billowed before the lights.

That which had been impossible for him at first had become possible. Everything had been removed that other men had tied to the words to secure them to themselves. Clean, clean he had taken each word and made it new for himself so that at last it was new, free from the world for himself—never to touch it—dreams of his babyhood—poetic sweet-heart. No. He went in to his wife with exalted mind, his breath coming in pleasant surges. I come to tell you that the book is finished.

I have added a new chapter to the art of writing. I feel sincerely that all they say of me is true, that I am truly a great man and a great poet.

What did you say, dear, I have been asleep?

CHAPTER VI.

In spite of the moon in mid sky and the plaster of dully shining leaves on the macadam and all the other signs of the approach of fine weather there rang in his head: Such a cuddle muddle: Is that modern German poetry? I never saw such a lot of things mixed together under one title. These are modern times, Pa, airships and automobiles; you cover space—

And that's all right—

O America! Turn your head a little to the left please. So. Now are you ready? Watch my hand. Now: *Lohengrin* in

ITALIAN, SUNG AT MANHATTAN—San Carlo Company Revives Wagner Opera, with Anna Fitziu as Elsa.

Sweet kisses that come in the night—O argyrol!

Rain, rain, for three days and three nights.

In the night a cesura. Suddenly the fire bell begins to ring. I wake with a start and hear the small boy calling from the next room. Eight thousand people wake and count the strokes of the black bells. It is not our signal. Someone has been set afire. The engines pass with a crash and roar of the exhausts. Their siren whistles shriek with a fortissimo rise and fall. In a thousand beds men of forty, women of thirty eight, girls in their teens, boys tired from football practice and little boys and girls down to babyhood wake and think the same thoughts. They listen and count the number of strokes, and sink back saying to themselves: Fire! Presently all but the few who are immediately affected are again asleep. The fire has burnt itself out. Slowly the sun has been crossing Europe and will soon appear fresh from the sea with his benison. The tie of that black thought in the night will be broken. The opportunity will be lost forever. Each will rise and dress and go out into the rain on whatever errand the day has chosen for him.

Rain all day long. The sun does not appear. The heat is suffocating. The rattle of the torrent fills the ears. Water is everywhere.

In the night a wind wakens. It comes from the southwest about midnight and takes the trees by their heavy leaves twisting them until they crack. With a roar the wind batters at the houses, shaking them as if it were a heavy hand. And again for the second night running eight thousand men and women and boys and girls wake and listen or get up to close windows and to look out at the trees leaning with snapping branches, tossing and seething with a sound of escaping steam. It has grown cold. Pull up the covers. It has grown cold. Sixteen thousand hands have drawn the covers closer about the bodies. The wind is cold.

The sun has come back. The air is washed clean. Leaves lie plastered upon the streets, against the tree trunks, upon the very house sides. The bird bath is filled to overflowing. A lame man is hurrying for the train.

They had talked for hours. The new project was beginning to take form. It was the evening of the second day. There stood the train puffing out great volumes of dense smoke which no sooner arose than it was caught in the wind and sent flying out ahead of the train. I wish to God I were on that train wherever it might be going. Oh well, remarked the younger man and said good-bye, which is what it is to be a man.

He was too old, remarked the voice in the room next to the one in which the woman was lying, he never should have gone out in that rain. Too cold! At times it seems possible, even now. She took the hair between her thumb and index finger of the right hand and using her left hand swiftly stroked the little hair strands back toward the head to make it stand out. Ratting it, I told her. It ruins the hair. Oh well I haven't much left, it might as well be broken.

She wore blue stockings under a very quiet dress but the world has not beheld a more maddening spectacle. Devoted to the art of writing, he read with his mind watching her and his mind in the sky seeking, seeking some earth to stand on when the boys were tearing up the soggy turf with their cleats. What to do? There it is. The wind hesitated whether or not to impregnate her. So many things were to be considered. In the years since his passage over Ponce de León's soldiers on the beach—the wind footloose, gnawing the leaves had witnessed flying footballs that it had blown out of bounds. He had not a word to stand on, yet he stood, not knowing why. Fear clutched his heart. Visions of uprooted trees passed over his heart as he shook her heavy skirt about her knees. But she, oblivious to it all, walked with downcast eyes—looking at her feet or smiling pleasantly at one here and there in the crowd that was shouting and pressing to see the players.

In the night all nature was asleep as she lay with her young cheek pressed against her pillow and slept. The boys tossed and turned from the stiffness in their joints and from the bruises received in the game. But she lay quiet and asleep, the breath coming slowly in regular flow from her hollow nostrils moving them slightly back and forth.

Under the covers her young form could be made out, the left shoulder, the hips and the legs and feet, the left knee slightly bent and fallen to the mattress before the other. Not a sound in the room for a million years. Still she lay there asleep.—The wind has turned into hail.

Spring flowers are blossoming in the wind. There is the tulip, the jonquil and the violet—for it is September and no man shall know his defeat. So there are spring flowers that grew up through the ice that will be present later. It is of ice that they have made the flowers.

Yet sometimes it seems that it would still be possible. And this is romance: to believe that which is unbelievable. This is faith: to desire that which is never to be obtained, to ride like a swallow on the wind—apparently for the pleasure of flight.

The swallow's bill is constructed in such a way that in flying with his mouth open tiny insects that enter are ensnared in hair-like gills so that he is fed.

Here are a pretty pair of legs in blue stockings, feed. Yet without the thought of a possible achievement that would make it possible to command the achievement of certain— The boys kick the ball and pay no attention. The boys kick the ball up into the wind and the wind hurriedly writes a love note upon it: Meet me tonight. Say you are going to the Library and I will have my car at the corner of Fern Street. I have something to tell you. There is one word you must hear: You.

There is one word you must hear. It will come out at my lips and enter in at your ears. It might be written with letters on white paper but it is a word that I want you to have out of the lips into your ear. And she answers: I will be there. So he does not keep his appointment. Off he goes in search of a word.

But she goes home and weeps her eyes out. Her pillow is wet with her tears—

What do you think! He has left his wife, and a child in the high school has been ill a week, weeping her eyes out and murmuring his name. Is it not terrible?

It is the wind! The wind is in the poplars twiddling the fading leaves between his fingers idly and thinking, thinking of the words he will make, new words to be written on white paper but never to be spoken by the lips to pass into her ear.

Quietly he goes home to his wife and taking her by the shoulder wakes her: Here I am.

CHAPTER X.

ARNOLD, this wind is, the wise and sagacious captain. Henchman of the wind. The wind is a lion with hooked teeth. The saber-toothed tiger inhabited the region west of the Alleganies throughout the pleistocene age. With a snarl it wrenches the limbs of the trees from their places and tosses them to earth where they lie with the leaves still fluttering.

Vacuous; full of wind. Her whole pelvis is full of intestine but aside from the ptosis I find nothing really wrong. The uterus appears to be normal. The bleeding may come from a cyst. At least there is no good reason for removing —for a hysterectomy. There it is. It. Like some tropical fruit color of the skunk cabbage flower. There it is, that mystical pear, glistening with the peritoneum. Here the cavern of all caverns. Alpha if not omega. Talk politely and obey the law. But do not remove it.

Oh my country. Shall it be a hysterectomy? Arnold there is a wind with a knife's edge.

And Remy says the spring of curiosity is broken at thirty. Nothing left at fifty but the facts of bed and table. He has the lilt of Heine at his best and in places quite equals the work of the author of Danny Deever. The cat-gut had slipped out of the needle. The young interne held the point of the suture between his fingers and the nurse approached the needle as accurately as she could. But the man's hand trembled slightly. For a moment they tried to complete the connection but failing in their attempt the nurse took the end in her other hand and soon had the needle threaded. The young doctor looked up as much as to say thank you.

Such a wind. At fifteen they seem noble, desirable beyond dreams. In the winter the trees at least remain stems of wood that resist with a will, whose branches rebound against the impact of sleet. At thirty they are what they are. The boy rebels and she with her hair in distressed tangles about the disorderly boudoir cap, at mid-day, whines and snatches at him as he jerks and defies her. It is beyond her strength to control a boy of nine. Clutching her dressing sack—oh slobbery morsel—about her breast-less form with one hand she rushes as far as she dares to the porch edge, glancing furtively about for chance gentlemen or neighbors and tries to overtake the youngster. No, the young man has really escaped. He goes to school filthy again and what will they think of his mother.

At fifteen they are slender and coquettish and they cry if you are rough with them. Great burly fellow, she seemed to him all that he was not, the quintessence of Ibsenism, the wind among the reeds. Or perhaps the reed in the wind. Something to love, to take into the arms, to protect—If you can find any reason for doing a hysterectomy doctor, do it. Her husband is good for nothing at all. She at least is a power in her family. She is not like the native American women of her class, she is a Polock. You never saw such courage.

The schooner left Southampton bound for New York with a cargo of rails—steel rails. But the English emigrants were not like these modern messes. Those round, expressionless peasant faces of today. See that one there with the little boy at her side. Castle Garden. At last we are to be in America, where gold is in the streets. Look at that face. That is the kind of immigration we want. Look at the power in that jaw. Look at that nose. She is one who will give two for every stroke she has to take. Look at the intensity of her gaze. Well, she's English, that's the reason. Nowadays they have no more of that sort. These Jews and Polocks, Sicilians and Greeks. Good-bye America!

The head nurse's legs under her practical short skirt were like mighty columns. They held the seriousness of her looks, her steady, able hands. A fine woman.

CHAPTER XI.

THE AMERICAN background is America. If there is to be a new world Europe must not invade us. It is not a matter of changing the y to i as in Chile. They are bound.

The background of America is not Europe but America.

Eh bien mon vieux coco, this stuff that you have been writing today, do you mean that you are attempting to set down the American background? You will go mad. Why? Because you are trying to do nothing at all. The American background? It is Europe. It can be nothing else. Your very method proves what I say. You have no notion what you are going to write from one word to the other. It is madness. You call this the background of American life? Madness?

As far as I have gone it is accurate.

It is painting the wind.

Ah, that would be something.

Mais ça, are you a plain imbecile? That is a game for

children. Why do you not do as so many of your good
writers do? Your Edgar Lee Masters, your Winesburg,
Ohio. Have you not seen the photographs of men and
women on your walls? They are type, as distinct as a
Frenchman or a German. Study these men, know their
lives. You have a real work to do, you have the talent, the
opportunity even. This is your work in life. You Americans, you are wasteful, mad—

Our background.

You would paint the wind. Well, it has been tried—many
times, and do you know where that leads?

I know where it has led.

But do you know? Have you seen, felt, heard what they
have seen, felt, heard, our Villons—

Apollo was out of breath but the nymph was more tired
than he. The chase must soon have ended when she falling
to her knees half from the will to be there half from fatigue
besought her mistress Diana to save her from the God's
desire. And she was changed into a laurel bush.

All about the hills where they stood the hard waxen
leaves of the laurel glistened above the dead leaves of the
hardwood trees, the beech, the maple, the oak.

You imagine I am French because I attack you from the
continental viewpoint. You are wrong. I am from the country of your friends Moussorgsky, Dostoiefsky, Chekov. At
least if you will not yield me the point that America cannot
be new, cannot do anything unless she takes the great heri-
tage which men of all nations and ages have left to the
human race.

You mean that I should not be an American but—Turge-
nef, enjoy you more if, well, if you were more comprehen-
sible, a little more particular, *vous comprenez?* You sweep
out your arms, you—I see no faces, no details of the life,
no new shape—

The druggist's boy cannot be distinguished from his
master when he says, Hello, over the phone—Is that what
you mean?

Well, you are very much children, you Americans.

It is not to be avoided as far as I can see.

Let us have now a beginning of composition. We have had enough of your improvisations.

I am consumed by my lusts. No American can imagine the hunger I have.

It is the itch, monsieur. It is neurasthenia. Desire is not a thing to speak of as if it were a matter of filling the stomach. It is wind, gas. You are empty my friend. Eat. Then and then only.

Like all men save perhaps the Chinese you are most transparent when you imagine yourself most protected.

Her bosom reached almost to her knees. That morning in the October garden she had picked a violet for him and placed it in his coat. Watching the feet of men and women as they touched the pavement a strong odor of violets crossed his path.

He turned and saw the massive Jewess waddling by. It had been good perfume too.

These Polocks. Their heads have no occiput. They are flat behind. It is why when they put on their American hats the things slip down about their ears. The nigger's head isn't that way. You know how the bump goes out behind in so many of them. The club sandwich on her plate kept sliding apart, the top slice of bread would slip. Then she took the pieces in her fingers and poked the lettuce in under the sheet. On her breast was a black pin. It formed a circle. She looked up with her mouth full of food and resting both elbows on the table chewed America thoughtfully while she held the state of Maryland in her firm fingers. The ends of each finger were stubby, the nails cut short and as clean as well manicured nails could well be. Clatter, clatter, clatter. He could see himself in the plate glass behind her. He was conscious of his hat which he had not removed. He was at this table with these five women—one of them young, ready—and he had not removed his hat. There was in fact no place to put it.

I am begging, frankly. Ten cents a ticket. I have to raise fifty dollars by the end of next week. We want to fit up a room in our hall where the colored working girls can come and rest. On Thursdays we serve tea. Then they go back to the office. When the impact is over the man must think. I tell you I do not contemplate with relish seeing my children bred out of all these girls. Is it wrong? Well, I thought you said you had an appetite. Impregnate eighty of them, right and left as you see them here in this room. It would not be impossible. I cannot think of my children running about in the environment in which these have to live. My dear sir, you are a fool. You are lying to yourself—As to the girls, I frankly desire them. I desire many, many, many.

There she sat on the bench of the subway car looking idly about, being rushed under the river at great speed to the kitchen of her mother's flat. Malodorous mother. Or wrinkled hard-put-to-it mother. Savior of the movies. After the impact his great heart had expanded so as to include the whole city, every woman young and old there he having impregnated with sons and daughters. For everyone loved him. And he knew how to look into their eyes with both passion and understanding. Each had taken him to her soul of souls where the walls were papered with editorials from the Journal and there he had made himself father to her future child. As they went upstairs he saw how her heels were worn—Who will understand the hugeness of my passion?

But he had understood. The truth lay under the surface. Why then not—No two can remain together without training. Who better than that one who is practiced. The faithful husband of the clothing store madam is used to her. They functionate well together. He puts his hat in the right place. His money in the right bank. His arm fitted in just the posture best suited to their mutual height and width. All their practices were mated.

But he was an outsider. He was new to all. Her shoes are stitched up the back.

Card-index minds, the judges have. Socialism, immorality and lunacy are about synonyms to the judge. Property is sacred and human liberty is bitter, bitter, bitter to their tongues.

Walk up the stairs there little girl. But she is naked! These are all doctors. So the little tot struggled up the very high clinic steps, naked as she was, and all the doctors looked at her. She had some spots on her body that had been there a year. Had I been her father I would know why I am a fool.

Naked and free, free to be damned in to hell by a chance vagrant to whom she had taken a fancy. Her father did not know her. Did not even know that she existed. Cared less. We will look after her said the head doctor.

III

Fiction

from **A Voyage to Pagany**

EVANS walked, though very tired, for several hours on the principal streets of the city, up the avenue de l'Opera, etc., seeing the famous dancers on the portico, all verdigris, and dirtied by the birds. Lit dimly from below he saw the lyre of Apollo featured at the peak of the opera façade and remembered the story: When the poet Verlaine had died and from his poverty-stricken room they were bearing his body up the avenue, a state funeral, to bury it, as they approached the Opera, suddenly the great golden lyre was seen to totter in its fastenings and fall!

He looked at the lyre, refastened in its place.

On the boulevard des Italiens, Evans admired the toylike clocks in the windows of several jewelry stores, their tiny pendulums going, visibly, at a great pace back of a hole in the face—something he had not seen before. But he was filled with a strangeness inexplicable—satisfying—by it all. It was, as far as he could gather it, walking. How much one escapes by just being here, how much of lying, how much of stupidity!

He went for supper to a small place next to the Theater du Vieux Colombier. There the waiter brought his Chateaubriand, serving him a portion of it from the plate and putting the remainder of the steak aside, on a shelf—which Evans let him do, half-suspecting he was stealing it, which exactly, he was doing, and did.

A crier came in from the theater announcing the last act of the play.

Waking next morning at the Beausoir, Evans looked out of the window as three planes went by slowly overhead in

133

flying goose formation. The sky was clear, the sun was shining. He flung open the window and saw an old fellow in baggy underwear walking about his room across the court.

Paris! He felt ridiculously delighted. He pried into every corner of his room, the small familiar violin-shaped *bidet* was there. This made him think of Mme. de Pompadour. He smiled contentedly.

Without ringing he dressed and went out. Brioche and coffee on the sidewalk at the corner. Fresh butter. A woman at the *caisse*, prim, neat, keen-eyed. Snappy.

On the street an old woman was selling mimosa from a bunch in her hand.

There was the usual morning market on the boulevard Raspail. Evans crossed over, watching the orderly line of people waiting for the bus, each pulling his serial ticket from the bunch fastened to the post, each waiting his turn. Orderly and intelligent. He needed some fresh collars. Walked over to the Bon Marché. They were having a white sale.

Collars, he said to a floor walker standing in frock coat and high collar facing the door.

To the right in the rear.

All about the floor were heaps of linen and cotton sheets, pillow cases, etc. Even at this hour the place was crowded with women in shawls, poker-faced housewives, going about from place to place. But the heaps of stuff were on the floor, the floor was dirty. Towels were being trampled, the edges of sheets were black here and there.

A wash cloth.—He had a devil of a time to remember what it was in French. Yes. He found what he wanted and found a girl to take it up for him.

Follow me, she said. He did so—delighted, grinning to himself.

She took him to the *caisse*. There they checked off the purchase, took his money and entered the transaction in longhand in a great ledger. He was amazed.

The boy who sold the collars asked him the size, which Evans could not, of course, give in centimeters—so they guessed at it. You have a neck *à peu près* the same as my own.

You have the damnedest way of selling things in this city, said Evans. I should think you'd pass out with all this running back and forth, to and from the cashier's desk.

Yes, I've heard they do it better in New York. He smiled. I'd like to take that place in.

Why don't you? said Evans.

Some day, perhaps, but what can you do?

He was a good-looking kid in a stiff collar and a frock coat. He certainly was earning his money.

And I suppose they—of course—they were balancing as they went.

What a country!

Then he went out with his collars, a wash cloth, a nail brush and a leather purse that smelled to be of goat's hide, in a bundle in his hand.

Delight was his on this January morning. Everything seemed to function with economy and precision: the eggs in flat baskets in the stores, fruit, the neatly cut and tied bundles of meat, the children with blue jumpers over their clean clothes, going to school.

He stopped in at the Post Office on the rue de Rennes and sent a *pneu* to his sister: he had not—purposely—told her when he would arrive.

Then, going back to the hotel to rid himself of his bundle, he ran directly into his friend Jack, looking a little stouter, a good bit wiser, but dressed with the same engaging nonchalance as ever. The two friends, the older and the younger, greeted each other enthusiastically.

Never had Evans forgotten the balance of spirit, the distinguished attack upon life which had charmed him with Jack Murry from the moment of their first meeting in New York. The firm, thin-lipped lower face, jaw slightly thrust out, the cold blue eyes, the long, downward-pointing, slightly-hooked straight nose, the lithe, straight athletic build. The whole picture was there—almost intact.

How would it be inside? for they had had great plans together for rescuing life from the thicket where it is caught in America, the constant pounding on the head. They had worked hard to get to an expression—and Jack had left—to marry.

That night at 42nd Street when they had parted and Evans knew it was all up, tears had stood in their eyes. Jack had showed him his new clothes, they had spoken of continuing a scheme for publishing good writing—and Jack had sailed next day.

Oh well, that's America, Evans had written down in his mind.

Now here was Jack. They shook hands a long time. Dropping the bundle at the hotel, they set out on foot talking as they strode.

You must meet—so and so and so. Van Cleve is not in Paris just now.

They stopped for a moment at the Dome while Evans told Jack his plans. Then they set out again walking and it was important. They went past La Closerie des Lilas.—There's Harland, said Jack. We won't stop now. See him later.

They were no business partners, no members of a cabinet, not even members of a team. How would they get on? How do men ever get on without some business together? Brothers never do. In the same ship, the same regiment—maybe. There is the Field Marshal, the General, the Major, the Colonel, the Captains, the Sergeants and the privates or it is on a ship. The order keeps them down. The order kills it all. But, as Walsh said, you can't even get drunk with a guy any more without having the name pasted on you.

Evans thought of his English father. How the devil do you love a man anyway? Either you slop over or fight or else you avoid each other. He had admired his father, in some things; loved him—for a few things. But here in Paris, nothing to do—he felt uneasy with Jack.

To hell with what anybody else says, anyway. Evans loved his friend, as some one who brought over to him a section of life where *he* was weak to get at it, too shy, superstitious, too stately reverential.

He loved his younger friend for the bold style of his look at life. Often, when Jack demolished situations and people with one bark, Evans smiled to himself at the rudeness of it, the ruthlessness with which so much good had been mowed down. But he himself never could have done that. Jack struck at the false and, in the thicket of good where it lay, it perished—along with a number of other things. But when Jack ignorantly had smitten, he Evans freely could breathe.

God bless Jack, he had said to himself a thousand times, I love him. I stand for him.

But when it came to saying anything to Jack about it— nothing doing. They walked in together and through the Luxembourg gardens, down between the lines of chestnut trees toward 12 rue de l'Odéon, to get the mail.

Evans saw the French children of the better classes playing around the basin. He didn't admire their dolled-up appearance. It isn't the lack of births that keeps the French population down, it's that so damned many of them die before they are five years old. The French are the worst people in the world for bringing up kids.

They went on past the gloomy buildings of the Senate.

If we had anything to do together—anything—

Already Jack was getting on his nerves.

Merely to walk and to talk—What?

The modern ideal is the prize ring. Men socking men on the jaw. A gentlemanly art. That's all.

But if you want to know a man, if you find him excellent, why you've got to have something to do together. You've got to work.

Why do you have to do anything? Why the hell do you have to work anyway?

Jack and Evans, wide apart as to ages, were not so far apart in general appearance. Evans needed Jack. Jack had rescued him in America, rescued him from much stupidity, from dullness, at a certain time when he needed just that. Evans thought he had aided Jack to get going.

What remained of all that now? One can't go on just beating the air. Was it still there after these three years past?

Each knew the other's antecedents pretty well. Perhaps there was nothing left.

Evans had begun to be depressed without knowing why, at first.

There was no mail at the bookshop. Coming out they hopped into a taxi.

What in God's name did I come here for?

My generation has done one thing, Jack started off, it isn't afraid to be called anything. It—they're not going to be frightened into anything either, by a lot of spineless—just tell them to move along when they get too thick.

Evans didn't know.

He was disturbed, avowedly. The connotations of his affection for Jack with nothing he could do about it—nothing to do—the slipping, slipping way the world has of getting out from under a difficulty and presenting the wrong face of an object, while it gives you, yes, perhaps what you ask, distressed him heavily.

They were lounging in the taxi. Evans looked out across the place St. Sulpice at the façade of the great church which had given the square its name.

How get in? Where was Jack? Why else then was he, Evans, a writer? He *would* do something about it, *something* at least.

Being a writer he could at least make it into a book, a poem, a novel. But he didn't want to make it into anything. He wanted Jack and he did not want a makeshift. He wanted to be let in, he wanted to let Jack in.

He grew angry because as he thought, they wanted to make him do what he wasn't even interested in doing, or if he didn't do that, they wouldn't let him speak to Jack.— You might as well pick up a sailor; but you can't find this—

What was it he found in young Murry? What does anybody find in anybody? Something he can't get except through that somebody. The luck of it gave that one the chance to look in and see; to look through.

Evans wanted to be let in.

Was it literature? To hell with literature. Was it to know the details of Jack's life? Evans didn't know he had any. Was it his soul? What the hell is that? It's to get *through* something. To get down to it, or up to it. There wasn't any act, that Evans knew, that would do any good for that. Not that he knew of.

Yes, you shouldn't be afraid, but you shouldn't let them hand you a sack of guts either—or kid you into thinking you want it. Some day, maybe he'd have to come to that but not yet a while, not while there was any chance of getting through whole.

Maybe Jack didn't need him any longer.

A sudden coldness went over Evans. Jack suddenly faded far away. Evans looked at him coldly and asked himself what Jack had ever done to warrant his, Evans', liking —except to be decorative, as he was.

But to get down to what? That was what it amounted to. What to do, not in desperation and whining self-pity but— whole. How are we going to get to know each other again? said he aloud.

What do you mean? said Jack. Then he went on, You've got to see a whole lot of things over here, people first. They all want to know you, they've read your stuff. Like it.

Evans had forgotten where they were going. Oh yes, to the bank. They stopped the taxi. Jack got his cash and they went on to sit for a while at the Café de la Paix.

Then as J. spoke of his plans for publishing, Evans' mood began again to revive.

So it was the desire to get down to some sort of sense about writing, then, that was the cement for their friendship and there Evans decided to stop for to-day. Jack had a

fresh mind on paper. He was distinguished—as a writer. It
made no difference to Evans that he hadn't done anything
much as yet. Evans knew better than that he should fail—
and that's love. Yes, he still loved Jack.

That ended that. He got up positively—Let's go. Jack
liked that and they set off. They took another taxi, Evans
improvising to himself on the streets, staring out.

Now they were coming back again to Montparnasse, and
again Evans saw the façade of St. Sulpice with its severe
front and wondered what in God's name it signified. *La
Cathédrale Englouti*—signified Debussy. He said that. But
there, square stone blocks ornamented with carvings.
What? You looked at it. Devout people were going in at the
doors. Devout? What? Is it a poem? So is the grass. Leaves
of Grass: America, because the people are common as grass
—and as green; nothing showy; on the ground. True
enough, but what of that? Does that help?

Love. Everybody talks about love. It's the commonest
thing in the world. There are no two kinds of love. Love is
love. The moralist will tell you that. You love someone,
that is all. If you love a girl, you want to have a baby. If you
love a man, you want to have—what? If you love a girl,
you don't want to have a baby at all. You just have one.
You love her and after a while you have a baby. He
thought of Panurge and the lady of Paris—called her a
name.

It's love and how do these medieval church fortresses
help? Love. Where is it on them? I don't see any love. Yes,
it's one kind, a kind of official love, museums of love!
That's what churches are.

This amused him—Museums of love presided over by
men to watch the cases so that you don't take anything
precious. I wonder if the jewels in the Louvre are real and
if they still look as large as ever.—His mind flew off.

He looked out of the windows of the taxi, and wondered
which of these old houses of the Latin Quarter it was in
which his uncle had first slept soundly.

He saw the Musée du Luxembourg.—Paris is love, Paris is the living cathedral of the world. But what of to-day? He did not pray for help. He was interested and felt glad he was there.

CHAPTER V. THE SUPPER

THE third day of his stay in the French capital Evans called, as he would think of it in the following weeks, just Paris. He had had a wildly sleepless night. But in the morning he received a note he had been expecting. It read: Arrived safely. All set. Wednesday evening at the Quai d'Orsay. Signed, Lou.

All right. America to the fore. And with that he put all trouble behind him, arose and went out into the air.

This was the night for which Jack had promised him the literary banquet. At noon he was to lunch with his sister and their aunt. Now he went for a stroll toward the *Champs Elysées*.

As he crossed the river before the *Chambre des Députés* he leaned to watch more closely the fish-catching. The poles were so long, the men so staid-looking, the fish so bright and shiny and so small that he could not but laugh.

Again as he walked he saw men and women greeting each other familiarly with kisses on the street. It was the Paris that charmed him. Just the sense one had of being there—just Paris. But it seemed absurd that the greatest thrill he had that morning was when, still early, he stumbled by chance upon the *place François Premier*.

This tiny gray plaza, but a step from the great *Arc de Triomphe*, did for him exactly what he wanted France that day to do. Standing there he found himself all unconsciously addressing the low gray houses, with the small plot of grass around the statue in the center, as if it were a person.—Where did you come from, you beautiful creature "with the cross between your horns?"—Thrills coursed up and down his spine, tears came to his eyes as if he had been a starved man looking upon a fruitful oasis. It seemed ridiculous even to him to be thus standing there crying; he looked around hurriedly to see if there were any from whom he should hide his tears. But the cobbled streets abutting upon the little symmetrical place were all empty.

And still he stood and looked at the low gray houses ranged around in a hexagonal symmetry and, feeling broken down, low, peasant-plain, he put a pear, which he had just bought, again to his lips like a country bumpkin and looked, asking himself what it was all about. Was it just an *asile*, an escape from roar to quietude and symmetry? This did not seem quite enough. As far as he could tell, it said *Braque*. It linked completely with the modern spirit. It was France, cold, gray, dextrous, multiform, and yet gracious—its smallness, in their case, endeared it to him. It came all pressed up ready to understand, to be understood, to carry away like the bundles they handed you so graciously in the department stores.

He walked thoughtfully on, eating his pear.

But at the bridgehead facing the *Ecole Militaire*, he stopped again at a piece of brilliance unequalled in his experience: there passed a high-powered motor car, a limousine of great size and most immaculate blackness, with two men in staid untrimmed livery on the front seat. But the car shone, the glass flashed brilliantly as if specially polished, and inside Evans saw two boys about twelve and fourteen years of age, blossoms of a stagnant birth rate, males exquisitely finished, sitting in position on the back seat with eyes as brightly burning as the car was brightly polished, but restrained, symmetrical, one like the other: design, intelligence and a cold fire. . . .

At the Trianon, where Jack had arranged for the supper, the regular patrons of the little restaurant with the strong cellar smell in the entrance corridor, were departing. In the back room six or eight small tables were placed end to end

before the upholstered wall-bench to one side and in a
moment eight or ten of the guests arrived. Others followed
—more than were invited for this is the custom, it seems, in
Paris. These were mostly English and Americans who Jack
thought might be interested in Evans; at least, he wanted to
honor Evans by having them meet him. For the few things
Dev had contributed now and again to the lesser known
literary papers had been frequently admired.

Evans was a man who enjoyed writing. He wrote
because he loved it and he wrote eagerly, to be doing well
something which he had a taste for, and for this only did he
write. As far as wishing to advance his acquaintanceship by
his writing, or to advance himself, it never entered his
mind. If they liked it, he was entranced; if not, he didn't
blame them. So that now he felt uneasy. But none let him
be so for long.

With the American cocktails the conversation became
general and before many minutes it became uproarious.
Evans need not have worried about himself. They asked
him for a speech, which he could not make. He said something stupid in his embarrassment, however—something he
never forgave himself for saying, and Jack heard it. Something about the honor that is done corpses in Paris—where
all men on the street doff their hats when a funeral is passing.

But it was a magnificent dinner, wine flowed fast and
expensively. Jack sang Bolliky Bill. Others sang. H. tried
vainly to shout a sailor story across the table. Some ate for
the week, perhaps. But some were silent and looking.

Evans drank. Some one kissed him. He grasped the arm.
He was being swallowed. He playfully nipped the tender
skin of his admirer below the elbow with his teeth—Is not
this what is required?

But he knew Jack was watching him.

To him it all meant nothing, something that might be for
some one else; he drank, he was restless. He was glad it was
over.

Back to the Dome went many of the guests, others turning home early. For the former, after several highballs, taxis were chartered when out they all piled at a nigger joint on the other side of the river.

Jack forgot everyone and stood from then on at the bar. He drank.

Evans drank and danced with Delise whom they had picked up at the Dome. He had at once formed a passionate attachment for this sleek-haired American woman. The minute he had looked at her clear eyes, Evans had determined to keep close to her. She was wildly hilarious that night. Before many minutes she was on the table taking off her stockings. One foot at a time she held in the air removing the shoe, then the stocking, then putting back the shoe she repeated the process with the other leg. Dev was jammed in between two others on the cushion side of the table next the wall. Delise jumped down forcing herself next to him and turning at once looked full into his eyes while the others, seeing how things stood, found other interests. They two became oblivious to everyone as he began to kiss her again and again.

No one paid any attention.

Delise jumped to her feet in another instant and seeing Jack at the bar, she ran over and grabbed him by the hand. Out into the middle of the floor she drew him and there they danced—wildly. Several well-groomed men at another table applauded her loudly. She danced like mad, her bare legs flying. Jack followed her as a foil till he was tired and went back to the bar.

Dev, slightly drunk, could not get up and go, he could not. He looked and admired her. One of the gentlemen outside the party got up. Delise accepted his offer. They danced to the nigger jazz all over the place. An American sailor and a French girl now got on the floor; this was the girl Dev knew was going to the tuberculosis sanatorium in the morning.

Delise left the floor and acknowledging the gentleman's bow carelessly she came back to Dev's table, panting, placing her arms out flat on the cold surface and her head over them, panting. Dev stroked her hair.

Dev thoughtfully kissed the back of her neck, tenderly, lovingly—with greatest admiration and tenderness.

What a delightful thing—drunkenness. He grew furious at the damned stupidity of his people. Whose people? Look, he thought, at this beautiful girl, this armed, able woman. Look! compare her with that, that God damned hell hole of a country.—He wanted to be profane. Instead he kissed her arms, admiringly, tenderly again, with intensity, with peculiar heat such as he knew, he knew—but who else would understand it in him? He was a timid fool—not at all; only *he* knew, or could ever know.

He kissed her drunkenly. But she looked up with an understanding smile and taking him with her they were on the floor together, nobody watching them.

But Evans was a poor dancer. The fire was not in him for that. Maybe it was his age. Once he had danced. Delise soon left him and then all moved out once more to the taxis. It was three A.M. Where shall we go now? To the Dingo.

There, there was a crowd at the bar. They sat, Dev and Delise, to themselves in a corner and Dev patted her face between his hands, the drink bothered him a little but it gave, it gave much. There was an English woman in the corner gathering up her man, her man in a dress suit, silly, paralyzed, helpless, drunk. But Dev shook his own head a little to clear his vision and—caressed Delise. She was quiet.

Why are there not more men like you, dear? she said. He looked hard at her clear eyes. You are tender, kind. Nobody else knows how to be so kind.—Dev only kissed her. She leaned over the table into his arms; tenderly he held her as if it were the whole world he were holding. Amazed, puzzled, wishing nothing else, knowing it was nothing.

Leaning closer she confided to him her jealousy over Garda. Her feeling that when Maurice smiled at her, at Garda, that she, Delise, couldn't bear it. Why are you so good, why are you so good? Why do I tell you this? she kept saying. You ask for nothing.—She leaned over and nipped the graying hair at his temples with her sharp white teeth. You don't ask for anything. What is it?

Dev felt—as he always felt: what? And that's all he could say. What? What? I love you. I love to kiss you, dearest. But what? What?

Then he drank, drank and slept with his head on his arm. Delise had gone to another table and was leaning upon another's shoulders. Later, all went out to a little place near the Gare Montparnasse. They had fried eggs with the laborers who came there for breakfast.

Jack didn't eat. He was drunker than Evans. He was peevish.

They left the others and walked home in the dawn. Jack felt quarrelsome.

The trouble with you, Dev, he said, is that you're a damned fool. Didn't know you were so soft.

Yes.—But it cut deep. The whole thing was clear to Evans. The assinine attempt at a speech, and so forth, and so forth, and so forth. Anyhow, he felt that way. To hell with all of them then.

Why don't you *do* something?—and there were worse things said.

The Venus

WHAT THEN is it like, America?

It was Fräulein von J. talking.

They were on their way to take the train to Frascati, the three of them—she, her companion, and Evans.

In reply, he shook his head, laughing—and they hurried on to catch the car.

She could speak English well enough, her companion could not, Dev's German was spasmodic coming in spurts for a moment or two but disappearing as suddenly leaving him tongue-tied. So they spoke English and carried their lunch. A picnic. He was delighted.

This day it was hot. Fräulein von J. seemed very simple, very direct, and to his Roman mood miraculously beautiful. In her unstylish long-sleeved German clothes, her rough stockings and heavy walking-shoes, Evans found her, nevertheless, ethereally graceful. But the clear features, the high forehead, the brilliant perfect lips, the well-shaped nose, and best of all the shining mistlike palegold hair unaffectedly drawn back—frightened him. For himself he did not know where to begin. But she looked at him so steadily for some strange reason, as if she recognized him, that he was forced at last to answer her.

The tram was packed to the doors with passengers. Just before starting three treelike Englishwomen had come rushing up calling out distractedly in English that the tram must not go, that somebody was coming— Do you see her? Oh, what can have happened? She had the correct information, et cetera—until finally Clara arrived just in the moment of the tram's departure and clambered aboard desperately, not a minute too soon. So that now they stood in the aisles, the four of them, sweating and glowering at the Italian men, who oblivious to such violence had long since comfortably settled themselves in their seats.

Fräulein von J. was placed immediately before Evans looking at him absorbedly like a child. Not knowing what else to do or to say, he too looked (as the tram went through some bare vineyards) straight back into her clear blue eyes with his evasive dark ones. She lifted her head a little as if startled, flushed (he thought) just a trifle but did not change her gaze. So they continued, to look fixedly among the backs and across the coats of the Englishwomen in the aisle, who were jabbering away disturbedly about the threatening weather. She did not stir to look away but seemed to rest upon his look with mild curiosity and no nervousness at all. It was, as usual, his look which faltered.

Hearing the talk of the Villa this and the Villa that, about to be visited, Evans felt that he wished he could lose this crowd and was more than pleased when Fräulein von J. suggested that as soon as they should get to Frascati they head for the open country, delighted to find that her mood suited his own so well.

At the market place of Frascati, where a swarm of guides and carriages swooped down upon them, the three pic-nickers moved off at right angles to the direction taken by the rest, up a road that led between two walls around behind the town. They did not know where they were or indeed anything about the place or its beauties—they didn't care. Fräulein wanted to see the Italian springtime, that was the most definite of their spoken desires and Dev, sick of antiquities and architectural beauties, was more than willing to follow. The companion disliked Italian gardens anyway, lacking as they do the green profusion of the northern trees. With this they started, beginning at once to see violets along inside the fences, violets they could not reach. Following a brook which ran beside them, contrariwise down the hill, they trampled on, heading for open country.

What is it like, America? And so Dev began to tell her— Not like this—and all the time somehow he was thinking of his sister. Where is Bess? I wish she were here! till walking and talking, leaving the town behind them, they came quite out into the fields with a hill on the left and a little village off in the distance across the valley before them. They were in a worn dirt gully high hedged on both sides with banks cut into narrow paths by goats' hoofs. Before them four absorbed children gathering violets rushed forward in the path by ones and twos rivalling each other in their efforts to pounce upon the finer groups of flowers.

The children paid no attention whatever to the three hikers, not even by so much as one glance. Running ahead with cries of delight, each racing to exceed the others, they soon disappeared through gaps in the hedge. Evans was over and over startled by the German girl's delicate colouration and hair and eyes. Also, her hands were lovely, her ankles, firm—like the Venus, thicker than the stage or dance-hall type, but active too—just suggestive enough of the peasant to be like a god's.

You have not told me yet, what it is like, America.

It is like, Dev began, something muffled—like a badly trained voice. It is a world where no man dare learn anything that concerns him intimately—but sorrow—for should we learn pleasure, it is instantly and violently torn from us as by a pack of hungry wolves so starved for it are we and so jealous of each of us is our world.

I think I know what you mean, she replied, it is that we are all good citizens on top and very much better than that inside. It makes me think of the *Johannesfeuer.* You know Sudermann's play?

America is a pathetic place where something stupefying must always happen for fear we wake up. Yes, I have read the play.

By this time they had come quite around behind Frascati

hill. Here they had lunch in a diminutive, triangular grove of oaks where there was a grassy bank with a few daisies on it, and the tall trees bending overhead. Then climbing through a fence they took the road again up to the right around the hill climbing steeply now on a stony path. It was a hard walk this part of the way and before long they were tired, especially Frau M. who was glad to stop near the top and rest.

But after a few words in German which Dev missed, Fräulein von J. cried, Come on! and they two went on alone about two hundred yards ahead up to the woody summit, to a place from which they could see Frau M. below them lying under an ash-tree. Here there were a few stones of some ancient construction almost gone under the wood soil and rotted chestnut leaves. It was a chestnut grove cut and counter cut by innumerable paths which led north over the brow of the hill—to Frascati, no doubt. But now at this early season, the place was deserted. The random, long, dart-shaped dry leaves covered the ground all about them, two foreigners resting on the old stones. Elsa waved to Frau M. from where she sat, then she turned again to Evans, Tell me what you are. You do not mind? I want to know everything. What is America? It is perhaps you?

No, Dev shook his head.

Is it something to study? What will it do? Shall we go there to learn? she asked in rapid succession.

Dev shook his head.

But you will return to it?

Yes.

Why?

Habit.

No, it is something.

It is that I may the better hide everything that is secretly valuable in myself, or have it defiled. So safety in crowds—

But that is nothing. That is the same as in Europe.

America seems less encumbered with its dead. I can see nothing else there. It gives less than Europe, far less of

everything of value save more paper to write upon—nothing
else. Why do you look at me so? Dev asked her.

Because I have seen no one like you in my life, few Americans, I have talked to none. I ask myself, are you an
American?

And if I am—

Then it is interesting.

He said, To me it is a hard, barren life, where I am
"alone" and unmolested (work as I do in the thick of it)
though in constant danger lest some slip send me to perdition
but which, being covetous not at all, I enjoy for the seclusion and primitive air of it. But that is all—unless I must add
an attraction in all the inanimate associations of my youth,
shapes, foliage, trees to which I am used—and a love of
place and the characteristics of place—good or bad, rich or
poor.

No, she continued, it is not that.

Evans felt at that moment, that there was very little in
America. He wanted to be facetious but the girl's seriousness was not a thing to be fooled. It made him pensive and
serious himself.

He could say—that it was just a place.

But you must not tell me that America is nothing, she
anticipated him, for I see it is something, and she looked
at him again with her little smile. You seem to me a man like
I have not seen before. This is America?

I am a refugee, Dev continued, America is or was a beginning, to clean out the—

Then, she replied, it is as in Germany. I did not think so
when I saw you.

And I, Dev answered, did not think so when I saw you.

Why am I in Rome, do you think? she queried next.

He did not know.

To become a nun.

And with a shock he remembered the German youths in
their crimson gowns whom he had seen filing down the
Quirinal, down the long steps; the Scotch youths playing

soccer in the Borghese Gardens Sunday afternoon with their gowns tucked up, or doffed, garters showing and running like college athletes for the ball. He remembered too, the Americans with the blue edge to their gowns, the Spanish, the French.

Yes, she continued, that is it. I am in Rome to feel if the church will not offer me an answer. I was fourteen years old when the war ended. I have seen the two things—to throw myself away or to take hold again. I have seen the women running in the stadiums, I have seen them together. If we were peasants, we could be nearer—but we must lose it all, all that is good. I am a German, an East Prussian. My mother is dead. My father is a general—of course. What shall I do? I do not want anything— Tell me what is America. You must say. Is it just a place to work?

Dev nodded.

You see that I am young—I am young, of course. You come to me carrying a message. I do not know what to do. I believe you will tell me. I am not a fool—and I am not gifted either. There is nothing for me. Is there? I cannot walk about letting my hair loose to surprise men because it is so yellow. You perhaps, yes, if you please—and she smiled —but not those whom I do not want. I cannot marry. It makes me sick to marry. But I want, I want. I do not care that I am a virgin or not. No. No. That is childish. I cannot remain as I am—but I must—until this (and she tapped her forehead) is satisfied. You have said something to me. What do I say to you?

Dev thought "running wild" that if they should do as he wished they would both end that night in the jail at Frascati hungry and very much disturbed—possibly—but no more than that. Fool.

They speak to me of my body. It is beautiful. For what? Of what use to me?

She talked quite coolly.

Within a few years I must lose this. Why not? and I have nothing else unless it is a mind to have, to have and nothing that I want. Not painting, not music, philosophy, tennis—for old men, for young men, for women? No. America, that seems something new.

You would find nothing in America, Evans quickly interposed. The girls there cannot go half a mile out of town for fear a Negro might rape them, or their complexions be spoiled by the weather or the Japanese come too close or they be buried in snow or baked in summer; or they marry their business managers or secretaries and live together two or three in apartments. Their thoughts are like white grass so heavily have they been covered by their skins — and so heavily covered are they to protect them from the weather that when they are uncovered they do not exist. One must snatch another up quickly from the general supply, from a patent container. — Evans was ashamed of this speech of which as a fact Fräulein von J. understood not one word. But the few women he had admired were not pretty and the pretty ones he did not admire. — Never think of America, he concluded. The men are worse than the women.

Are you then one?

Evans had no reply.

When I saw you, I saw something unusual, I am never mistaken. I saw something different from what I see every day, neither throwing away nor taking hold to the old horrible handle, all filthy — Is it America? I asked, but you tell me nothing. It is because you will not do so.

America, he began again haltingly, is hard to know.

Yes, she answered, because she had made him serious so that he must speak his mind or say nothing.

I think it is useful to us, he continued, because it is near savagery. In Europe, you are so far from it that maybe you will have to die first before you will live again. But Dev was not such a fool — Europe, I do not know, he corrected himself. I am seeing a few superficial moments only.

But he had a quick pupil. That is enough, replied Fräulein von J. I see now what I saw at the beginning. You are a savage, not quite civilized — you have America and we have not. You have that, yes it is something.

It is very difficult, said Dev. I am not a typical American. We have a few natives left but they would not know me—

You are holding on to something, she said.

It is very difficult, Dev went on—something very likely to be lost, this is what— So he took out the flint arrowhead he had in his pocket and showed it to her.

She was impressed. She held it hard in her hand as if to keep its impression there, felt the point, the edge, tried it, turned it over.

Yes, she said, I have seen the same thing from our own fields, more finished work—but it is very far, very far. No one believes it is real. But this you carry in your coat? It is very strange. Where did you find it?

In a corn-field in Virginia, there are many of them there.

Are there many Americans who know this that you are saying?

Dev shook his head. I have seen but a few. There are pictures pressed into my mind, which have a great power of argument. Summer pictures mostly, of my part of the country, one of the old pioneer houses fast to the ground. There is nothing like them in Europe. They were not peasants, the people who built them, they were tragic men who wasted their wits on the ground—but made a hard history for me—not for me only, I think; they were like all the earlier peoples but it has been so quick and misplaced in America, this early phase, that it is lost or misinterpreted—its special significance.

You think then it might be useful to—me? Yes, that was what I saw in your eyes. She looked again. Yes, it is so.

She shook her head gently from side to side in marveling realization. Come, she said, I was right. What an America is that! Why then did you not look at me all this week? I was troubled. I wondered what was the matter with me.

Dev said he had been excited studying something he wanted among the antiquities.

But a feeling almost of terror, Dev thought, mixed with compassion perhaps, came now into her eyes as she continued to look at him.

It must be even more lonesome and frightening in America than in Germany, she said. She shook her head. She seemed as if looking off into a new country and to be feeling the lonesomeness of it.

America is marvelous, replied Dev, grossly prosperous—
She shuddered, No. So were we. So will we be soon again. She was frightened. How can you stay where you are? Why do you stay there? You make the church impossible—but you are alone. I will pray for you.

They started to get up quietly from their serious mood and were rather startled to find themselves still in the surroundings of this pagan grove. Not too sure were they that they knew each other as well as they had been feeling they did for the few moments of hard sympathetic understanding just past, projecting themselves out; each feeling, each trying hard, to get at the other's mood. They laughed, and Dev gave her his hand but she did not move away.

It is very difficult, she said, for us to support ourselves after we have passed the semi-consciousness of the peasant, and his instinct. We fall back, do we not? You are brave, she said, to want to find some other way—and one that is American. It seems curious to me.

Moving to rejoin Frau M. they saw that it was getting on into the afternoon and that they must be stepping along if they would be back in Rome by nightfall.

You believe in America like a church, mused Fräulein von J. almost to herself.

Dev did not think so.

Do you believe then that the church is an enemy to your belief?

Yes.

She looked away.

Oh come on, said Dev, let's get out of this.

Life Along the Passaic River

ABOUT NOON of a muggy July day, a spot of a canoe filled by the small boy who no doubt made it, lies west of the new 3rd St. Bridge between Passaic and Wallington, midstream opposite the Manhattan Rubber Co.'s red brick and concrete power plant. There's a sound of work going on there, and a jet of water spouts from a pipe at the foundation level below the factory onto the river's narrow mud bank which it has channeled making a way for itself into the brown water of the two hundred foot wide stream. The boy is drifting with the current but paddling a little also toward a couple of kids in bathing suits and a young man in his shirt sleeves, lying on what looks to be grass but is probably weeds across the river at the edge of an empty lot where they dumped ashes some years ago, watching him. These youngsters who make boats out of barrel hoops and a piece of old duck, wherever they find it, live by the river these hot summer days. It's a godsend to them.

They're all over the city as soon as they can walk and say, Paper! even when perhaps it's the only thing they can say. Pre-kindergarten stuff, watching the next corner below their brother's where he can keep an eye on them and at the same time cover twice the ground, coming tearing uphill encumbered by the news under the left arm to get change for a quarter. Or along the canal where they back the freights in, by the cobbled street in front of the wholesalers, sorting over half-rotten oranges and fennel and stuffing the outer leaves of lettuce heads into a burlap bag. Struggling home with firewood on a misassorted set of four wheels. Or

156

clown-grey with ashes from the dumps and another wagon
of the sort woggling under a sack of reclaimed coals, a
morning's work. Blind, crippled, orphaned. Classroom per-
verts driving the teacher mad. Vaccinating herself with a
piece of sharp tin to obey the order, remain in line, and cir-
cumvent the sloth of her parents. Objecting to being called
out of their names: Don't call me Dick Baker. Here they are,
on the steps of the Y.M., about a hundred of them from
black Wops right on through to white-haired Polacks, a
regular zoo, lined up before the main entrance having their
pictures taken. Restless. With the sun in their faces making
them blink. Just sitting there waiting.

Most of the younger men who have jobs wear blue shirts
and sit on the pavement along the wall outside the factory
smoking during the noon hour. But this one was standing on
a corner on the way north out of town. Not bad looking.
The kind you don't mind picking up, just about of age, in an
unpressed suit and a soft hat. No violent jerking with the
thumb and hand. Just the eyes. Thanks. He gets in. Cigarette? I don't mind. How far you going? Westover. Where's
that? Not far, just up here a way. I'll tell you when we come
to it. Takes a light. Looking for work? Just came off the
road. Selling? No, just dropped off the freights for a while,
leaving again tomorrow morning. This your home town?
Yes. How far'd you get? The coast. You don't say. How are
things out there? Worse than here. No work? Shakes his
head. I was up and down the whole coast and back again
through the country. Have you a trade? Yes, baker's appren-
tice. But I don't like the ovens and the hours. Not for me.
Tell me something: How does a fellow eat when he's travel-
ling that way? Back doors. Hm. Can you always get something? Most always, I didn't eat so bad. But there must be
times—Sure. Once in a while. I went forty-eight hours twice
without eating. How was it? Not bad. I always take good
care of myself. Lots of them gets sick; the hospitals are full
of them all over the country. Not me. I never been sick a

day. The next corner. Here? That's it. You mean here? Sure.
There's a good swimming hole back in the woods there. Just
the day for a swim too, I envy you. Why don't you join us?
—Courteous, with every air of travel and experience—I
haven't a suit. You don't need any.

All the streets of the Dundee section of Passaic have men
idling in them this summer. Polacks mostly, walking around
—collars open, skinny, pot-bellied—or sitting on the steps
and porches of the old-time wooden houses, looking out of
place, fathers of families with their women folk around
them. You see a few niggers, but they're smiling. Jews, of
course, trying to undersell somebody else or each other and
so out of the picture. But the Polacks look stunned, mixed
up, don't know what it's all about. Not even enough coin to
get drunk on. They'll do for the whole bunch. The kid in
the boat is probably a Polack. Anyhow, it doesn't make any
difference, the Polacks will do.

I'll bet the boat isn't four feet long, doesn't look as if it
would hold even a child. It's almost up to the gunwales as it
is in the small waves of the river. It's only been a few years
since the river water was so full of sewage and dye-waste
from the mills that you didn't want to go near it, much less
swim in it as they do now—or boat on it. It was a good job
to build the Passaic Valley Sewer and clean up that stink
hole. And in a way, although they need the money, it's a
good job to get the Polacks out of the factories even if it is
because there's no work for them. And it's a good job to
have the kid paddling that way on the river and the other
kids off to camp. It's what they need. You can see it by the
looks on their faces. They've needed it a long time. You can
see that too on their faces.

They're a husky bunch, mostly. Take for instance the one
in the derby hat who was coming up the street just now—a
six-footer, looking like the usual bum in the vaudeville shows
you'd think might be leaning down any minute to get his
hooks onto a cigar stub. No hurry. And as he gets near

the 1927 open car parked at the curb with the two wooden-faced guys sitting in the front seat staring off into space, loafing, suddenly he gives a hoarse yell at them as much as to say, To hell with you! without looking up, and goes on slowly by, a kind of threatening, cursing growl with plenty of lung power behind it as if he might be chasing kids he'd caught stealing peanuts from a stand. The two hardly noticed him, didn't even move. And he didn't even raise his face either but went on by as if he'd never said a word. Looked drunk. What are you going to do with a guy like that. Or why want to do anything with him. Except not miss him.

Yeah, I know. The kid in the boat is only a kid and don't know a thing more than he's doing. You can't expect a big Polack in a derby to go paddling a canoe on the river just for the hell of it. He's up against it; he's got to be what he is. O.K. Let him stay lit then. Something like that. Maybe it'll slow things up and let them sink in a little after a while. Take that other thickhead they made a place for down at the finishing mill, in Joe Hick's department; they do everything for him and he turns on them and abuses them. Fine! That'll make 'em think. But some of the younger guys, a few girls and kids of all ages from around four to ten, go down and fish for crabs all day long where the old docks are mostly rotted away and the reconditioned excursion boat Mary Ann is tied up. They've started running it to Coney Island every Sunday, a dollar the round trip, the first time such a thing has been tried around here for the past quarter of a century. Not a bad racket at that and a good trip, well worth the dollar—if you've got it.

It's all right in the sun, but the sun can't do everything. It can't make up for what's past. Even the kid in the boat, when he comes in, take a look at him. He's sun-burned all right; but the shape of his head is funny, his chest's too high, and he's got that old look to his face you see sometimes. The same goes for the young guys in the street passing the ball, waiting for Sunday so they can get out on the lot and show their stuff. It's the way they live, from the start up. Two rooms. Three kids in one bed. And all that. Take the girls for instance, take a good look. Not so bad, some of them. But they try to get their big feet into shoes three sizes too small for them and think they're making a hit. Anybody that knows anything spots them the minute they make the first move. It's written all over them. No use trying to kid yourself about things like that. If your shoes fit you and they're made of good leather, if you know what good leather is, and you have straight heels on them, you're getting somewhere. What did you say? The girls' feet look like flat tires in most of the things they don't know enough not to buy and to wear. Try and stop them doing it.

Look at this one lying on the autopsy slab at the hospital; you can see the whole thing. Twins. About five months on the way. Just a kid she was, nineteen, with a lot of soft yellow hair piled up in shiny coils, and her mottled face half leaning toward it. Good legs. A fine pair of breasts. Well-shaped arms. She's dead all right, and if you get what I mean, that's not such a bad thing either. But good God, what for? And the way she did it! all burned down her neck that way. Some guy got to her—someone that couldn't marry her maybe. Her mother gave it to us straight when she says the kid never stepped out nights like some of the other girls. Maybe that's why it happened. She was always home, the only one the old woman could count on to do anything around there. But anyway somebody has her. She's caught. So what? You can imagine, a religious girl like that. Who's going to give her fifty dollars for a doctor even if she knows enough to find one and go to him? She knows it won't make any difference anyway. She's sunk. So she drinks the stuff while her family's left her to attend a funeral. If you can make sense out of that, go to it.

It's all right to be wise, but you got to watch that too. There's no way to learn it easy. And it brings plenty trouble.

All you gotta do is rake in the old coin. Is that so? Last week two of those kids were out in a boat on the river a mile below the city when the oar of one of them struck something half sunk in the water. The body of a man. They pushed it in to shore and quickly called up the police. The head and arms had been cut off and the feet too when they came to look—though that didn't make him any deader. A few hours later they found another body stuck somewhere further up stream. Nobody knows who they were. Dumb all right. But there's no kidding even about a couple of dead punks when you can't find out who did it—so's to send their kids to college. Sure. What are they gonna do? Somebody's got to put up a fight and break into the rich racket. It can't always be the same guys. Somebody's got to get the good screws. They ain't nobody's suckers. All they say is: There it is. Somebody's gonna get it. Why not me? They're not taking it from nobody. If their kids wanna go to college, they can send 'em. And they'll have the best there is there. Sure. Just a lot of gorillas, a lot of mugs. Who says so? That don't bother them none. And if that's all the kids is gonna learn, phooie for them. And if they don't learn nothing else it's because they ain't never gonna know nothin'. And there ain't nobody can't teach 'em.

When they had the big strike at the textile mills, and that bright boy from Boston came down and went shooting off his mouth around in the streets here telling us what to do: Who paid for having their kids and women beat up by the police? Did that guy take a room down on Monroe St. and offer his services for the next ten years at fifty cents a throw to help straighten out the messes he helped get us into? He did not. The Polacks paid for it all. Sure. And raised up sons to be cops too. I don't blame them. Somebody's got to take the jobs. Why get excited? But they ain't moved away none; that's what I'm saying. They're still here. Still as dumb as ever. But it's more than that guy ever give up or could think to do to help them.

Just the same old crap. What are you gonna do with more money when you get it? Take a trip to the old country? You'll come back. It's no different there from here, except worse because it's lasted longer. Then what are you gonna do? Nobody's gonna teach it to you; you got to learn it yourself. Maybe though the kids'll get wise quicker and do something—if they get the breaks with the factories still more interested in dumping sewage cheap than keeping the river clean, and fighting it through the courts every time the Commission tries to finish the job right and puts the screws to them. That kind of thing.

Farther downstream at the County Bridge where they are replacing the rotten piling and timber-work of the bridge apron, twenty or more men lean every day on the iron guard rail and beside them small boys and little girls in beach pyjamas soiled across the behind, looking through the latticed grill work, watching the work going on below. The telephone cable got fouled in some way, and they had to send a diver down to free it for repairs. He worked from a scow tied under the middle span. You can see the diver now, in his undershirt, bareheaded and beginning to be bald, kneeling on the scow deck with his deflated suit laid out before him, the helmet—toward the bridge—and the clumsy bootlike feet being the only parts of it to keep their shape. Sailor fashion he's sewing up a tear in the fabric of one leg while the line on the bridge, Polacks mostly, lean their bellies against the hot iron-work looking down at him, learning something. A whole lot of things. Teaching them too, maybe.

It's an eye opener what you have time for these days. Somebody with nothing else to do but take a walk for himself found a coin, said to be gold! along the riverbank above the bridge this week. So it's been a regular mob of them walking up and down there ever since, thinking where there's been one piece maybe you'll find another, if you look long enough. And someone did find another coin, copper! today, with the date 1864 on it. But where there used to be a tree, a big tree, some years ago there's the remains of it now, a stump lying on its side with roots sticking up into the air ten feet or more above the riverbank. Tired of walking in the mud and finding nothing, a Polack, another one in his shirt sleeves, a man of about thirty I imagine, has climbed up among these roots to sit, holding on among them as in a saddle, where he can look down and watch the others prowling around with crooked sticks in their hands poking up the mud.

Not many gets away with the big stuff, straight, if you can call it straight, or crooked. The young men, in their twenties or early thirties, when they have a hard job on their hands often use shirts with the sleeves ripped out at the shoulders to give themselves more arm room. Swell looking muscles. What for? What good are they to a man when someone lands a slug of lead between his ribs? And you don't get to be a Delegate lifting quarter-ton bales onto a truck all day long either. You might as well take and trim the rim off an old soft hat the way they do sometimes, to keep their hair slicked down while working, that is, if you don't travel. Then you can run a scollop around the edge and cut the top full of airholes, stars, circles, and all that. And good luck to you. You got to say, sometimes, the older men, out of work and sitting around with their families, may be getting the breaks after all, as far as that goes. The kids will run out like the four orphans from the asylum—in the dark and storm—when they saw the railroad tracks undermined. They flagged the train with their coats, standing between the rails, determined not to give ground at any cost. And as a reward asked to be taken to see The Babe knock it, just once, out of the lot. Cuckoo! Cuckoo as a funny strip. But at that it's not so funny.

The Use of Force

THEY WERE new patients to me, all I had was the name, Olson. Please come down as soon as you can, my daughter is very sick.

When I arrived I was met by the mother, a big startled looking woman, very clean and apologetic who merely said, Is this the doctor? and let me in. In the back, she added. You must excuse us, doctor, we have her in the kitchen where it is warm. It is very damp here sometimes.

The child was fully dressed and sitting on her father's lap near the kitchen table. He tried to get up, but I motioned for him not to bother, took off my overcoat and started to look things over. I could see that they were all very nervous, eyeing me up and down distrustfully. As often, in such cases, they weren't telling me more than they had to, it was up to me to tell them; that's why they were spending three dollars on me.

The child was fairly eating me up with her cold, steady eyes, and no expression to her face whatever. She did not move and seemed, inwardly, quiet; an unusually attractive little thing, and as strong as a heifer in appearance. But her face was flushed, she was breathing rapidly, and I realized that she had a high fever. She had magnificent blonde hair, in profusion. One of those picture children often reproduced in advertising leaflets and the photogravure sections of the Sunday papers.

She's had a fever for three days, began the father and we don't know what it comes from. My wife has given her things, you know, like people do, but it don't do no good.

164

And there's been a lot of sickness around. So we tho't you'd better look her over and tell us what is the matter.

As doctors often do I took a trial shot at it as a point of departure. Has she had a sore throat?

Both parents answered me together, No . . . No, she says her throat don't hurt her.

Does your throat hurt you? added the mother to the child. But the little girl's expression didn't change nor did she move her eyes from my face.

Have you looked?

I tried to, said the mother, but I couldn't see.

As it happens we had been having a number of cases of diphtheria in the school to which this child went during that month and we were all, quite apparently, thinking of that, though no one had as yet spoken of the thing.

Well, I said, suppose we take a look at the throat first. I smiled in my best professional manner and asking for the child's first name I said, come on, Mathilda, open your mouth and let's take a look at your throat.

Nothing doing.

Aw, come on, I coaxed, just open your mouth wide and let me take a look. Look, I said opening both hands wide, I haven't anything in my hands. Just open up and let me see.

Such a nice man, put in the mother. Look how kind he is to you. Come on, do what he tells you to. He won't hurt you.

At that I ground my teeth in disgust. If only they wouldn't use the word "hurt" I might be able to get somewhere. But I did not allow myself to be hurried or disturbed but speaking quietly and slowly I approached the child again.

As I moved my chair a little nearer suddenly with one cat-like movement both her hands clawed instinctively for my eyes and she almost reached them too. In fact she knocked my glasses flying and they fell, though unbroken, several feet away from me on the kitchen floor.

Both the mother and father almost turned themselves

inside out in embarrassment and apology. You bad girl, said the mother, taking her and shaking her by one arm. Look what you've done. The nice man . . .

For heaven's sake, I broke in. Don't call me a nice man to her. I'm here to look at her throat on the chance that she might have diphtheria and possibly die of it. But that's nothing to her. Look here, I said to the child, we're going to look at your throat. You're old enough to understand what I'm saying. Will you open it now by yourself or shall we have to open it for you?

Not a move. Even her expression hadn't changed. Her breaths however were coming faster and faster. Then the battle began. I had to do it. I had to have a throat culture for her own protection. But first I told the parents that it was entirely up to them. I explained the danger but said that I would not insist on a throat examination so long as they would take the responsibility.

If you don't do what the doctor says you'll have to go to the hospital, the mother admonished her severely.

Oh yeah? I had to smile to myself. After all, I had already fallen in love with the savage brat, the parents were contemptible to me. In the ensuing struggle they grew more and more abject, crushed, exhausted while she surely rose to magnificent heights of insane fury of effort bred of her terror of me.

The father tried his best, and he was a big man but the fact that she was his daughter, his shame at her behavior and his dread of hurting her made him release her just at the critical moment several times when I had almost achieved success, till I wanted to kill him. But his dread also that she might have diphtheria made him tell me to go on, go on though he himself was almost fainting, while the mother moved back and forth behind us raising and lowering her hands in an agony of apprehension.

Put her in front of you on your lap, I ordered, and hold both her wrists.

But as soon as he did the child let out a scream. Don't, you're hurting me. Let go of my hands. Let them go I tell you. Then she shrieked terrifyingly, hysterically. Stop it! Stop it! You're killing me!

Do you think she can stand it, doctor! said the mother.

You get out, said the husband to his wife. Do you want her to die of diphtheria?

Come on now, hold her, I said.

Then I grasped the child's head with my left hand and tried to get the wooden tongue depressor between her teeth. She fought, with clenched teeth,. desperately! But now I also had grown furious—at a child. I tried to hold myself down but I couldn't. I know how to expose a throat for inspection. And I did my best. When finally I got the wooden spatula behind the last teeth and just the point of it into the mouth cavity, she opened up for an instant but before I could see anything she came down again and gripping the wooden blade between her molars she reduced it to splinters before I could get it out again.

Aren't you ashamed, the mother yelled at her. Aren't you ashamed to act like that in front of the doctor?

Get me a smooth-handled spoon of some sort, I told the mother. We're going through with this. The child's mouth was already bleeding. Her tongue was cut and she was screaming in wild hysterical shrieks. Perhaps I should have desisted and come back in an hour or more. No doubt it would have been better. But I have seen at least two children lying dead in bed of neglect in such cases, and feeling that I must get a diagnosis now or never I went at it again. But the worst of it was that I too had got beyond reason. I could have torn the child apart in my own fury and enjoyed it. It was a pleasure to attack her. My face was burning with it.

The damned little brat must be protected against her own idiocy, one says to one's self at such times. Others must be protected against her. It is social necessity. And all these things are true. But a blind fury, a feeling of adult shame, bred of a longing for muscular release are the operatives. One goes on to the end.

In a final unreasoning assault I overpowered the child's neck and jaws. I forced the heavy silver spoon back of her teeth and down her throat till she gagged. And there it was —both tonsils covered with membrane. She had fought valiantly to keep me from knowing her secret. She had been hiding that sore throat for three days at least and lying to her parents in order to escape just such an outcome as this.

Now truly she *was* furious. She had been on the defensive before but now she attacked. Tried to get off her father's lap and fly at me while tears of defeat blinded her eyes.

A Night in June

I was a young man then—full of information and tenderness. It was her first baby. She lived just around the corner from her present abode, one room over a small general store kept by an old man.

It was a difficult forceps delivery and I lost the child, to my disgust; though without nurse, anesthetist, or even enough hot water in the place, I shouldn't have been overmuch blamed. I must have been fairly able not to have done worse. But I won a friend and I found another—to admire, a sort of love for the woman.

She was slightly older than her husband, a heavy-looking Italian boy. Both were short. A peasant woman who could scarcely talk a word of English, being recently come from the other side, a woman of great simplicity of character—docility, patience, with a fine direct look in her grey eyes. And courageous. Devoted to her instincts and convictions and to me.

Sometimes she'd cry out at her husband, as I got to know her later, with some high pitched animalistic sound when he would say something to her in Italian that I couldn't understand and I knew that she was holding out for me.

Usually though, she said very little, looking me straight in the eye with a smile, her voice pleasant and candid though I could scarcely understand her few broken words. Her sentences were seldom more than three or four words long. She always acted as though I must naturally know what was in her mind and her smile with a shrug always won me.

Apart from the second child, born a year after the first, during the absence of the family from town for a short time, I had delivered Angelina of all her children. This one would make my eighth attendance on her, her ninth labor.

Three A.M., June the 10th, I noticed the calendar as I flashed on the light in my office to pick up my satchel, the same, by the way, my uncle had given me when I graduated from Medical School. One gets not to deliver women at home nowadays. The hospital is the place for it. The equipment is far better.

Smiling, I picked up the relic from where I had tossed it two or three years before under a table in my small laboratory hoping never to have to use it again. In it I found a brand new hypodermic syringe with the manufacturer's name still shiny with black enamel on the barrel. Also a pair of curved scissors I had been looking for for the last three years, thinking someone had stolen them.

I dusted off the top of the Lysol bottle when I took it from the shelf and quickly checking on the rest of my necessities, I went off, without a coat or necktie, wearing the same shirt I had had on during the day preceding, soiled but—better so.

It was a beautiful June night. The lighted clock in the tower over the factory said 3:20. The clock in the façade of the Trust Company across the track said it also. Paralleling the railroad I recognized the squat figure of the husband returning home ahead of me—whistling as he walked. I put my hand out of the car in sign of recognition and kept on, rounding the final triangular block a little way ahead to bring my car in to the right in front of the woman's house for parking.

The husband came up as I was trying to decide which of the two steep cobbled entry-ways to take. Got you up early, he said.

Where ya been? his sister said to him when we had got into the house from the rear.

I went down to the police to telephone, he said, that's the surest way.

I told you to go next door, you dope. What did you go away down there for? Leaving me here alone.

Aw, I didn't want to wake nobody up.

I got two calls, I broke in.

Yes, he went away and left me alone. I got scared so I waked him up anyway to call you.

The kitchen where we stood was lighted by a somewhat damaged Welsbach mantel gaslight. Everything was quiet. The husband took off his cap and sat along the wall. I put my satchel on the tubs and began to take things out.

There was just one sterile umbilical tie left, two, really, in the same envelope, as always, for possible twins, but that detail aside, everything was ample and in order. I complimented myself. Even the Argyrol was there, in tablet form, insuring the full potency of a fresh solution. Nothing so satisfying as a kit of any sort prepared and in order even when picked up in an emergency after an interval of years.

I selected out two artery clamps and two scissors. One thing, there'd be no need of sutures afterward in this case.

You want hot water?

Not yet, I said. Might as well take my shirt off, though. Which I did, throwing it on a kitchen chair and donning the usual light rubber apron.

I'm sorry we ain't got no light in there. The electricity is turned off. Do you think you can see with a candle?

Sure. Why not? But it was very dark in the room where the woman lay on a low double bed. A three-year-old boy was asleep on the sheet beside her. She wore an abbreviated nightgown, to her hips. Her short thick legs had, as I knew, bunches of large varicose veins about them like vines. Everything was clean and in order. The sister-in-law held the candle. Few words were spoken.

I made the examination and found the head high but the cervix fully dilated. Oh yeah. It often happens in women who have had many children; pendulous abdomen, lack of muscular power resulting in a slight misdirection of the forces of labor and the thing may go on for days.

When I finished, Angelina got up and sat on the edge of the bed. I went back to the kitchen, the candle following me, leaving the room dark again.

Do you need it any more? the sister-in-law said, I'll put it out.

Then the husband spoke up, Ain't you got but that one candle?

No, said the sister.

Why didn't you get some at the store when you woke him up; use your head.

The woman had the candle in a holder on the cold coal range. She leaned over to blow it out but misdirecting her aim, she had to blow three times to do it. Three or four times.

What's the matter? said her brother, getting weak? Old age counts, eh Doc? he said and got up finally to go out.

We could hear an engineer signaling outside in the still night—with short quick blasts of his whistle—very staccato —not, I suppose, to make any greater disturbance than necessary with people sleeping all about.

Later on the freights began to roar past shaking the whole house.

She doesn't seem to be having many strong pains, I said to my companion in the kitchen, for there wasn't a sound from the labor room and hadn't been for the past half hour.

She don't want to make no noise and wake the kids.

How old is the oldest now? I asked.

He's sixteen. The girl would have been eighteen this year. You know the first one you took from her.

Where are they all?

In there, with a nod of the head toward the other room of the apartment, such as it was, the first floor of an old two-story house, the whole thing perhaps twenty-five feet each way.

I sat in a straight chair by the kitchen table, my right arm, bare to the shoulder, resting on the worn oil cloth.

She says she wants an enema, said the woman. O.K. But I don't know how to give it to her. She ain't got a bed-pan or nothing. I don't want to get the bed all wet.

Has she had a movement today?

Yeah, but she thinks an enema will help her.

Well, have you got a bag?

Yeah, she says there's one here somewhere.

Get it. She's got a chamber pot here, hasn't she?

Sure.

So the woman got the equipment, a blue rubber douche bag, the rubber of it feeling rather stiff to the touch. She laid it on the stove in its open box and looked at it holding her hands out helplessly. I'm afraid, she said.

All right, you hold the candle. Mix up a little warm soapy water. We'll need some vaseline.

The woman called out to us where to find it, having overheard our conversation.

Lift up, till I put these newspapers under you, said my assistant. I don't want to wet the bed.

That's nothing, Angelina answered smiling. But she raised her buttocks high so we could fix her.

Returning ten minutes later to my chair, I saw the woman taking the pot out through the kitchen and upstairs to empty it. I crossed my legs, crossed my bare arms in my lap also and let my head fall forward. I must have slept, for when I opened my eyes again, both my legs and my arms were somewhat numb. I felt deliciously relaxed though somewhat bewildered. I must have snored, waking myself with a start. Everything was quiet as before. The peace of the room was unchanged. Delicious.

I heard the woman and her attendant making some slight sounds in the next room and went in to her.

Examining her, I found things unchanged. It was about half past four. What to do? Do you mind if I give you the needle? I asked her gently. We'd been through this many times before. She shrugged her shoulders as much as to say, It's up to you. So I gave her a few minims of pituitrin to intensify the strength of the pains. I was cautious since the practice is not without danger. It is possible to get a ruptured uterus where the muscle has been stretched by many pregnancies if one does not know what one is doing. Then I returned to the kitchen to wait once more.

This time I took out the obstetric gown I had brought with me, it was in a roll as it had come from the satchel, and covering it with my shirt to make a better surface and a little more bulk, I placed it at the edge of the table and leaning forward, laid my face sidewise upon it, my arms resting on the table before me, my nose and mouth at the table edge between my arms. I could breathe freely. It was a pleasant position and as I lay there content, I thought as I often do of what painting it was in which I had seen men sleeping that way.

Then I fell asleep and, in my half sleep began to argue with myself—or some imaginary power—of science and humanity. Our exaggerated ways will have to pull in their horns, I said. We've learned from one teacher and neglected another. Now that I'm older, I'm finding the older school.

The pituitary extract and other simple devices represent science. Science, I dreamed, has crowded the stage more than is necessary. The process of selection will simplify the application. It touches us too crudely now, all newness is over-complex. I couldn't tell whether I was asleep or awake.

But without science, without pituitrin, I'd be here till noon or maybe—what? Some others wouldn't wait so long but rush her now. A carefully guarded shot of pituitrin—ought to save her at least much exhaustion—if not more. But I don't want to have anything happen to her.

Now when I lifted my head, there was beginning to be a little light outside. The woman was quiet. No progress. This time I increased the dose of pituitrin. She had stronger pains but without effect.

Maybe I'd better give you a still larger dose, I said. She made no demur. Well, let me see if I can help you first. I sat on the edge of the bed while the sister-in-law held the candle again glancing at the window where the daylight was growing. With my left hand steering the child's head, I used my ungloved right hand outside on her bare abdomen to press upon the fundus. The woman and I then got to work. Her two hands grabbed me at first a little timidly about the right wrist and forearm. Go ahead, I said. Pull hard. I welcomed the feel of her hands and the strong pull. It quieted me in the way the whole house had quieted me all night.

This woman in her present condition would have seemed repulsive to me ten years ago—now, poor soul, I see her to be as clean as a cow that calves. The flesh of my arm lay against the flesh of her knee gratefully. It was I who was being comforted and soothed.

Finally the head began to move. I wasn't sorry, thinking perhaps I'd have to do something radical before long. We kept at it till the head was born and I could leave her for a moment to put on my other glove. It was almost light now. What time is it? I asked the other woman. Six o'clock, she said.

Just after I had tied the cord, cut it and lifted the baby, a girl, to hand it to the woman, I saw the mother clutch herself suddenly between her thighs and give a cry. I was startled.

The other woman turned with a flash and shouted, Get out of here, you damned kids! I'll slap your damned face for you. And the door through which a head had peered was pulled closed. The three-year-old on the bed beside the mother stirred when the baby cried at first shrilly but had not wakened.

Oh yes, the drops in the baby's eyes. No need. She's as clean as a beast. How do I know? Medical discipline says every case must have drops in the eyes. No chance of gonorrhoea though here—but—Do it.

I heard her husband come into the kitchen now so we gave him the afterbirth in a newspaper to bury. Keep them damned kids out of here, his sister told him. Lock that door. Of course, there was no lock on it.

How do you feel now? I asked the mother after everything had been cleaned up. All right, she said with the peculiar turn of her head and smile by which I knew her.

How many is that? I asked the other woman. Five boys and three girls, she said. I've forgotten how to fix a baby, she went on. What shall I do? Put a little boric acid powder on the belly button to help dry it up?

Jean Beicke

During a time like this, they kid a lot among the doctors and nurses on the obstetrical floor because of the rushing business in new babies that's pretty nearly always going on up there. It's the Depression, they say, nobody has any money so they stay home nights. But one bad result of this is that in the children's ward, another floor up, you see a lot of unwanted children.

The parents get them into the place under all sorts of pretexts. For instance, we have two premature brats, Navarro and Cryschka, one a boy and one a girl; the mother died when Cryschka was born, I think. We got them within a few days of each other, one weighing four pounds and one a few ounces more. They dropped down below four pounds before we got them going but there they are; we had a lot of fun betting on their daily gains in weight but we still have them. They're in pretty good shape though now. Most of the kids that are left that way get along swell. The nurses grow attached to them and get a real thrill when they begin to pick up. It's great to see. And the parents sometimes don't even come to visit them, afraid we'll grab them and make them take the kids out, I suppose.

A funny one is a little Hungarian Gypsy girl that's been up there for the past month. She was about eight weeks old maybe when they brought her in with something on her lower lip that looked like a chancre. Everyone was interested but the Wassermann was negative. It turned out finally to be nothing but a peculiarly situated birthmark. But that kid is

176

still there too. Nobody can find the parents. Maybe they'll
turn up some day.

Even when we do get rid of them, they often come back
in a week or so—sometimes in terrible condition, full of
impetigo, down in weight—everything we'd done for them
to do over again. I think it's deliberate neglect in most cases.
That's what happened to this little Gypsy. The nurse was
funny after the mother had left the second time. I couldn't
speak to her, she said. I just couldn't say a word I was so
mad. I wanted to slap her.

We had a couple of Irish girls a while back named
Cowley. One was a red head with beautiful wavy hair and
the other a straight haired blonde. They really were good
looking and not infants at all. I should say they must have
been two and three years old approximately. I can't imagine
how the parents could have abandoned them. But they did.
I think they were habitual drunkards and may have had to
beat it besides on short notice. No fault of theirs maybe.

But all these are, after all, not the kind of kids I have
in mind. The ones I mean are those they bring in stinking
dirty, and I mean stinking. The poor brats are almost dead
sometimes, just living skeletons, almost, wrapped in rags,
their heads caked with dirt, their eyes stuck together with
pus and their legs all excoriated from the dirty diapers no
one has had the interest to take off them regularly. One
poor little pot we have now with a thin purplish skin and
big veins standing out all over its head had a big sore place
in the fold of its neck under the chin. The nurse told me
that when she started to undress it it had on a shirt with a
neckband that rubbed right into that place. Just dirt. The
mother gave a story of having had it in some sort of home in
Paterson. We couldn't get it straight. We never try. What
the hell? We take 'em and try to make something out of
them.

Sometimes, you'd be surprised, some doctor has given the
parents a ride before they bring the child to the clinic. You

wouldn't believe it. They clean 'em out, maybe for twenty-five dollars—they maybe had to borrow—and then tell 'em to move on. It happens. Men we all know too. Pretty bad. But what can you do?

And sometimes the kids are not only dirty and neglected but sick, ready to die. You ought to see those nurses work. You'd think it was the brat of their best friend. They handle those kids as if they were worth a million dollars. Not that some nurses aren't better than others but in general they break their hearts over those kids, many times, when I, for one, wish they'd never get well.

I often kid the girls. Why not? I look at some miserable specimens they've dolled up for me when I make the rounds in the morning and I tell them: Give it an enema, maybe it will get well and grow up into a cheap prostitute or something. The country needs you, brat. I once proposed that we have a mock wedding between a born garbage hustler we'd saved and a little female with a fresh mug on her that would make anybody smile.

Poor kids! You really wonder sometimes if medicine isn't all wrong to try to do anything for them at all. You actually want to see them pass out, especially when they're deformed or—they're awful sometimes. Every one has rickets in an advanced form, scurvy too, flat chests, spindly arms and legs. They come in with pneumonia, a temperature of a hundred and six, maybe, and before you can do a thing, they're dead.

This little Jean Beicke was like that. She was about the worst you'd expect to find anywhere. Eleven months old. Lying on the examining table with a blanket half way up her body, stripped, lying there, you'd think it a five months baby, just about that long. But when the nurse took the blanket away, her legs kept on going for a good eight inches longer. I couldn't get used to it. I covered her up and asked two of the men to guess how long she was. Both guessed at least half a foot too short. One thing that helped the illusion besides her small face was her arms. They came about to her

hips. I don't know what made that. They should come down
to her thighs, you know.

She was just skin and bones but her eyes were good and
she looked straight at you. Only if you touched her anywhere, she started to whine and then cry with a shrieking,
distressing sort of cry that no one wanted to hear. We
handled her as gently as we knew how but she had to cry
just the same.

She was one of the damnedest looking kids I've ever seen.
Her head was all up in front and flat behind, I suppose from
lying on the back of her head so long the weight of it and
the softness of the bones from the rickets had just flattened
it out and pushed it up forward. And her legs and arms
seemed loose on her like the arms and legs of some cheap
dolls. You could bend her feet up on her shins absolutely
flat—but there was no real deformity, just all loosened up.
Nobody was with her when I saw her though her mother
had brought her in.

It was about ten in the evening, the interne had asked me
to see her because she had a stiff neck, and how! and there
was some thought of meningitis—perhaps infantile paralysis.
Anyhow, they didn't want her to go through the night without at least a lumbar puncture if she needed it. She had a
fierce cough and a fairly high fever. I made it out to be a
case of broncho-pneumonia with meningismus but no true
involvement of the central nervous system. Besides she had
inflamed ear drums.

I wanted to incise the drums, especially the left, and
would have done it only the night superintendent came
along just then and made me call the ear man on service.
You know. She also looked to see if we had an operative
release from the parents. There was. So I went home, the
ear man came in a while later and opened the ears—a little
bloody serum from both sides and that was that.

Next day we did a lumbar puncture, tapped the spine
that is, and found clear fluid with a few lymphocytes in it,
nothing diagnostic. The X-ray of the chest clinched the

diagnosis of broncho-pneumonia, there was an extensive involvement. She was pretty sick. We all expected her to die from exhaustion before she'd gone very far.

I had to laugh every time I looked at the brat after that, she was such a funny looking one but one thing that kept her from being a total loss was that she did eat. Boy! how that kid could eat! As sick as she was she took her grub right on time every three hours, a big eight ounce bottle of whole milk and digested it perfectly. In this depression you got to be such a hungry baby, I heard the nurse say to her once. It's a sign of intelligence, I told her. But anyway, we all got to be crazy about Jean. She'd just lie there and eat and sleep. Or she'd lie and look straight in front of her by the hour. Her eyes were blue, a pale sort of blue. But if you went to touch her, she'd begin to scream. We just didn't, that's all, unless we absolutely had to. And she began to gain in weight. Can you imagine that? I suppose she had been so terribly run down that food, real food, was an entirely new experience to her. Anyway she took her food and gained on it though her temperature continued to run steadily around between a hundred and three and a hundred and four for the first eight or ten days. We were surprised.

When we were expecting her to begin to show improvement, however, she didn't. We did another lumbar puncture and found fewer cells. That was fine and the second X-ray of the chest showed it somewhat improved also. That wasn't so good though, because the temperature still kept up and we had no way to account for it. I looked at the ears again and thought they ought to be opened once more. The ear man disagreed but I kept after him and next day he did it to please me. He didn't get anything but a drop of serum on either side.

Well, Jean didn't get well. We did everything we knew how to do except the right thing. She carried on for another two—no I think it was three—weeks longer. A couple of times her temperature shot up to a hundred and eight. Of course we knew then it was the end. We went over her six or eight times, three or four of us, one after the other, and nobody thought to take an X-ray of the mastoid regions. It was dumb, if you want to say it, but there wasn't a sign of anything but the history of the case to point to it. The ears had been opened early, they had been watched carefully, there was no discharge to speak of at any time and from the external examination, the mastoid processes showed no change from the normal. But that's what she died of, acute purulent mastoiditis of the left side, going on to involvement of the left lateral sinus and finally the meninges. We might, however, have taken a culture of the pus when the ear was first opened and I shall always, after this, in suspicious cases. I have been told since that if you get a virulent bug like the streptococcus mucosus capsulatus it's wise at least to go in behind the ear for drainage if the temperature keeps up. Anyhow she died.

I went in when she was just lying there gasping. Somehow or other, I hated to see that kid go. Everybody felt rotten. She was such a scrawny, misshapen, worthless piece of humanity that I had said many times that somebody ought to chuck her in the garbage chute—but after a month watching her suck up her milk and thrive on it—and to see those alert blue eyes in that face—well, it wasn't pleasant. Her mother was sitting by the bed crying quietly when I came in, the morning of the last day. She was a young woman, didn't look more than a girl, she just sat there looking at the child and crying without a sound.

I expected her to begin to ask me questions with that look on her face all doctors hate—but she didn't. I put my hand on her shoulder and told her we had done everything we knew how to do for Jean but that we really didn't know what, finally, was killing her. The woman didn't make any sign of hearing me. Just sat there looking in between the bars of the crib. So after a moment watching the poor kid beside her, I turned to the infant in the next crib to go on with my rounds. There was an older woman there looking in at that baby also—no better off than Jean, surely.

I spoke to her, thinking she was the mother of this one, but she wasn't.

Before I could say anything, she told me she was the older sister of Jean's mother and that she knew that Jean was dying and that it was a good thing. That gave me an idea—I hated to talk to Jean's mother herself—so I beckoned the woman to come out into the hall with me.

I'm glad she's going to die, she said. She's got two others home, older, and her husband has run off with another woman. It's better off dead—never was any good anyway. You know her husband came down from Canada about a year and a half ago. She seen him and asked him to come back and live with her and the children. He come back just long enough to get her pregnant with this one then he left her again and went back to the other woman. And I suppose knowing she was pregnant, and suffering, and having no money and nowhere to get it, she was worrying and this one never was formed right. I seen it as soon as it was born. I guess the condition she was in was the cause. She's got enough to worry about now without this one. The husband's gone to Canada again and we can't get a thing out of him. I been keeping them, but we can't do much more. She'd work if she could find anything but what can you do with three kids in times like this? She's got a boy nine years old but her mother-in-law sneaked it away from her and now he's with his father in Canada. She worries about him too, but that don't do no good.

Listen, I said, I want to ask you something. Do you think she'd let us do an autopsy on Jean if she dies? I hate to speak to her of such a thing now but to tell you the truth, we've worked hard on that poor child and we don't exactly know what is the trouble. We know that she's had pneumonia but that's been getting well. Would you take it up with her for me, if—of course—she dies.

Oh, she's gonna die all right, said the woman. Sure, I will. If you can learn anything, it's only right. I'll see that you get the chance. She won't make any kick, I'll tell her.

Thanks, I said.

The infant died about five in the afternoon. The pathologist was dog-tired from a lot of extra work he'd had to do due to the absence of his assistant on her vacation so he put off the autopsy till next morning. They packed the body in ice in one of the service hoppers. It worked perfectly.

Next morning they did the postmortem. I couldn't get the nurse to go down to it. I may be a sap, she said, but I can't do it, that's all. I can't. Not when I've taken care of them. I feel as if they're my own.

I was amazed to see how completely the lungs had cleared up. They were almost normal except for a very small patch of residual pneumonia here and there which really amounted to nothing. Chest and abdomen were in excellent shape, otherwise, throughout—not a thing aside from the negligible pneumonia. Then he opened the head.

It seemed to me the poor kid's convolutions were unusually well developed. I kept thinking it's incredible that that complicated mechanism of the brain has come into being just for this. I never can quite get used to an autopsy.

The first evidence of the real trouble—for there had been no gross evidence of meningitis—was when the pathologist took the brain in his hand and made the long steady cut which opened up the left lateral ventricle. There was just a faint color of pus on the bulb of the choroid plexus there. Then the diagnosis all cleared up quickly. The left lateral sinus was completely thrombosed and on going into the left temporal bone from the inside the mastoid process was all broken down.

I called up the ear man and he came down at once. A clear miss, he said. I think if we'd gone in there earlier, we'd have saved her.

For what? said I. Vote the straight Communist ticket.

Would it make us any dumber? said the ear man.

A Face of Stone

He was one of these fresh Jewish types you want to kill at sight, the presuming poor whose looks change the minute cash is mentioned. But they're insistent, trying to force attention, taking advantage of good nature at the first crack. You come when I call you, that type. He got me into a bad mood before he opened his mouth just by the half smiling, half insolent look in his eyes, a small, stoutish individual in a greasy black suit, a man in his middle twenties I should imagine.

She, on the other hand looked Italian, a goaty slant to her eyes, a face often seen among Italian immigrants. She had a small baby tight in her arms. She stood beside her smiling husband and looked at me with no expression at all on her pointed face, unless no expression is an expression. A face of stone. It was an animal distrust, not shyness. She wasn't shy but seemed as if sensing danger, as though she were on her guard against it. She looked dirty. So did he. Her hands were definitely grimy, with black nails. And she smelled, that usual smell of sweat and dirt you find among any people who habitually do not wash or bathe.

The infant was asleep when they came into the office, a child of about five months perhaps, not more.

People like that belong in clinics, I thought to myself. I wasn't putting myself out for them, not that day anyhow. Just dumb oxen. Why the hell do they let them into the country. Half idiots at best. Look at them.

My brother told us to bring the baby here, the man said. We've had a doctor but he's no good.

How do you know he's no good. You probably never gave him a chance. Did you pay him?

Sure we paid him.

Well what do you want me to do? To hell with you, I thought to myself. Get sore and get the hell out of here. I got to go home to lunch.

I want you to fix up the baby, Doc. My brother says you're the best baby doctor around here. And this kid's sick.

Well, put it up there on the table and take its clothes off then. Why didn't you come earlier instead of waiting here till the end of the hour. I got to live too.

The man turned to his wife. Gimme the baby, he said.

No. She wouldn't. Her face just took on an even stupider expression of obstinacy but she clung to the child.

Come on, come on, I said. I can't wait here all day.

Give him to me, he said to her again. He only wants to examine it.

I hold her, the woman said keeping the child firmly in her arms.

Listen here, I spoke to her. Do you want me to examine the child or don't you. If you don't, then take it somewhere.

Wait a minute, wait a minute, Doc, the man said smiling ingratiatingly.

You look at throat, the mother suggested.

You put the baby up there on the table and take its clothes off, I told her. The woman shook her head. But as she did so she gradually relented, looking furtively at me with distrustful glances her nostrils moving slightly.

Now what is it.

She's getting thin, Doc 'think somethink's the matter with her.

What do you mean, thin?

I asked her age, the kind of labor she had had. How they were feeding the baby. Vomiting, sleeping, hunger. It was the first child and the mother was new at nursing it. It was four and a half months old and weighed thirteen and a half pounds. Not bad.

I think my milk no good, said the woman, still clinging to the baby whose clothes she had only begun to open.

As I approached them the infant took one look at me and let out a wild scream. In alarm the mother clutched it to her breast and started for the door.

I burst out laughing. The husband got red in the face but forced a smile. Don't be so scared, he said to his wife. He, nodding toward me, ain't gonna hurt you. You know she hasn't been in this country long, Doc. She's scared you're gonna hurt the baby. Bring it over here, he said to her and take off his clothes. Here, give 'im to me. And he took the infant into his own hands, screaming lustily, and carried it to the table to undress it. The mother, in an agony of apprehension kept interfering from behind at every move.

What a time! I couldn't find much the matter and told them so. Just the results of irregular, foolish routine and probably insufficient breast milk. I gave them a complemental formula. He chiseled a dollar off the fee and—just as he was going out—said, Doc, if we need you any time I want you to come out to the house to see it. You gotta watch this kid.

Where do you live, I asked.

He told me where it was, way out near the dumps. I'll come if you give me a decent warning, I told him. If you want me call me in the morning. Now get that. You can't expect me to go running out there for nothing every time the kid gets a belly ache. Or just because she thinks it's dying. If you call me around supper time or in the middle of a snow storm or at two o'clock in the morning maybe I won't do it. I'm telling you now so you'll know. I got too much to do already.

O.K., Doc, he said smiling. But you come.

I'll come on those conditions.

O.K., Doc.

And sure enough, on a Sunday night, about nine o'clock, with the thermometer at six below and the roads like a skating rink, they would call me.

Nothing doing, I said.

But Doc, you said you'd come.

I'm not going there tonight, I insisted. I won't do it. I'll ask my associate to make the call or some good younger man that lives in that neighborhood but I won't go over there tonight.

But we need you Doc, the baby's very sick.

Can't help it. I tell you I'm not going. And I slammed up the receiver.

Who in the world are you talking to like that, said my wife who had put down her book as my voice rose higher. You mustn't do that.

Leave me alone, I know what I'm doing.

But my dear!

Four months later, after three months of miserable practice, the first warm day in April, about twenty women with babies came to my office. I started at one P.M. and by three I was still going strong. I hadn't loafed. Anybody left out there? I asked the last woman, as I thought, who had been waiting for me. Oh yes, there's a couple with a baby. Oh Lord, I groaned. It was half past three by then and a number of calls still to be made about the town.

There they were. The same fresh mug and the same face of stone, still holding the baby which had grown, however, to twice its former size.

Hello Doc, said the man smiling.

For a moment I couldn't place them. Hello, I said. Then I remembered. What can I do for you—at this time of day. Make it snappy cause I've got to get out.

Just want you to look the baby over, Doc.

Oh yeah.

Listen Doc, we've been waiting out there two hours.

Good night! That finishes me for the afternoon, I said to

myself. All right, put it up on the table. As I said this, feeling at the same time a sense of helpless irritation and anger, I noticed a cluster of red pimples in the region of the man's right eyebrow and reaching to the bridge of his nose. Like bed-bug bites I thought to myself. He'll want me to do something for them too before I get through I suppose. Well, what's the matter now? I asked them.

It's the baby again, Doc, the man said.

What's the matter with the baby. It looks all right to me. And it did. A child of about ten months, I estimated, with a perfectly happy, round face.

Yes, but his body isn't so good.

I want you should examine him all over, said the mother.

You would, I said. Do you realize what time it is?

Shall she take his clothes off? the man broke in.

Suit yourself, I answered, hoping she wouldn't do it. But she put the infant on the table and began carefully to undress it.

No use. I sat down and took out a card for the usual notes. How old is it?

How old is it? he asked his wife.

Ten months. Next Tuesday ten months, she said with the same face on her as always.

Are you still nursing it.

Sure, she said. Him won't take bottle.

Do you mean to say that after what I told you last time, you haven't weaned the baby?

What can she do, Doc. She tried to but he won't let go of the breast. You can't make him take a bottle.

Does he eat?

Yeah, he eats a little, but he won't take much.

Cod liver oil?

He takes it all right but spits it up half an hour later. She stopped giving it to him.

Orange juice.

Sure. Most of the time.

So, as a matter of fact, she's been nursing him and giving him a little cereal and that's all.

Sure, that's about right.

How often does she nurse him?

Whenever he wants it, the man grinned. Sometimes every two hours. Sometimes he sleeps. Like that.

But didn't I tell you, didn't I tell her to feed it regularly.

She can't do that, Doc. The baby cries and she gives it to him.

Why don't you put it in a crib?

She won't give it up. You know, that's the way she is, Doc. You can't make her do different. She wants the baby next to her so she can feel it.

Have you got it undressed? I turned to the mother who was standing with her back to me.

You want shoe off? she answered me.

Getting up I went to the infant and pulled the shoes and stockings off together, picked the thing up by its feet and the back of the neck and carried it to the scales. She was right after me, her arms half extended watching the child at every movement I made. Fortunately the child grinned and sagged back unresisting in my grasp. I looked at it more carefully then, a smart looking little thing and a perfectly happy, fresh mug on him that amused me in spite of myself.

Twenty pounds and four ounces, I said. What do you want for a ten month old baby? There's nothing the matter with him. Get his clothes on.

I want you should examine him first, said the mother.

The blood went to my face in anger but she paid no attention to me. He too thin, she said. Look him body.

To quiet my nerves I took my stethoscope and went rapidly over the child's chest, saw that everything was all right there, that there was no rickets and told them so— and to step on it. Get him dressed. I got to get out of here.

Him all right? the woman questioned me with her stony

pale green eyes. I stopped to look at them, they were very curious, almost at right angles to each other—in a way of speaking—like the eyes of some female figure I had seen somewhere—Mantegna—Botticelli—I couldn't remember.

Yes, only for God's sake, take him off the breast. Feed him the way I told you to.

No will take bottle.

Fine. I don't give a damn about the bottle. Feed him from a cup, with a spoon, anyway at all. But feed him regularly. That's all.

As I turned to wash my hands, preparatory to leaving the office the man stopped me. Doc, he said, I want you to examine my wife.

He got red in the face as I turned on him. What the hell do you think I am anyhow. You got a hell of a nerve. Don't you know . . .

We waited two hours and ten minutes for you, Doc, he replied smiling. Just look her over and see what the matter with her is.

I could hardly trust myself to speak for a moment but, instead turned to look at her again standing beside the baby which she had finished dressing and which was sitting on the table looking at me. What a creature. What a face. And what a body. I looked her coldly up and down from head to toe. There was a rip in her dress, a triangular tear just above the left knee.

Well— No use getting excited with people such as these— or with anyone, for that matter, I said in despair. No one can do two things at the same time, especially when they're in two different places. I simply gave up and returned to my desk chair.

Go ahead. What's the matter with her?

She gets pains in her legs, especially at night. And she's got a spot near her right knee. It came last week, a big blue looking sort of spot.

Did she ever have rheumatism? You know, go to bed with swollen joints—for six weeks—or like that.

She simply shrugged her shoulders.

Did you have rheumatism? he turned to her.

She don't know, he said, interpreting and turning red in the face again. I particularly noticed it this time and remembered that it had occurred two or three times before while we were talking.

Tell her to open up her dress.

Open up your dress, he said.

Sit down, I told her and let me see your legs.

As she did so I noticed again the triangular rip in the skirt over her left thigh, dirty silk, and that her skin was directly under it. She untied some white rags above her knees and let down her black stockings. The left one first, I said.

Her lower legs were peculiarly bowed, really like Turkish scimitars, flattened and somewhat rotated on themselves in an odd way that could not have come from anything but severe rickets rather late in her childhood. The whole leg while not exactly weak was as ugly and misshapen as a useful leg well could be in so young a woman. Near the knee was a large discolored area where in all probability a varicose vein had ruptured.

That spot, I told her husband, comes from a broken varicose vein.

Yeah, I thought so, she's got them all up both legs.

That's from carrying a child.

No. She had them before that. They've always been that way since I've known her. Is that what makes her have the pains there?

I hardly think so, I said looking over the legs again, one of which I held on the palm of either hand. No, I don't think so.

What is it then? It hurts her bad, especially at night.

She's bow-legged as hell in the first place. That throws the strain where it doesn't belong and look at these shoes—

Yeah, I know.

The woman had on an old pair of fancy high-heeled slippers such as a woman might put on for evening wear. They were all worn and incredibly broken down. I don't see how she can walk in them.

That's what I told her, the man said. I wanted her to get a pair of shoes that fitted her but she wouldn't do it.

Well, she's got to do it, I said. Throw away those shoes, I told her, and get shoes with flat heels. And straight heels. I tried to impress her. What they call Cuban heels, if you must. New shoes, I emphasized. How old is she, I asked the man.

His face colored again for reasons I could not fathom. Twenty-four, he said.

Where was she born?

In Poland.

In Poland! Well. I looked at her, not believing him.

Yeah, why?

Well. Twenty-four years old you say. Let's see. That's different. An unusual type for a Jew, I thought. That's the probable explanation for her legs, I told the husband. She must have been a little girl during the war over there. A kid of maybe five or six years I should imagine. Is that right, I asked her. But she didn't answer me, just looked back into my eyes with that inane look.

What did you get to eat?

She seemed not to have heard me but turned to her husband.

Did she lose any of her people, I asked him.

Any of them? She lost everybody, he said quietly.

How did she come to get over here then?

She came over four years ago. She has a sister over here.

So that's it, I thought to myself looking at her fussing, intensely absorbed with the baby, looking at it, talking to it in an inarticulate sort of way, paying no attention whatever to me. No wonder she's built the way she is, consider-

ing what she must have been through in that invaded territory. And this guy here—

What are we going to do about the pains, Doc?

Get her some decent shoes, that's the first thing.

O.K., Doc.

She could be operated on for those veins. But I wouldn't
advise it, just yet. I tell you. Get one of those woven elastic
bandages for her, they don't cost much. A three inch one.
And I told him what to get.

Can't you give her some pills to stop the pain?

Not me, I told him. You might get her teeth looked at
though if you want to. All that kind of thing and—well,
I will give you something. It's not dope. It just helps if
there's any rheumatism connected with it.

Can you swallow a pill, I turned to her attracting
her attention.

She looked at me. How big? she said.

She swallows an Aspirin pill when I give it to her sometimes, said her husband, but she usually puts it in a spoonful
of water first to dissolve it. His face reddened again and
suddenly I understood his half shameful love for the woman
and at the same time the extent of her reliance on him.

I was touched.

They're pretty big pills, I said. Look, they're green.
That's the coating so they won't dissolve in your stomach
and upset your digestion.

Let see, said the woman.

I showed a few of the pills to her in the palm of my hand.

For pains in leg?

Yes, I told her.

She looked at them again. Then for the first time since
I had known her a broad smile spread all over her face.
Yeah, she said, I swallow him.

The Burden of Loveliness

As he was screwing the cap onto the tank my friend glanced up at me sidewise with a smile on his swarthy young face.

Wha's a matter, Doc? You look kinda down this morning.

Not especially.

You like the picture? I had taken an advertising leaflet from a box hanging near one of the pumps while he was working.

More legs. They use legs to advertise pretty nearly everything now but I never saw them used this way for gas before.

We get a new set every month.

Come to think of it though it's about the best thing they could use to advertise gas with—and vice versa, if you know what I mean.

Come on, come on, Doc. You talk like an old man. Three dollars is right.

Three dollars! Boy, oh boy. There it goes.

Wha's a matter, somebody been holdin' out on yuh, Doc?

If it did them any good, that's what gets me.

What do you mean?

Perfect suckers for the smooth guys who rock them to a fare-thee-well while they pass up the honest man who is trying to save them money. And if you say anything . . .

Yeah, I had a woman here this morning. Just a little bill, four dollars, and I sent it to her. You act as if you were afraid we're going to leave town, she said. Just because I sent her a bill. Some of them don't like that. Others are entirely different. They like to be reminded.

194

And still others act sometimes as if their heads had got stepped on while they were being born.

Boy, you got it bad this morning, Doc. How are your tires? Shall I put a little air in them?

Wait a minute! I said, as a swanky open air car pulled into the station on the opposite runway from where I was standing. An expensively dressed young woman was driving it, alone in the front seat.

Not bad, huh? Hey, Jack! to one of the helpers under a car on the hydraulic jack at the far end of the station, take care of the doctor. Pull over there, will you, Doc? I'll be with you in a minute.

Take care of yourself.

O.K., said the boy coming from under the car he was greasing, wiping his hands on a piece of waste. My friend left me to take care of his new client.

Nice day, sir, said the boy in his neat mechanic's uniform, his curly hair neatly parted. He pulled the air hose out and hooked it under a rear wheel.

Yes, a nice day for a murder, I said.

He looked at me. How much pressure do you want? Thirty-five?

Thirty-eight wouldn't do any harm.

Yes, sir. He began putting air into one of the tires.

Dance much, Sonny?

What's that, sir?

Do you take the girls out much to dances these fine October days?

No, *sir*. Not me, and he walked around to the front of the car, flinging the hose after him as he crouched and loosened a valve cap.

Why not?

Costs too much money.

Lots of pretty girls around nowdays would count it a treat to get their fingers in that curly hair of yours.

Yeah, I know. But it's a funny thing. Did you ever look at one of those girls' faces up close? He paused a moment where he was kneeling on the concrete and turned his face at me.

No, not especially. Why?

Well, what the hell's pretty about it? He was serious and for the first time that morning I laughed heartily.

Good boy, I said. You'd make a swell doctor.

No, seriously? he said.

Don't talk to him, Doc, said the older man coming up. He's one of those weak-in-the-head guys you were telling me about a little while ago. He doesn't even know the difference between a G string and a clothesline. We were kidding the shirt off him the other day and he's still worrying about it. Did you get a good look at her?

Who?

That woman that pulled in here just a minute ago. You were the one who first noticed her.

No, to tell you the truth I kind of forget her. She wasn't bad though, at that.

Oh, you should have looked. She's something.

Well, go ahead. We got nothing to do. Let's have it.

Sure you don't know her? 'Cause I wouldn't want to . . .

I don't know who the hell she is.

Say, Doc, look here a minute. He was standing toward the front of the car pointing down at the tires. Not much tread left on that one. We're having a special on them this week.

You mean a sale?

No, the regular price. But we're allowing you something on your old ones. Your tires are an unusual size; they're hard to get. I have a customer could use these right now. Get you a couple of dollars a piece for them.

Nothing doing. I haven't got the money.

It's up to you, only you really owe it to yourself to be careful, you know.

Yeah, I know. Fifty bucks, I suppose.

They'd cost you fifty-two but I can get you four dollars off for the old shoes.

Fifty bucks, eh? Huh! What I could do with fifty bucks. I haven't spent fifty bucks on myself for so long I've forgotten what it feels like. I need a new suit of clothes right now.

Yeah, I know. My wife keeps bothering me for new clothes. But I told her, nothing doing. Not till I get a new suit for myself. She can't see that. Why, the other day I had her down at Bamberger's. I followed her around. She bought some curtains, this and that. I've forgotten it all. Then she started down for the dress-goods department. Where are you going? I sez. I'm going to buy a dress, she told me. She'd been ordering things right an' left and telling them to send them to the house. Things we needed. Do you know how much you've spent already? I asked her. Why no, she says. So I took out my little piece of paper I'd been jotting it down on as I was following her around and I told her: sixty-three dollars and thirty-eight cents. She almost hit the ceiling. What! she says. I'm going right back and cancel those orders. Oh no, you're not, I says. Those are things we gotta have. But no dress for you today. You should have seen her face.

A woman's got to have clothes. If they can't get something new to wear . . .

I know, but I felt sorry for her. They don't have it so easy. How about those tires? Shall I save two for you?

Forty-eight dollars, eh? Say what about that woman who was just in here you were going to tell me about?

She's the wife of one of the big bosses in this town.

So what?

You should have taken a look. A beautiful woman, really. One of these little ones, you know, pocket edition, just perfect.

Well, what about it?

Well, you see I got a friend up here. This was several

years ago. He was running a shoe store for one of the big companies and the women used to come in there—you know, looking for bargains. And he'd talk to them . . .

Just at that moment a large flock of blackbirds began passing over us and we both looked up at them. You could hear them crackling the way they do, as they flew by, thousands of them.

Well, you know this town's the place for that sort of thing. Anything goes. So he used to take these women in the back room, any number of them. It was a regular thing with him. They understood it. And what do you think he'd give them for it.

I don't know. A couple of bucks?

No.

Maybe they were looking for something themselves and paid him for it.

He'd give them maybe twenty-five cents off on a pair of shoes or maybe the trimmings they have in the windows sometimes when they have displays, all that sort of junk.

Colored silk I suppose and things like that, I said.

He had 'em by the dozen. But then there was this little girl that used to come in sometimes. Just a kid. But she was beautiful, perfect. Pretty face, nice manners, the most beautiful curly yellow hair you ever saw. And very quiet.

Did he tell you all this?

Yes, we used to pal around a lot together before I was married. Well, after she'd been coming in there for about a month or so he kind of put it up to her. Sure, she was willing. You know he was kinda surprised. She seemed to be different from the others and he didn't feel right about it. I guess he was kind of in awe of her. Something like that.

Talked himself out of it, eh?

Naw, he had her all right, but only a couple of times, once in a while. Maybe three or four times in the course of a year, but most of the time he only wanted to play with her, you know. She was so beautiful.

What do you mean, play with her?

He just wanted to look at her. He said she had the smoothest body he ever imagined. . . .

Oh, so that's it.

Everything about her, you couldn't find a thing wrong with her. He just liked to touch her. Oh, he'd hold her and all that but the best he got out of her was just to sit and look at her. He said he never saw anything like it.

Nice fellow.

Then after a while he kind of missed her. He didn't notice it at first but when he did he just thought nothing more about it. But about a year later he met her on the street one day. She hadn't been in the store for all that time.

She was glad to see him and they stood there talking a while. Then he asked her, Why don't you come to see me anymore? No, she said, I'm going steady now, that's all finished. Why don't you just come around once more for old time's sake? he kind of pleaded with her. No, she said, not any more.

Nothing he could say would make her change her mind. Just once more, he said. There's no harm in it, is there? Then she told him.

What did she tell him?

No, she said. No more. You didn't know how to take care of me when you had me. Now it's too late.

Boy! Was that telling him.

I don't blame her. It must be tough, you know, being that good-looking. A fellow never thinks of it that way. But when you look at it from a woman's side, they don't have it so easy. How about those tires?

All right. Can I pay you ten a week?

The place is yours, Doc. I'll put two of them aside and any time you can leave the car here for a couple of hours we'll fix it right up.

And now she's married.

Yeah, now she's married. He gives her everything she asks for. Awful nice woman to talk to.

The Zoo

Go THAT WAY, the Missus said, pointing or rather waving with her whole hand downtown. It isn't very far, ten or twelve blocks, on this—she motioned again—side of the park. You can walk.

Yes, I can walk, said the stocky new Finnish girl, Elsa, and looking at the Missus with her big blue eyes, she smiled brightly.

Um, said the Missus. Well, then walk. And come back by five o'clock. Five o'clock! She held up her hand with the five fingers spread wide. Five. You understand?

Elsa was hurt. Yes, I understand good. One, two, three, four, five. Five o'clock.

All right then, said the Missus. Out with you. And she held open the door of the apartment for the new maid to wheel the little go-cart through it. No, take that down first, right to the street. Then come back for the baby. I strong! Yes, I know, said the Missus, but be careful.

Saturday afternoon, cool air, but not too cool, the trio came at last to the high wire enclosure of the zoo and began following a group of children running ahead and calling back to a heavy-set man and woman to hurry. They were in before they knew it. And before they knew it they were standing in front of a rather narrow outdoor cage, containing an ape with a banana in his hand. He was sitting there peeling and eating it, darting looks about right and left from time to time though he was quite alone in the cage.

Elsa's mouth fell open in amazement. Lottie looked up at her and then at the animal. The beast finished the banana,

200

threw down the skin and came to the front of the cage as though looking for more. Elsa turned to the people around her. There were six or eight of them watching. They seemed to think it very funny.

Flossie apparently didn't see anything.

Squirrels were running about over the grass. The maid with her two small charges went up and down among the outdoor enclosures. She saw wolves like dogs with fierce eyes, narrow-snouted foxes, and deer with astonishing, many branching horns, elk and bears in big strong cages against some rocks. But many of the cages were empty due to the beginning chill that was in the air and she did not quite dare venture as yet into the various houses here and there about her on either hand.

She looked through the window of one low building half-covered with ivy where a peacock, all white, at large on the premises, was sitting quietly. Not two feet beyond it through the glass Elsa saw an enormous snake! She could only see part of it. She shuddered from head to foot. Not there, at any rate and hurried on dragging the children with her.

Why not go in? The Missus hadn't told her not to. Anyhow it was beginning to get cold walking around, and though the baby was happy and contented, maybe it would be warm in there. She would go. Here was one with cages outside and places for the birds to go inside, too. She would go in there to see the birds. She went to wheel her carriage through the door but a guard stopped her.

Can't go in there with baby carriages. There, he said, pointing. So Elsa was practically forced to do what the others were doing. She stood the carriage aside, carefully took the baby into her arms, told Lottie to come on and went through the door. She stopped short. The smell was appalling. Dead fish, dead something, anyhow foul, it gripped you in the throat, you could taste it. She made a face, looked right and left at others about her, but after a long moment, seeing many lively fowl before her, went ahead.

Once you got a little used to the fetid odor of the place, the din hit you. Shrieks and catcalls on all sides. The baby clung to the girl's neck. In a big central cage were ducks, and terns and gulls, some huddled on the sandy cage bottom, incredibly colored, others with their beaks open laughed loudly, so it seemed, with piercing volleys of calls about the cage, moving aside carefully as a big gray bird with a pouch under his chin took off from the pool and landed heavily among them wobbling forward a few additional steps before he could come to a stop. Some birds were brooding on barkless pieces of dead branches hung from above, two by two, all letting their droppings go when they would. Immediately in front of Elsa and the children a white, long-legged bird was feeding, sloshing his bill, spoon-shaped at the end, right and left sidewise through a pail of half-liquid stuff before him.

The little servant circled the cage. About it were other birds in cages along the wall. She couldn't believe it. Long red and green legs that slowly moved about the narrow confines of the enclosure flexing and straightening—so long and thin you'd think they'd snap. Eyes and pointed bills . . . No! she turned uneasily, holding her breath—without appearing to hurry. Come, Lottie, she said. Let us go.

It was better in the air again. There was a water creature lying on its back or its belly, she couldn't tell which, on the rocks near a cold-looking pool. She went on, looking up at the sky quickly to see how much of the afternoon remained to her. As she passed along the edge of the pool there was a swirl of the water and a sharp pointed snout arose and barked once then the thing turned and with the speed of a serpent plunged under and was gone again.

Well, maybe that was enough. Perhaps she'd better go home. It was a long walk and the sun was already beginning

to fade from its midday position in the sky. Still—maybe
so, why not?

You want to go? she asked Lottie and the baby.

Go, go! the baby said earnestly.

You want to sit in the carriage? the little maid asked
Lottie. Yes, that was what she wanted, Lottie assured her.
So Lottie was seated at the foot of the little go-cart and,
reassured, Elsa decided to continue her investigations a
little further.

Going quietly along now, the flaxen-haired girl steered
away from the crowd.

The house of the pachyderms admitted carriages; Elsa
saw a woman working one up the three steps to the entrance
and followed eagerly. Warm in here and high, and there
were sparrows chattering up under the roof beam. And
there was an elephant! Alone behind its bars one hind foot
chained to an iron ring in the floor. There was a crowd
before his cage.

Elsa saw what was going on. There was a man at the back
tossing in hay with a fork and the enormous beast seemed to
want to be loosened. But the man bowed his head and
backed out through a small door at the rear and the elephant
quieted down again. He didn't seem to want the hay but
took a wisp of it in his trunk, rolled it up into a little
bundle, raised it swingingly to his mouth and then as grace-
fully lowered his trunk again with the hay still in it, two
or three times, before he ate it.

Elsa watched every move, looked at the eye and the ears
of the beast without stirring. Still swinging its stocky trunk
as it rocked from foot to foot, the enormous beast suddenly
uncurled it forward, through the bars toward the people
standing there, opening the tip of it like a small hand
begging. Elsa strained forward to see beyond the backs
of the people before her as a child placed a peanut in the
opening. The elephant, without a movement, still held the
trunk there waiting.

The little blue-eyed maid woke as if from a dream when she heard Lottie say, I want to get down, and felt her struggling on her arm. She hadn't realized that she was holding her. Sighing as if she had forgotten to breathe for the last five minutes, Elsa suddenly recollected her duty toward her charges and turned away from the crowd once more.

But what astonished the little maid more than anything else was the head of the hippopotamus. Unlike the birds and many of the other beasts, here was something, alert as it seemed, that did not move. There was no more than a faint turning of the eye from time to time and a slow shift of the head hardly to be perceived. This was something beyond the imagination! The skin of an eel, the ears of a pig, but the mouth! The bulk of the head and the breadth of it! Incredible! The thing didn't yawn, it didn't rise or move. . . . Elsa looked into the faces of the people about her and discovered no wonder. She looked at the children and moved on.

These things lived naturally in all their deformity in the same world as she. What are they for? She did not know. The less than pig eyes of the rhinoceros and his broken horns! It made her shudder. And she was startled by their stillness, too. They hardly moved. Yet with that leathery bulk of insensitivity before her, she heard a distant rhythmic . . .! Was it a cat had got into the place? She looked about. Again, an almost imperceptible small sound. No, it was the beast itself! It was the rhinoceros, mewing like a kitten.

The elephant, to the admiration of the crowd which grew silent at this point, let go its bladder—as though someone had dumped a barrel of stale cider down a drain.

Come, Lottie! said the girl.

It was an exciting game. In one house there was a very small dainty-footed deer, no bigger than a terrier, walking quickly up and down inside the bars while another, the same, was lying curled up, its head upon it flanks asleep in the straw. Kangaroos, red and gray, powerful and delicate, one of them sitting upright upon its fat tail, the forefeet with their narrow wrists dangling idly.

Zigzag went the little maid about the room, the wild swine with coarse black hair, curling tusks and knobs of crusted filth, she thought, between them where he couldn't scratch. Was it from that or—in the next cage again beyond belief—that there came such an overpowering stench!

Elsa wanted to go but could not resist the desire to see this other thing. No head at all, just a slithering body tipped with a snout a yard long, armed with filthy eyes, tapering from a shaggy neck, the head no more than a slight bulge in the snout itself—on the body of, almost a bear! she thought.

Whew! that's terrible! she said aloud.

Lottie was already moving away.

Coated with long dangling wiry hair that swept the floor as the beast paced up and down, filthy with dust and straws, the tail a bulky hanging mass of long, spiny hairs dragging on the bottom of the cage—and powerful forelegs armed by one fierce long claw—whew! Terrible.

I'm tired, said Lottie. So Elsa loaded her once more into the foot of the carriage and started for home. But first—it was still so early—passing another building the little maid thought, Why not?

No, no, no! said Lottie.

Yes, said Elsa. So she parked the carriage. It was getting to be an old thing now, took the baby in her arms, Lottie by the hand in spite of her hanging back, and went in behind some others. It was just before three o'clock; she saw it by her big watch which she always carried by a chain in her pocket.

Timid but responsible at the same time, Elsa saw at once that she was among the lions. She got just inside the door and there she stood. On the right were the cages, while along the other side of the room, up three steps, was a row of benches all occupied.

Most of the people were at the other end of the room whither several newcomers hurried, leaving the little blonde maid and the two children almost alone. The people on the benches were looking at her. She didn't understand.

But near her in the first, no, the second, cage, next to two big black cats with green eyes, was an enormous shaggy-maned lion pacing alone up and down inside bars. Now he would come toward the young girl with the two children then turn away again to the far corner of his cage, stop, press his heavy head forward into the bars, trying to look around the corner, up beyond, then drop his head, turn and come down the face of the bars again. Back he would go once more. Look and return. Elsa didn't move.

Then the beast stopped. Cocked his ears. Stared. Opened his jaws. And split the air with a terrifying voice of thunder.

The baby clung to the maid's neck and began to whimper. Lottie clung to her skirts. Elsa herself was spellbound— standing almost alone, not knowing whether to retreat or go farther.

I want to go home! said Lottie whimpering. The baby, loosening the little maid's neck a moment, turned her head around a little way timidly to see what had happened. Several ladies were laughing. Elsa flushed crimson.

This was no place for a child, said one of the women on the benches to her companion. Can you imagine a mother sending two small children out with a maid like that—in this crowd?

Pretty little thing, said the other. As much of a child as they are. This is going to be fun.

Then a commotion began at the other end of the room. There, they're going to feed them.

There was a scurry and a hubbub followed by fierce guttural roars. An attendant was going down the aisle between the spectators and the cages poking something in under the bars. Growls and roars, half-muffled, savage and repeated, menaced the ear. And then the big lion let go once more.

Lottie, bewildered, put her hands up to her ears and ran— forward into the room as Elsa clutched the baby which suddenly had again clutched her. The two ladies were pointing and laughing as Elsa went to grab Lottie and missed, caught her and tried to get hold of her hand. . . .

Another deafening roar.

In terror the little maid and the children escaped through the door nearest them.

She must really go home now. She must. But to prove to Lottie that she mustn't be afraid . . . You want to see the monkeys? Then we go home. All right we see the monkeys.

Monkeys are funny in all languages—she'd try here—on her way to the exit—the last place and then go.

As she had hoped, they were funny, very funny. Even more than that, shocking. So that you felt the blood come into your face watching them. Never mind. Nobody else seemed to.

You could hardly follow them, quick as birds. So surprised they always looked. Frightened. Fear is written in all their faces. And their faces never change. Hands and feet and tails made for getting away.

She didn't hurry this time, she had learned what to do— but there were already too many people inside. Nevertheless, nothing ventured nothing won; she'd go ahead.

Monkeys on all sides! Little ones blinking and clinging to the bars, calling, looking furtively at their fellows, eating, scratching or walking slowly about. After all, Elsa was doing no more than the others about her. There were a number of men and women with children of all ages.

Monkeys! Oh, look, monkeys! Wouldn't you get lost in the cage with the monkeys?

This is the monkey house, what else do you expect to find here?

Look at the old man up there thinking!

Elsa didn't know what they were saying exactly. But as she followed the direction of the pointing fingers, sure enough . . . ! She stared with her mouth open where, on a perch, at the very top of a cage which she had thought empty, was the dark and huddled figure of a man-like ape. He was black-haired and looking down at the crowd below him had, his hand supporting the lower part of his face, half-covering his mouth, the appearance of thinking.

Monkeys are interesting people, said a tall woman to a man beside her. But Elsa could not get over her astonishment. No ungainly bird's legs, the colors of the rainbow, here, nor hippopotamus and rhinoceros heads of misshapen bone and blubber, hides like armor, not even the grace of a deer—but a sort of people in contour and motion.

The black, thoughtful creature rubbed his hand over his eyes while what seemed to be his wife along the same shelf, a little smaller, held a piece of paper in her hand putting it to her mouth now and then nibbling, then puffing out her lips and blowing her breath through them with a soft high-pitched clatter. She moved about more than her mate, but neither one was particularly active.

In this house the crowd was getting to be almost impassable. It was entrancing, the most exciting place in the whole gardens. Baboons, walking stiffly on all fours, whose behinds when they turned from the astonished Elsa were blue and crimson. A shriek of laughter went up from several young girls whenever the beast would turn away from them.

And opposite them long-armed gibbons swinging from the cage wall, to the trapeze, to the iron upright in the cage's middle in prodigious leaps, never failing, up and down and around with lightning agility.

Suddenly a great roar of laughter went up from the far end of the building. Then it quieted and as suddenly burst out again in gales of merriment. The call was irresistible. Elsa was drawn inevitably that way along with the rest.

As she came up, the thing was clapping its hands, excitedly, wildly. Then it leaped directly at the crowd! Elsa involuntarily shrank back, bumping into a fat woman who gave her a hard shove with her elbow. And the crowd let out another spasm of roars. The thing inside had disappeared into the back of its cage. Then it leaped again! It hit the bars with the whole weight of its body and clung there snarling and shaking from side to side.

What if it should get loose? Everybody was laughing, but Elsa could see that the beast was furious. He hated the crowd. He wanted to kill them. She could see that. Where was Lottie? Lottie! Lottie! Lottie! The child had disappeared from her hand. Lottie!

The beast was waving its arms and now it spit. It spit into the crowd which laughed and gave way suddenly. And there was Lottie all alone. Elsa ran forward and grabbed her by the hand. Come. And this time she was through.

An attendant came and drove the beast toward the back of the cage. Go on, he said to the people. Go on. Keep moving. Don't stand in front of the cages.

Elsa was tired when she got back to the apartment. So were the children. Well, did you like it? the Missus said.

No, schtinks! said the little maid. I see elephant and many things. Well, some day you can go again, said the Missus. No, said Elsa. Schtinks! I see once, I see too much.

from **White Mule**

SHE ENTERED, as Venus from the sea, dripping. The air enclosed her, she felt it all over her, touching, waking her. If Venus did not cry aloud after release from the pressures of that sea-womb, feeling the new and lighter flood springing in her chest, flinging out her arms—this one did. Screwing up her tiny smeared face, she let out three convulsive yells—and lay still.

Stop that crying, said Mrs. D, you should be glad to get outa that hole.

It's a girl. What? A girl. But I wanted a boy. Look again. It's a girl, Mam. No! Take it away. I don't want it. All this trouble for another girl.

What is it? said Joe, at the door. A little girl. That's too bad. Is it all right? Yes, a bit small though. That's all right then. Don't you think you'd better cover it up so it won't catch cold? Ah, you go on out of here now and let me manage, said Mrs. D. This appealed to him as proper so he went. Are you all right, Mama? Oh, leave me alone, what kind of a man are you? As he didn't exactly know what she meant he thought it better to close the door. So he did.

In prehistoric ooze it lay while Mrs. D wound the white twine about its pale blue stem with kindly clumsy knuckles and blunt fingers with black nails and with the wiped-off scissors from the cord at her waist, cut it—while it was twisting and flinging up its toes and fingers into the way— free.

Alone it lay upon its back on the bed, sagging down in the middle, by the smeared triple mountain of its mother's disgusted thighs and toppled belly.

The clotted rags were gathered. Struggling blindly against the squeezing touches of the puffing Mrs. D, it was lifted into a nice woolen blanket and covered. It sucked its under lip and then let out two more yells.

Ah, the little love. Hear it, Mam, it's trying to talk.

La, la, la, la, la, la, la! it said with its tongue—in the black softness of the new pressures—and jerking up its hand, shoved its right thumb into its eye, starting with surprise and pain and yelling and rolling in its new agony. But finding the thumb again at random it sobbingly subsided into stillness.

Mrs. D lifted the cover and looked at it. It lay still. Her heart stopped. It's dead! She shook the . . .

With a violent start the little arms and legs flew up into a tightened knot, the face convulsed again—then as the nurse sighed, slowly the tautened limbs relaxed. It did not seem to breathe.

And now if you're all right I'll wash the baby. All right, said the new mother drowsily.

In that two ridges lap with wind cut off at the bend of the neck it lay, half dropping, regrasped—it was rubbed with warm oil that rested in a saucer on the stove while Mrs. D with her feet on the step of the oven rubbed and looked it all over, from the top of its head to the shiny soles of its little feet.

About five pounds is my guess. You poor little mite, to come into a world like this one. Roll over here and stop wriggling or you'll be on the floor. Open your legs now till I rub some of this oil in there. You'll open them glad enough one of these days—if you're not sorry for it. So, in all of them creases. How it sticks. It's like lard. I wonder what they have that on them for. It's a hard thing to be born a girl. There you are now. Soon you'll be in your little bed and I wish I was the same this minute.

She rubbed the oil under the arm pits and carefully round the scrawny folds of its little neck pushing the wobbly head back and front. In behind the ears there was still that white grease of pre-birth. The matted hair, larded to the head, on the brow it lay buttered heavily while the whole back was caked with it, a yellow-white curd.

In the folds of the groin, the crotch where the genitals all bulging and angry red seemed presages of some future growth, she rubbed the warm oil, carefully—for she was a good woman—and thoroughly, cleaning her fingers on her apron. She parted the little parts looking and wondering at their smallness and perfection and shaking her head forebodingly.

The baby lay back at ease with closed eyes—lolling about as it was, lifted by a leg, an arm, and turned.

Mrs. D looked at the toes, counted them, admired the little perfect nails—and then taking each little hand, clenched tight at her approach, she smoothed it out and carefully anointed its small folds.

Into the little sleeping face she stared. The nose was flattened and askew, the mouth was still, the slits of the eyes were swollen closed—it seemed.

You're a homely little runt, God pardon you, she said—rubbing the spot in the top of the head. Better to leave that—I've heard you'd kill them if you pressed on that too hard. They say a bad nurse will stop a baby crying by pressing there—a cruel thing to do.

She looked again where further back upon the head a soft round lump was sticking up like a jockey cap askew. That'll all go down, she said to herself wisely because it was not the first baby Mrs. D had tended, nor the fifth nor the tenth nor the twentieth even.

She got out the wash boiler and put warm water in it. In that she carefully laid the new-born child. It half floated, half asleep—opening its eyes a moment then closing them and resting on Mrs. D's left hand, spread out behind its neck.

She soaped it thoroughly. The father came into the kitchen where they were and asked her if she thought he could have a cup of coffee before he left for work—or should he go and get it at the corner. He shouldn't have

asked her—suddenly it flashed upon his mind. It's getting
close to six o'clock, he said. How is it? Is it all right?

.. He leaned to look. The little thing opened its eyes,
blinked and closed them in the flare of the kerosene oil
lamp close by in the gilded bracket on the wall. Then it
smiled a crooked little smile—or so it seemed to him.

It's the light that hurts its eyes, he thought, and taking a
dish towel he hung it on the cord that ran across the
kitchen so as to cast a shadow on the baby's face.

Hold it, said Mrs. D, getting up to fill the kettle.

He held it gingerly in his two hands, looking curiously,
shyly at that ancient little face of a baby. He sat down,
resting it on his knees, and covered its still wet body. That
little female body. The baby rested. Squirming in the tender grip of his guarding hands, it sighed and opened its
eyes wide.

He stared. The left eye was rolled deep in toward the
nose; the other seemed to look straight at his own. There
seemed to be a spot of blood upon it. He looked and a cold
dread started through his arms. Cross eyed! Maybe blind.
But as he looked—the eyes seemed straight. He was glad
when Mrs. D relieved him—but he kept his peace. Somehow this bit of moving, unwelcome life had won him to
itself forever. It was so ugly and so lost.

The pains he had seemed to feel in his own body while
the child was being born, now relieved—it seemed almost
as if it had been he that had been the mother. It was his
baby girl. That's a funny feeling, he thought.

He merely shook his head.

Coffee was cooking on the back of the stove. The room
was hot. He went into the front room. He looked through
the crack of the door into their bedroom where she lay.
Then he sat on the edge of the disheveled sofa where, in a
blanket, he had slept that night—and waited. He was a
good waiter. Almost time to go to work.

Mrs. D got the cornstarch from a box in the pantry. She
had to hunt for it among a disarray of pots and cooking
things and made a mental note to put some order into the

place before she left. Ah, these women with good hus-
bands, they have no sense at all. They should thank God
and get to work.

Now she took the baby once more on her lap,
unwrapped it where it lay and powdered the shrivelling,
gummy two inch stem of the gummy cord, fished a roll of
Canton flannel from the basket at her feet and putting one
end upon the little pad of cotton on the baby's middle
wrapped the binder round it tightly, round and round, pin-
ning the end in place across the back. The child was hard
there as a board now—but did not wake.

She looked and saw a red spot grow upon the fabric. Tie
it again. Once more she unwrapped the belly band. Out she
took the stump of cord and this time she wound it twenty
times about with twine while the tiny creature heaved and
vermiculated with joy at its relief from the too tight belly
band.

Wrapping an end of cotton rag about her little finger,
Mrs. D forced that in between the little lips and scrubbed
those tender gums. The baby made a grimace and drew
back from this assault, working its whole body to draw
back.

Hold still, said Mrs. D, bruising the tiny mouth with
sedulous care—until the mite began to cough and strain to
vomit. She stopped at last.

Dried, diapered and dressed in elephantine clothes that
hid it crinkily; stockinged, booted and capped, tied under
the chin—now Mrs. D walked with her new creation from
the sweaty kitchen into the double light of dawn and
lamps, through the hallway to the front room where the
father sat, to show him.

Where are you going? For a walk?, he said.

Look at it in its first clothes, she answered him.

Yes, he said, it looks fine. But he wondered why they
put the cap and shoes on it.

Turning back again, Mrs. D held the baby in her left
arm and with her right hand turned the knob and came

once more into the smells of the birth chamber. There it
was dark and the lamp burned low. The mother was asleep.

She put out the lamp, opened the inner shutters. There
was a dim light in the room.

Waking with a start—What is it? the mother said. Where
am I? Is it over? Is the baby here?

It is, said Mrs. D, and dressed and ready to be sucked.
Are you flooding any?

Is it a boy? said the mother.

It's a girl, I told you before. You're half asleep.

Another girl. Agh, I don't want girls. Take it away and
let me rest. God pardon you for saying that. Where is it?
Let me see it, said the mother, sitting up so that her great
breasts hung outside her undershirt. Lay down, said Mrs. D.
I'm all right. I could get up and do a washing. Where is it?

She took the little thing and turned it around to look at
it. Where is its face? Take off that cap. What are these
shoes on for? She took them off with a jerk. You miserable
scrawny little brat, she thought, and disgust and anger
fought inside her chest, she was not one to cry—except in
a fury.

The baby lay still, its mouth stinging from its scrub, its
belly half strangled, its legs forced apart by the great diaper—and slept, grunting now and then.

Take it away and let me sleep. Look at your breasts, said
Mrs. D. And with that they began to put the baby to the
breast. It wouldn't wake.

The poor miserable thing, repeated the mother. This will
fix it. It's its own mother's milk it needs to make a fine baby
of it, said Mrs. D. Maybe it does, said the mother, but I
don't believe it. You'll see, said Mrs. D.

As they forced the great nipple into its little mouth, the
baby yawned. They waited. It slept again. They tried
again. It squirmed its head away. Hold your breast back
from its nose. They did.

Mrs. D squeezed the baby's cheeks together between her
thumb and index finger. It drew back, opened its jaws and

in they shoved the dripping nipple. The baby drew back. Then for a moment it sucked.

There she goes, said Mrs. D, and straightened up with a sigh, pressing her two hands against her hips and leaning back to ease the pain in her loins.

The mother stroked the silky hair, looked at the gently pulsing fontanelle, and holding her breast with the left hand to bring it to a point, straightened back upon the pillows and frowned.

The baby ceased to suck, squirming and twisting. The nipple lay idle in its mouth. It slept. Looking down, the mother noticed what had happened. It won't nurse, Mrs. D. Take it away. Mrs. D come here at once and take this thing, I'm in a dripping perspiration.

Mrs. D came. She insisted it should nurse. They tried. The baby waked with a start, gagging on the huge nipple. It pushed with its tongue. Mrs. D had it by the back of the neck pushing. She flattened out the nipple and pushed it in the mouth. Milk ran down the little throat, a watery kind of milk. The baby gagged purple and vomited.

Take it. Take it away. What's the matter with it? You're too rough with it.

If you'd hold it up properly, facing you and not away off at an angle as if—Mrs. D's professional pride was hurt. They tried again, earnestly, tense, uncomfortable, one cramped over where she sat with knees spread out, the other half kneeling, half on her elbows—till anger against the little rebellious spitting imp, anger and fatigue, overcame them.

Take it away, that's all, said the mother finally.

Reluctantly, red in the face, Mrs. D had no choice but to do what she was told. I'd like to spank it, she said, flicking its fingers with her own.

What! said the mother in such menacing tones that Mrs. D caught a fright and realized whom she was dealing with. She said no more.

But now, the baby began to rebel. First its face got red, its whole head suffused, it caught its breath and yelled in sobs and long shrill waves. It sobbed and forced its piercing little voice so small yet so disturbing in its penetrating puniness, mastering its whole surroundings till it seemed to madden them. It caught its breath and yelled in sobs and long shrill waves. It sobbed and squeezed its yell into their ears.

That's awful, said the mother, I can't have it in this room. I don't think it's any good. And she lay down upon her back exhausted.

Mrs. D with two red spots in her two cheeks and serious jaw and a headache took the yelling brat into the kitchen. Dose it up. What else?

She got the rancid castor oil and gave the baby some. It fought and spit. Letting it catch its breath, she fetched the fennel tea, already made upon the range, and sweetening it poured a portion into a bottle, sat down and rather roughly told the mite to take a drink. There, drat you. Sweet to unsweeten that unhappy belly. The baby sucked the fermentative warm stuff and liked it—and wet its diaper after.

Feeling the wet through her skirt and petticoat and drawers right on her thighs, Mrs. D leaped up and holding the thing out at arm's length, got fresh clothes and changed it.

Feeling the nice fresh diaper, cool and enticing, now the baby grew red all over. Its face swelled, suffused with color. Gripping its tiny strength together, it tightened its belly band even more.

The little devil, said Mrs. D, to wait till it's a new diaper on.

And with this final effort, the blessed little thing freed itself as best it could—and it did very well—of a quarter pound of tarrish, prenatal slime—some of which ran down one leg and got upon its stocking.

That's right, said Mrs. D.

CHAPTER III. TO GO ON BEING

Monday morning they put the baby in the front room where it would be most out of the way. You'd think she'd been here for a month, said Mrs. D, with her little hands and the face of her and the little bit of hair she has all smoothed down on her head.

There Joe found her when he returned that evening from the office. He walked to the crib and looked in. The baby was turned from him to the left with fists placed one before the other before her nose. He recognized the gesture and smiled, nodding his head in assent.

Mrs. D came into the room so he asked her how things had gone that day. It's slept the whole time through, was the reply he got. Good, said Joe.

Tuesday Mrs. D brought the baby out to its basket as soon as Joe had left and laid it on its blue down pillow. Sleep again. But now she'd stir, wrinkle up her face, pucker it, then curl her lips and cry.

But mostly she lay sleeping—as before, but breathing air now almost imperceptibly until she'd wake and root around for food or squirm or yell. She sneezed.

The aunt, who was there again, jumped up.

That's nothing, said Mrs. D, they all do that. It's the air she ain't used to inside her nose tickles her. Leave her alone. She's all right.

It pressed and ached and gnawed. Sleep, the one refuge she sought only to return to it and to remain there. But she could not. That well where she had swum like so much weed two days ago had lost its charm.

The woman rescued her, lifting and wiping, loosing and binding, carrying her to food, warmth to her feet—to soften and allay—what else? but could not alter her condition.

Prickled by the light she moved her head from side to side, then started, flooded with urine to the armpits, to find herself flying, stiffened for a fall, only to land safely from the hold of Mrs. D upon some bed or table.

The little divil. I think she's made of it. That's the third time I've changed her hand running. She waits till I've a dry one on her and then she soaks it, said Mrs. D.

The baby yawned and blinked and wrinkled up its brows. A kitten or a pup would have been crawling on its belly. Not she. She was not able. Her mouth against the tit, unlike an animal, she sucked indifferently. Yet she sucked a little, her belly tightened, the nipple fell from her mouth —too soon.

I don't think you've much milk coming, said Mrs. D to the mother. Nonsense, replied she. I nursed the first one for a year. I can't help that, said Mrs. D, I don't like the way she fights it. Let her wake up first, said the mother, take a wet cloth to her face the next time. All right, said Mrs. D.

Meanwhile, the light got to her more and more.

But that night Joe came up to the crib again and seeing her quiet stood looking down. He had heard that if you look too hard at a sleeping baby you'll wake it. He wondered if that were true. Apparently not, for the infant didn't budge. So he touched its forehead with his index finger.

The baby slowly smiled, a crooked little grin. It pleased Joe marvelously. So when the smile had gone, he tried the trick again. No one else was in the room.

This time the baby opened its mouth and turned its head about as if searching for the breast. This wasn't so good. Joe felt a little panic at this twist of things and drew back.

Then it began to cry a little, then flung up its arms and yelled. He moved quickly away and tried to look innocent as Mrs. D came in.

Its harsh, small voice stilled a little as the woman slid her hand under it to feel its bottom. Finding this dry, she turned to Joe and, reminding him that he was the father and that she had work to do, went off.

He sat by the crib and joggled it. It did no good. It seemed some petty engine letting off steam, the thing drove its breath so furiously. The face grew purple. After ten minutes, Joe went back to the kitchen and told the woman she'd have to go and see to it.

She's got an awful temper, said Mrs. D. Let her cry it out, it won't hurt her.

But Joe wasn't going back. How can an infant that age have a temper, said he, stalling. You'd better go and take it up.

What! It shows you've never seen many babies, said Mrs. D, working at the sink. That baby's got a temper. They could hear it down the hallway yelling still, convulsively. In about two days you begin to notice a difference in them. They're no two of them alike.

What are you doing to my baby? they heard the mother calling.

And with that the thing stopped its noise as unaccountably as it had started. Mrs. D went on with her cooking and Joe went into the toilet—for a change.

In the front room it lay—still once more—its thumbs clenched into its fists, its eyes closed.

In the baby's comprehensive mind—unconscious thoughts were put—weaving the future out of the past—as it lay and sucked its lips.

Nothing lasted for long—since she had no strength to bear it—a flash—a sound! Then it focused in space somewhere—by chance, this thing that was disturbing her and fell as a bolt and stuck in her right ear—a boring pain.

The fight was on.

She rolled her head, screwed up her face, gasping·and choking in her agony, her fists or fingers aimlessly striking across her brows.

It must have been about five A.M. on the fourth day. Mrs. D got up from where she had been lying asleep on the double bed beside the mother to go and see.

What's the trouble now, said the mother, why doesn't it go to sleep? It's been asleep all night, said Mrs. D seeing the gray dawn outside and lighting a candle, don't bother yourself now, I'll care for it. So she picked it up and took

it to the kitchen at the back of the house to dry and change
it. I'll be back in a minute, she added, for you to suck it—
if you're awake, she said again to herself under her breath
as she went down the corridor.

But the baby writhed and drew her nails about her eyes
and nose until small bloody scratches marked her cheeks
when Mrs. D had lit the kitchen lamp and closed the door
and turned to look at her.

Look at you now, you miserable little brat, she said to it.
You've got yourself all scratched to bits. So she picked up
the tiny reddish hands one at a time and looking closely at
the nails bit them off—it would be bad luck to cut them—
as well as she could, so the baby could no longer do herself
a damage.

The infant cried again and pumped its bony knees up
and down, knocking them together, crossing and recross-
ing its hands and wrists—that harsh, hoarse, grunting, barking, wheezing, scraping, frantic cry of an agonizing infant.

Shut up, you'll wake the whole house, she said to it again
going to the stove in her bare feet to get warm water with
which to wipe it. You'd think I was killing you the way
you carry on.

But nothing would stop it. Mrs. D stopped her work
instead and taking the thing up, unpinned, blanket and all,
joggled it up and down on one arm while she shifted the
kettle to the back of the range with the other.

When at last it sobbingly quieted, she laid it on the table
once more and would have finished changing it. But no
more it felt the hard surface than it began again—fairly
frantic now.

She put the sweetened bottle in its mouth. It sucked
eagerly, then as quickly threw back its head, opened its
mouth and gurgling with half swallowed water, cried and
choked again—until in alarm this time Mrs. D grabbed it
quickly up and turning it over, jounced it in her hands
once more until it could at least begin to breathe again.

Try once more. She looked carefully this time watching
the twisting, tormented face. Then—while the baby, more

from exhaustion than anything else, drowsed a moment, she went to the sink, found a piece of soap, took up a paring knife and began to whittle.

First she cut off the end of the soap cake a finger long. This she pared then sharpened, about an inch or two of it. Then wetting it at the faucet, she rubbed it with her fingers to take out the knife marks, smoothed it, and taking it in her hand, finally went to the baby, lifted up its flails of feet by their ankles no bigger than her finger and not half so strong, and gently pushed the soap plug into the little hole between the buttocks.

The baby startled, stiffened and the soap came out. Carefully Mrs. D inserted it again, well in this time, and held it there by pinching with her fingers. There, try and get by that, she said to the baby, yawning and pulling up a chair with her left hand to sit and wait.

The light was growing outside, a cat yowled blood-curdlingly—a yowl that was matched instantly by another half a tone higher and with a fiercer accent. Then an explosion of wild spits and yells and the rattle of some fallen metal object.

That's why the garbage gets all out of the cans, said Mrs. D. You'd think they'd keep their damned animals in the house at night. There, that'll fix you, she added to the baby, that'll fix you, she said again with satisfaction.

The dawn was rapidly approaching now. Joe was up and in the bathroom shaving. You could hear the water and the hoarse sound of the closet flushed. Mrs. D took the baby, new diapered and half sleeping, back to the mother to be nursed.

But the infant would not.

Get out of here, said Gurlie finally, go on into the kitchen and get breakfast. I can do this better alone. But Mrs. D could hear the battle going on as she worked. Joe heard it too.

What's the matter, he said to Mrs. D, coming into the kitchen.

What's the matter! said the latter pausing a minute to

look at him. What's the matter? The baby's crying.

Joe lifted his eyes quietly a moment to hers then sat down to his coffee. Without opening his mouth again, he finished this—hesitated—arose, then went to stand briefly before his wife's door without entering, realized that she was busy, looked as though he was going to enter, then went back to the kitchen and, turning, said to Mrs. D, Yes, it's crying.

Well, there's nothing I can do, he added to the wall and stove. So he went and took up his hat from the rack in the front hallway and came back once more to say to Mrs. D, Tell her I've gone. Then he opened the door and went downstairs.

She'll be glad to hear that, said Mrs. D to herself after the door had closed. The baby was still crying distractedly. But Mrs. D, having already had two samples of the mother's temper during the past two days, made up her mind she wouldn't go in the room till she was called this time, so she went back and began to wash the breakfast dishes.

The baby cried all that day except when Mrs. D without a word to anyone gave it twenty drops of paragoric in a spoon of sweetened water. The baby slept three hours that time. But when Joe returned that night it was again crying in the front room where they'd placed it.

He came in, heard the sound, went toward it, saw the baby beating itself about the face with its hands and looking, heard no other sound in the place. Puzzled, he stood there wondering at the thing, troubled and amazed. He couldn't make it out.

Gurlie, he called out. No answer. That's funny. He went to the bedroom door, opened it, looked in. His wife was fast asleep, her face flushed, her hair disheveled. He went to the kitchen. No one. He went back to the infant. It looked sick to him, drawn, miserable. Its voice was cracked and sometimes it didn't sound at all when it cried. Where was Mrs. D?

Then he heard the stairs creak. And in she came, a paper bag in hand.

Jesus, is it still yelling, was the first thing the woman said between puffing breaths. There's been the devil here today. I never saw a thing like that for screaming in all the length of my life—I'm glad you're here to hear it.

And as she went through the room, Joe caught a strong whiff of her beery breath. He nodded and went over to watch the baby.

The thing's sick, he made up his mind. He put his hand on its face and the skin was dry and hot. And through his chest he felt a tight knot drawn. Sick. A tiny thing like that, you almost didn't dare to lift it in your hands it seemed so frail. It wouldn't live. He could see that from the first. It wouldn't live.

Mrs. D came into the room again, having doffed her draggled hat. And would you believe it if I told you its mother's sleeping? She looked at Joe but once again he lifted that quiet grey eye to hers and she didn't face it.

The child's sick, he said to her.

Sick? said Mrs. D.

Do you think we should get a doctor?

A what? said Mrs. D. A doctor? What for?

It doesn't look to me as if it will live, said Joe.

Live? That? It'll live to be a hundred, said Mrs. D with a slightly shaky roar of laughter. I never saw the like of it for strength—for its size. It's had us crazy.

What's that? said the voice from the bedroom. Joe went at once—slowly, to the door, then tapping on it gently, opened it and went in.

Well, how are you? he said cheerfully, attempting a broad smile. But this didn't go well with Gurlie.

Is that thing still crying? she said.

Well, you can hear it, can't you? said he.

I think the baby is sick, said Joe, seriously. Or maybe you haven't enough milk for it.

What! said the wife. Look at this. And she sat up abruptly, pulled aside her buttoned gown and showed him her breasts, taut with engorgement and the milk in them, the nipples erect. Look at this. I wish you had them. I'm

soaked to the waist with them now. Not enough milk, did
you say? And she took the nipples between her fingers so
that a stream of milk spurted out, landing across the back
of his hand as he sat there. He looked down at it but did
not at once wipe it off.

Well, is it my fault? his wife went on. I have the milk for
it, but it won't suck. And you come here and blame me.

Ach! who's talking of blame? If the child is sick, why
don't you call a doctor?

What have we got the midwife for? That's her business.
Don't you bring any doctor to this house. You must have
money, the way you talk.

Well, said Joe then, settle it yourself. And he went out,
lingering a moment at the door as Mrs. D passed him coming in with the baby to put it to the breast once more.

This time it took hold and the milk gushed so fast into
its gullet that it choked it. It drew back and coughed, then
cried, then when they put it back it merely yelled and
turned its face aside. Joe shook his head and vanished.

For three days the house was an inferno. Each night
when Joe returned he found the baby weaker, thinner, its
scrawny face more shrunk and, worst of all, Gurlie's
breasts suddenly were empty. The aunt had come to offer
her assistance and advice. One blast from Gurlie and she
had retired not to return again till the fall.

The baby cried and slept, surreptitiously drugged by
heavy draughts of paragoric. Now it vomited from time to
time, even when it did swallow a stomachful, or even half
of that.

A vomiting baby always does well in the end, said Mrs.
D, but that wasn't going so well either, latterly. So she
looked around for someone to blame it on. Who else but
Joe? Mrs. D couldn't see Joe. She felt now that when the
baby cried somehow he was back of it—even though he
was at the office all day. His awkward, sensitive hands—
turned her sour. If I was your wife, she said to herself
when she looked at him, I wouldn't be baking cakes for
you when you come home, I'd have a nice big mud pie

ready for you. And for the thousandth time she went to care for the baby who was still crying.

Tempers grew shorter as the days increased. It began to look really serious until finally Joe decided he'd put an end to it. Coming up the stairs one night and hearing the pitiful hoarse blast of the baby's torment still going on, he turned back and walked across a few blocks to where he had seen a doctor's sign one day on a residence near the park.

There it was—T. Wesley Colt, M.D. A different meaning it had now that he came for business—half relief, half distrust.

Joe mounted the brownstone steps, rang the bell and when a young woman came to the door, removed his hat and asked for the doctor.

The doctor is at supper. If you will come back at seven o'clock.

It's for the baby, said Joe earnestly.

A male voice sounded inside: Close that door. Then a man appeared, a young man. What's this? he said.

Are you the doctor? said Joe.

Yes, said the man, what is it?

A baby.

Been sick a week, I suppose, said the doctor.

Yes, just about, said Joe.

Then you come to me at this time, don't you know I'm eating supper?

Ya, said Joe, I suppose so. I'd like my supper too, and he was going out when the doctor stopped him. Where is it?

104th Street.

Poor pickings, thought the doctor, but—All right, wait a minute, he said.

Joe felt grateful to the young man as they walked over the few blocks and climbed the stairs to the flat which had been turned into some sort of a savage den for him in the last few days. He felt that now he had come armed, he felt he had a protector, he opened the door and invited Dr. Colt to precede him.

The doctor walked in.

Gurlie was furious when Joe went to her in the bedroom. Keep him out there, she said, I don't want to see him. So they took the wobbly headed mite into the kitchen and laid it on a blanket on the table.

Mrs. D was in the midst of preparing what supper there was to be that night. She too was skeptical and angry, looking down from her height of years and experience on this young man, this intruder, who seemed to threaten to dethrone her.

I guess this is the first she's fallen asleep in the last three days, said Mrs. D.

Strip it, said the doctor.

He thinks maybe a pin's sticking it, thought Mrs. D. But she did as she was told, fumbling and fussing. Let me see that diaper, said the doctor. It was spinach green. How many a day of these?

Every time you change it, said Mrs. D. She strains, doctor, till it's a pity to look at her—and the color is terrible.

How many times is that? said the doctor.

Mrs. D looked at him with a blank expression. Well, she said, did you think I counted them?

Oh, that many, said the doctor. For a week, I hear, is that right?

Mrs. D looked at Joe with murder in her eyes. Now, doctor—then she stopped. About a week, said Mrs. D.

And what have you given it?

We've tried everything, said Mrs. D. The last was a cup of water with a mite of bee's honey in it.

Maybe that's what's the matter with it, commented the doctor, half to himself. Is the cord off yet?

Yesterday, said Mrs. D as she finished undressing the infant.

Dry?

Not yet, I have a raisin on it, she added casually.

A raisin?

With the seeds out of it, Mrs. D continued.

Sugar cured, eh? replied the doctor.

My mother was a nurse for forty-five years before me, said Mrs. D. But the doctor was not listening.

Now the doctor picked the little thing up in his hands and turned it over. Its skin was hot and dry, it wrinkled under his fingers; there was no fat there. He shook his head, then asked: Where's the mother?

In the bedroom, doctor, said Joe, resting.

May I see her? Then sensing Joe's hesitation, he added: All I want to see is her breasts, if there's any milk in them.

Joe went to ask her if she'd see the doctor.

All right, let him come, said Gurlie. So he came, looked at her breasts which were flat now, said, Thank you, sorry to bother you, and went out while she stared at him unsmiling.

What does it weigh?

Weigh? said Mrs. D. Oh, about five pounds and half or so, I'd guess. It's lost a good bit in the last five days.

Haven't you some scales in the pantry?

I think I could find them, said Joe. So he went fumbling around among the pans until in a drawer he drew out a large pair of fish scales with a hook at the bottom. Dr. Colt tied the baby up in a diaper, knotted the four ends back and forth and lifted the weight up an inch off the table. All looked to see what the sliding point would rest at on the brass face of the crude instrument.

Five pounds and a half, said Mrs. D triumphantly. Didn't I say so?

That's bad, said the doctor, a little over five pounds, about five and a quarter, as far as I can make out. The child's in poor condition. Dress it, he added after he had looked down its throat, felt of its belly, sounded its lungs and taken its temperature—105 rectal. The child's sick—very sick.

Will you please wash this—in cold water, he added handing the thermometer to Mrs. D.

She took it gingerly, wondering how to work it. So that's one of them new temperature sticks, she thought to herself turning it over in her hand.

The doctor told them to give the baby barley water for three days, told Mrs. D how to prepare it—told them to sponge the baby, to syringe it—to bind up the mother's breasts. And went off saying he'd see it again two days later when they had had a chance to carry out his instructions.

Sure, and now go home and have your supper, my boy, said Mrs. D. You've earned your money—for Joe paid him at the door. How much? asked Mrs. D. Ah, what does he know, a young lad like that?

No use. The baby cried the same. Barley water, said the mother disgustedly. Barley water! to a starving baby? But Joe insisted so they tried the barley water and the infant would not take it. And when it did it vomited and purged as green as ever.

No more doctors, said the mother angrily. The fools, anybody can do that.

Well, said Joe, what are we going to do then?

To this Mrs. D responded that, if they would give her a free hand, she could manage it, but if they were going to take things out of her hands continually, what was she there for anyhow?

I'd like to know that myself, said Gurlie quickly.

The baby was two weeks old now and had lost a pound or more. Each day after that when Joe came home from the office he'd weigh it, hoping against hope—until he gave it up—and gave the baby up for lost. The doctor was taboo. Give it anything, at last Joe said, get a can of condensed milk and give it that. Children like sugar, give it some of that.

And kill it, said the mother. Joe felt the force of that and had no answer.

The mother's breasts were entirely empty now, but not knowing what else to do, they came back with the baby to the breast as a last resort.

Or send it to Coney Island to the incubators, said Joe finally.

Mrs. D had pumped some milk out of both breasts and tried a spoon then a dropper—nothing doing.

They tried it till Gurlie was disgusted. One day she was sitting with chest cramped over, cross-legged on the bed, red faced, Mrs. D tapping her foot on the floor, till it almost drove the mother crazy. She turned on the nurse with a flash and damned her up and down with such animal violence that she drove her from the room in anger and surprise. Get out of here. You're no good. It's all your fault, you dirty good for nothing. Get out of here. What do we pay you for?

You haven't paid me a thing yet, said Mrs. D. But seeing the fierce light in the other woman's eyes, she quickly retired closing the door behind her and saying, Well, if she's not gone crazy with it, I'm a Jew. And kept to the kitchen the rest of the afternoon till Joe should come home for her to get her money. She was through.

Gurlie sighed a sigh of relief, took up the baby and put it to the breast again. It was thin, dry lipped, crying. As she touched it, it wrinkled up its wizened face and squeezed out the maddening mechanical cry of a starved child. Then it opened its mouth in an O and stretched its skinny neck, as if seeking to suck. The mother took it up for the ten thousandth time—she thought—and pulled out her breast. It went eagerly at the gross nipple but instead of sucking, it fumbled, did not close its jaws but panted eagerly without taking hold, rubbing its face back and forth on the breast aimlessly, then screwing up its face again and squawking feebly. It was infuriating to Gurlie.

She pinched up her breast once more, pushed it into the mouth and, putting her finger under the tiny thin-boned jaw closed that forcibly. The infant screamed through its forcibly closed gums, struggling and twisting to draw back and breathe. Gurlie persisted, her own chest bursting from the position she was in.

Then suddenly she threw the baby from her. It fell, of course, on the soft bed, bounced on its face and screamed anew.

The woman threw back the covers and got up. She was white with fury now. Leaving the child where it was, she got a coat and putting it on, went out into the other room, closing the door behind her and sat by the window.

Gott in himmel! she raved, holding her hands to her ears. Then she sat up cold as ice and looked at the sharp details of the sky and street—at the approach of evening. She felt big alone, she could have clutched the whole world up in one fist and smashed it to smithereens.

When Joe came in, she was still there. She turned with a hard look at him but he was not in a mood for it this time.

Where's the baby?

I don't know, she said. On the bed, I guess.

He went into the bedroom and finding it uncovered, turned back the edge of the quilt over it, seeing it was asleep.

What's happened today?

I don't know.

Where's the woman?

I don't know—and with that his wife arose and went into the bedroom and closed the door.

Joe went to the kitchen and found Mrs. D with two empty beer bottles on the table before her—but she was not drunk. I'm leaving, said Mrs. D, I'm through digging out anybody's dirty place for them.

How much do I owe you? said Joe.

Two dollars a day, for fourteen days, that's twenty-eight dollars, said Mrs. D.

Here you are, said Joe, handing her the money. Count it before you put it in your pocket.

I'd be honest enough to return it if you give me more than is coming to me, said Mrs. D. And with this she took off her apron and began to look around for her bag in which to pack her things.

When she had gone, Joe went back to the bedroom. There was no supper ready. I'm going down to get some delicatessen, he said. What's happened to the baby?

Gurlie, dull and indifferent, had not touched it where it lay. There it is, she said.

Nurse any better?

No.

Joe looked and the thing stirred a little without waking. Then he went out and returned with a can of condensed milk among other things he had bought. It was still sleeping.

He took up the can, read the directions, and opened it, ladled out a teaspoonful of the contents awkwardly, measured out the water, filled a bottle and, handing it to Gurlie, told her to put it in the baby's mouth. This she did indifferently. The thing sucked eagerly. Finished the bottle. Gaped for more. He went back to the kitchen and filled the bottle again. It emptied that. The third bottle it refused after a few sucks as its head rolled aside slowly with milk oozing from the corner of its mouth and, with a comical distorted look of contentment on its face, fell asleep again.

On the coverlet where the child's head had lain the whole afternoon there was a yellow drying spot. The abscess in its ear had broken.

The battle between the pigmy and the giants was now over. The child was fed with condensed milk and began to thrive, not perfectly, but at least it fed and grew.

Now it was time for the sister to return home. Five years of age. Where is my baby brother? she asked at once. I wanna see him. But when she saw the baby and was told it was a little baby girlie like herself, The nasty thing, she said and, before anyone could stop her, she slapped it with all her strength right in the face.

from **In the Money**

WHEN she got to the park with the children, Lottie walking and Flossie in her carriage, Gurlie continued idling along in the brilliant sunlight thinking to herself of the present and the future. Squirrels frisked about here and there and fat pigeons walked ahead of the carriage, zigzagging right and left, glancing back or pecking quickly at invisible crumbs about them. Gurlie didn't even see them, almost running them down now with the baby carriage wheels so tame they were. Lottie would stop, holding her breath, as a pigeon just moved enough sometimes for the carriage to pass. Then breathing again the child would resume her walk, catching up the step or two she had lost to her mother's side as they went along. You couldn't push them out of the way they were so fat, cozy and secure there.

It was very lovely in that part of the park with rolling rocky land and a small stream that always made Gurlie think of the days before there was ever a city there but a romantic forest where wild beasts and Indians lived undisturbed. She came out of that soon, preferring the sun in her face as she started southward toward the reservoir. Now there were many sunny bays and well kept patches of fresh grass along the winding path as she kept sauntering further. At one of these where there were two benches she stopped to rest. She was very warm from walking. Flossie was clamoring to get down so Gurlie spread a small blanket on the grass and let her sit on it. The ground was warm and dry when she put her hand down to feel it.

"Can I walk on the grass?" asked Lottie. "Yes," said Gurlie, "as much as you like." Finding it even drier than she had expected and quite comfortable, Gurlie herself sat

233

on the grass along with the children where there was a patch of clover and began to go over it carefully looking for four leafed ones.

"What are you looking for, Mammie?" "Oh go on and play." The baby was soon on her hands and knees and began to wander off.

"Look!" said a little girl who was passing with an older woman. "You *can* go on the grass." "No," said the woman, "I told you no. It's damp there and you'll catch cold." Gurlie didn't hear them. The little girl began to cry. "Mama," she called back over her shoulder. "I wanna play on the grass like them," pointing, "and Nana won't let me."

Gurlie looked up and saw the child with what appeared to be her grandmother while a few paces back a younger woman, probably the mother, was coming along up the little hill pushing a very heavy English baby coach with exaggerated effort. "Ugh!" she said, wobbling her shoulders heavily. "Let's sit down here." "No," said the older woman, "not here." With that the younger woman turned her carriage crosswise with the walk and collapsed into one of the benches. She would go no further.

The older woman stood a moment then sat down also. Gurlie twenty feet away with her back to them continued minding her own business. Three pigeons settled to the walk near the newcomers and the little girl was at once attracted. "I wanna peanut to feed the birdies." She began to burrow with her hand at the foot of the carriage. "All right, all right," said her mother. "Keep your hands out of there. You might be sorry."

The lady who was rather fat and slow in her movements took a few peanuts from a paper bag into her lap and cracked the shells. The little girl took one of the nuts before it was cracked and threw it violently at the birds who hopped a few feet away from her, went to the nut, eyed it and came back to the bench. "You see," said the woman to the little girl, "that's what you get for being in such a hurry, they won't eat it. Here. Hold out your hand to them"—but the little girl was afraid.

Gurlie could hear them but she did not turn round.

"Oh look!" said the woman to the old lady beside her. "Isn't that a cute baby? Look at it trying to walk. Ooops! there it goes." And indeed little Flossie did go down hard on her bottom trying to come toward the bench whence the new excitement was emanating. She crawled along now a few feet then sat back and grinned at the newcomers.

"I wanna play with the baby," said the little girl. "No," said the older woman. "I don't want you to go on the grass." The child looked at her mother then put one little foot on the grass and turned sideways to look at her grandmother who got up and grabbing her roughly by the arm jerked her back and shook her finger in her face. "No! I said, No!"

"Oh mother," said the younger woman. "Leave the child alone."

"Leave her alone, yes. If she has croup again tonight then who will be to blame? Then I'll leave her alone. Come on. I want to go." "Not yet," said her daughter. "I'm tired."

Now the little girl saw Lottie and walked along the asphalt walk until she was opposite her. There she stood and smiled putting her head sidewise and twisting her body a little sharply so that her little skirts rocked around her with a swish. Then her face got serious. Then she smiled a big smile but she didn't dare go on the grass to her new found friend.

The lady took her baby out of the heavy carriage and held it on her lap. It was quite a small baby and very sleepy, not more than seven or eight months old. She was arguing with the older woman who finally shrugged her shoulders and turned away. The young woman as Gurlie had done before spread a blanket also on the perfectly dry lawn and laid her baby on it while she herself sat on a corner of it. She seemed greatly amused at Flossie's gyrations.

"Oh," she said after a moment, "Pthuh! No, no, no! Look, lady," she said to Gurlie. "Look what your child's doing."

Gurlie looked. Flossie was sitting on the grass with her back to her mother perfectly quiet.

"Look!" said the woman. "She's eating something. It's a peanut I think." Gurlie called to her infant. "Spit it out. She's all right," she said to the woman. "It won't hurt her." The woman was scandalized. "Oh I'd be frightened," she said. "It might be a worm." Gurlie laughed but she got up and went to Flossie leaning down over her. "Nasty," she said and she put her finger in the baby's mouth. It was a little stone which Flossie was mouthing making half disgusted faces while she chewed. "Come here," said Gurlie and she put her back on the blanket. "Now stay there."

A great screaming and whacking went up at this from the other end of the little grass plot. The grandmother had the little girl and was shaking her as a terrier shakes a pillow. "Didn't I tell you not to go on the grass. You're the most disobedient child I have ever seen. Sit down there," and she plunked her on the bench where the child sobbed, looking toward Lottie in great shame and misery.

After a moment the old woman took the child by the wrist and walked off down the path. "I'm not staying here," she said to her daughter. "I'm going home." "Leave Sarah," the younger woman said. "I want her with me." So the older woman went off down the path alone. The young woman shook her head as Gurlie looked up at the scene, as much as to say, Isn't it awful? "Come here," she said to her child. "Come here. Blow!" She wiped her daughter's little face. "So. Now run and play with the little girl. But don't run away. And don't sit on the grass. Remember." The child was shy now and didn't want to go. But she went slowly just the same.

"It's awful," said the woman in the general direction in which Gurlie was sitting. "Old people get to be such fools. They forget that the world is changing. Look at that!" she added suddenly. "Quick!"

Flossie was struggling and shaking her head, pinching up her eyes and opening her mouth as wide as she could. What a face! "What in the world has she got?" said the woman who had run to her. "It's a cigarette!"

Sure enough Flossie had found a cigarette butt in the grass and had been chewing it bitterly and in silence.

"Let her learn," said Gurlie. "But she's too little, she don't know." "Let her learn then," said Gurlie. "If she doesn't like it she can spit it out."

"But look," said the woman. "A cigarette butt. Somebody else has been sucking it. It's dirty. It'll poison her." "She shouldn't eat it then," said Gurlie.

The woman looked at her. "I'd be afraid."

"Where are those children?" "Leave them alone," said Gurlie. As a matter of fact the two older girls had merely stepped in among some low spruce branches where there was a carpet of red needles covering the dry ground. The little girls were busy gathering handfuls of the stuff and bringing it out through the low branches gingerly to make a little heap of it on the grass beyond.

"Do you have your mother living with you?" said the woman to Gurlie.

"No," said Gurlie. "Where is she going?"

"Oh she'll come back," said the woman. "She always does that. That's an awfully cute little girl you have. Have you any other children?"

"No," said Gurlie. "Is that a boy?" "Yes," said the woman as if apologetically. "Boys are so different. Look how he's sleeping. Ain't that cute. I love to look at them when they're sleeping. But he can be a devil. She always picks him up. When my husband's home he lets her do it. At home I'm the only one that lets him cry."

Two small boys broke through the trees where Lottie and her friend were playing, stopped a minute, kicked over the pile of spruce needles they had gathered and ran off laughing and turning backward to see the effect of their raid. They disappeared down the path.

The girls came to their mothers, "Look what those bad boys did."

"Oh go on," said Gurlie. "Pick them up again. That'll give you something to do." The other little girl looked at Gurlie with her mouth open and went off with Lottie to pick up some more of the spruce needles.

"You don't worry about things, do you?" said the woman to Gurlie.

Gurlie laughed at her. "You're German, aren't you," said Gurlie. "You're all alike you Germans. I wish I could find a four leafed clover."

"You don't worry about nothing, do you?" said the woman. Gurlie looked at her. "I don't let things worry me," she said. "If you read the Bible you'll know everything that's going to happen."

"Is that right?" said the woman. "But I don't know what to do about my mother."

"Oh," said Gurlie. "That'll be all right."

"Yes, I suppose it will. But she's driving us crazy. She's good, but I think she's sick. She walks around at night and if the baby cries she picks him up before I can even get there. I don't own my own baby. I suppose she thinks of her own children, there was seven of us and we were always sick. I'm sorry for her, but you can't talk to her."

"Why don't you send her away?" said Gurlie.

"I would if I knew where to send her," said the woman. "We're all wrecks. I had enough. She picks on my little girl something terrible. But I'm not going to let her spoil my baby."

"Haven't you got anyone else in the family you can send her to?"

"No, they're all on the other side." "Well, send her over there then," said Gurlie. "She won't go. I tried to make her go last year. They lost all they had over there and she won't go back."

"Doesn't she sew or knit?" said Gurlie.

"Oh she can't sit still long enough for that. She just wants to clean all the time. She says I'm dirty. She says nobody knows how to keep house in this country. I tell her this isn't Germany but that don't make no difference to her. She says the same things all the time."

"Doesn't she read?"

"No. I wish I could be like you. Are you German?" "No," said Gurlie and began to look into the grass again. The woman looked down at the little patch of clover which Gurlie was examining and then leaned over a little to look up into Gurlie's eyes, then looked down at the clover again. There were a few small white blossoms in the patch and a bee came and began to walk nervously over one of them.

"Look, there's a bee," said the woman, "he'll sting you." Gurlie laughed. "They won't hurt you." "They sting, don't they?" "No," said Gurlie and pushed the bee away with her hand. "Oh!" said the woman drawing back. As she did so she turned her head and jumped up. There was little Flossie again with her hands in her mouth. "Crackie, cookie, crackie!" she said as the woman came at her.

A pleasant old man who was strolling by at the moment, looked down at her smiling. "Dada," she said. "Bring her here," said Gurlie to the woman. "Shoe," said the baby looking at the man's feet. "She's got something in her mouth again," said the woman, fetching Flossie to her mother. "I didn't want to take it out. You better do it."

"Give her to me," said Gurlie. "Spit it out." The baby only closed her mouth the harder and bowing her head a little looked up at her mother with reluctant eyes. Gurlie put her finger into the baby's mouth and fished around in her cheeks until she found something which turned out to be a piece of peanut shell.

"Does she always do that?" said the woman. "I don't think it's good for them to eat things like that. Won't she get convulsions? I know banana peels will give them convulsions."

The man who stopped a moment to look at the baby walked quietly away.

"My poor baby's got a birthmark," the woman began again apropos of nothing at all.

"Where?" said Gurlie. "On his face?" "Yes," said the woman. "I wish I knew what to do about it. Look, you can see it from here."

"I can't see anything," said Gurlie. She got up slowly and rubbed her knees. "Oof!" she said straightening herself. She went with the woman to see the sleeping child. There he lay fast asleep on the blanket, his head turned to one side, his arms spread symmetrically out, bent at the elbows, his hands palms up, completely relaxed. You could see him breathe.

The woman turned the sleeping child's face up so Gurlie could see it. There was a mottled red streak going up across the forehead from the base of the nose into the hair which was very blond and thin, and the left eyelid was also a deep winey red. "That's nothing," said Gurlie. "That'll go away. Lots of children have that. I'll bet he has another spot like it at the back of his neck."

"That's right," said the woman. "You do know, don't you? What makes them? The one at the back of his head will be covered by hair but this one——"

"You ought to know, they call them *storch biss* in German."

"You mean the stork is supposed to bite them when he brings them, is that it? Look, he's waking up."

The baby yawned and stretched, stiff legged. "Isn't he wonderful?" said the mother. Gurlie nodded. The infant opened two deep blue eyes. "He's getting so fresh now. They get so *fresh* at this age. Watch him!" Gurlie was watching. He was really a very nice little boy.

"He's perfect, except for that birth mark. And they didn't circumcise him good either. We're not Jews but my husband wanted it done so they did it. They didn't do a good job, they left too much skin. I wouldn't know except I've seen other little boys. It's just like a little acorn on the end but you can't see his unless I pull back the skin. That ain't right."

The baby opened his eyes wide now and smiled self-consciously. Then he grew excited and, stiff legged, began to kick his feet up and down on the blanket. "He loves to do that," said the woman. "Mother puts a pillow for him. She's afraid he'll hurt his heels."

Now the baby twisted his body round until he had turned over then raised his head and looked at them, smiling. "He crawls backward," said the mother. "Why do babies always do that—maybe it's because their arms are stronger than their legs. But he's so different from his sister. With her I had troubles but he eats everything." She picked him up. "Agh, agh, agh!" said he standing on his toes. "He always wants to stand on his toes," said the mother.

"Sometimes when he's lying there he'll raise himself up on his heels and bang himself down, hard, many times. Can he hurt his kidneys?"

The woman wet her right index finger with her tongue and plastered a small blond curl down on the baby's forehead.

Gurlie returned to where she had been sitting.

Left to themselves the two older girls had fetched spruce needles again until they had gathered enough of them to make two little patches which they called beds and there they were now stretched out flat on their backs, perfectly happy, talking together in low voices when back came the old lady in a fury.

"Get up from that ground," she said to the little girl while Lottie sat up, leaning back on her hands in terror. The little playmate was jerked to her feet.

"Don't spank me! Don't spank me!" she cried to the old lady. "Please! don't spank me!" But whang! she got it on one side, and now on the other. Whang! Then the woman turned on her daughter and let her have it till she, as well as Lottie was in tears.

Gurlie paid no attention except to glance at the old woman scornfully. Flossie crawled to her and sat down right in the center of the clover. Gurlie lifted her up and as she did so suddenly glanced back at a spot where the leaves had been turned over by the pressure of the baby's foot. No, only two threes that had been pressed together so that it looked like a four but when you pulled them apart the extra leaf slipped away and became part of the other one.

Lottie's little friend was being towed weeping loudly away. She had been told to hold onto the edge of the carriage, which she did crying lustily the while—not looking where she was going but stumbling over her own feet and the edge of the path they dragged her off to her fate.

"Come, Lottie, we'd better be going now," said Gurlie to her older daughter. She lay back for a moment on the soft grass with her hands under her head and looked up at the sun. The baby leaned over her and rested her head sidewise on her mother's breast. Lottie too came beside her mother and stood looking down at her.

CHAPTER XIII. HOTEL ROOM SYMPHONY

A HOTEL ROOM is a purgatory between desires, a window to leap from, a prison cell, the neatness of a well trimmed coffin, reminiscent of life—that was here last night, in this bed, a remainder seeking to keep some slight warmth to itself after *that* has passed by, disappeared. A few clean sheets, a new pillow case, the pillow knocked up to a resemblance of freshness by the old sour faced bedmaker—her eyes too indifferent to look for anything but pennies and dimes—especially dimes since they are thin and small and easily lost—that fell out of the pocket of the pants taken off carelessly, a good hairpin, used at once as she sweats and dusts and changes.

Even the rain isn't more than dust here—except for its patter. Futile to rouse anything. No use more than to streak the already grimy windows—Why bother with anything? thought Joe. For what? Let them have it? Especially when it is easily your own. That is the time to open the palms of the hands and let it slide away—so that the hands may be clean again. Empty. Clean.

Empty. Joe looked out through the rain over the city of Washington and saw the dome of the Capitol. Barefooted in his underwear. This was the big day. Hard to imagine. Compared with the world of his imagination or even with the two, four, six, eight world of affairs, his own little business seemed as unimpressive to him, infantile even, as dirty socks on the back of a chair.

Infantile. What good is it? If it were lying there on that table, so that by reaching out my hand for it I should possess myself of the wealth of the world—I wouldn't stir a finger. I'd shave and go down for breakfast.

So he turned on the hot water in the basin and prepared to shave—or find some other pretext. It's all right for some people though, without brains or consciences. If they didn't have money they wouldn't have any excuse for building churches. Somebody would have to crack their heads open with a hammer, make a crack in the bone. Then you could with a small piece of metal, a strong screwdriver wouldn't be a bad thing, pry it open a little and put some sense in. Take out the lever and it would close itself. Then they'd know the value of money, and so forth.

No use. You have to be an actor. You have to get all excited and make them think you want something desperately. You *have* to. They have to see it in your face, that you want money. Because it is important. That's why. Because with money you can buy everything. Joe laughed out loud. You can buy everything! Even a load of horse shit. He laughed.

But if you don't make a good show you disappoint people. They don't think you know. They hate you. Yes they do, they hate you. You're their enemy. You have to respect money. You owe it to them. You owe it to them because you're sorry for them, you have to show them that they're right. Money is, by God, valuable. It means everything. Then you have honored humanity and you don't have to feel sorry for them. You don't have to give a damn whether they ... He cut himself trying to shave down into the sharp cleft of his chin.

Joe didn't feel impressed. "Be at the White House offices at 9:45. Your appointment is for 10 sharp. I'll meet you there." It was signed by the Postmaster General himself. The President of the United States wanted to see him. Just to *see* me, said Joe. That's all. He doesn't believe me. He wants to see me. Then what will he know? He isn't a woman to know by instinct what I am.

Joe had read the papers. He knew what had taken place and the President's attitude toward him. Roosevelt had been quoted as saying: "I don't like this man Stecher. I don't like his way of doing business." Payne had been splendid, no question—but why? It wasn't particularly out of any good feeling or understanding of the situation. Not at all. Merely that the setup had put him, Payne, and his department, in a bad position. If he, Joe Stecher, hadn't played his game so as to put the pressure on when its effect would be most telling—what chance would he have had? Self-interest is a great benefactor, thought Joe. Anyhow, that's how it was and I know it.

And those Associates! Babes in the wood. Joe felt kindly toward them. What a lot of *narren*. They go about with their mouths open like children at a circus. You walk up to them and put a nickel in their mouths. They don't even see you. And they begin to play a tune. And so earnest! They know they are right. They are upholding the honor of the printer's trade. Joe smiled to himself.

But the bastards can make trouble. They made enough of it for me—without knowing what they were doing.

He knew how the President had listened to them. It was all in the papers. The President of the United States had listened to them and told them that he was heartily in favor of what they had to say. Then the Postmaster General had wept, so the papers said. My business made the Postmaster General stand before the President of the United States and cry, they say. A lie perhaps. Anyhow, sounds good.

Why not a good healthy lie? "Yes, Mr. President, you are completely right," that's what Joe wanted to say to the

President when he met him. He wanted to look him in the eye and say, "Mr. President, you are right. You are always right. This Joe Stecher is a thief and a blackguard. I would cancel that contract for the money order blanks at once by executive order, no matter what it costs. Don't trust him. Don't let that man get away with his crooked business. And if you don't believe me," Joe would say, "you call the chief of the Money Order Division that you have so unjustly dismissed after his long service, call the officials of the Mohawk Press, they'll tell you. This man Stecher is a crook."

While he said this, Joe would watch the President and he would see the look of self-satisfaction come to his face. He would see virtue triumph and the authority of the United States of America rise up in power before him and he, Joe Stecher, would—laugh! He'd laugh till his back crumbled. But he mustn't show it. He'd have to be a good poker player. He'd stand there without a trace of feeling under his moustache, he'd thank the President for his insight and initiative and—go home and—well, all right. Better not mention it.

Anyhow, whichever way you go, a man has to eat his breakfast once he's shaved, dressed—his shoes! My God he'd better get a shine. Probably in the basement somewhere.

At 9:45 Joe presented his card at the Executive Offices, was told to go in and sit down. Took off his raincoat, his rubbers, stood his umbrella in the stand and took the newspaper from his pocket to read. A quick glance about was all he needed: an office like any other—with unimportant differences.

"I was opposed to giving this contract to you, Mr. Stecher," the President was saying. The Postmaster General was beside them.

"Yes, Mr. President," said Joe. "I saw that in the papers."

"You did. I didn't like your way of going about it."

"Mr. President," broke in the Postmaster General.

The President held up his hand. "But my friend Payne seems to believe in you. You're said to be the ablest printer in the United States at this time, so I've been given to believe."

Joe made no move. "Thank you," he said.

"I want to ask you a question. My policy has been——"

Ah ha! thought Joe. So that's it.

"It's my policy to handle government work in government offices, under direct government control whenever it is possible to do so."

Sounds nice! thought Joe.

"What's that?"

"Nothing," said Joe. "I didn't say anything, sir."

"We have a Public Printer, why isn't the Money Order business in his hands?" There was a pause. "Well?" said the President.

"Do you want my opinion, sir?" asked Joe.

"Yes, that's what I asked you."

"He couldn't print them," said Joe.

"Why not?"

"He hasn't the equipment or the knowledge."

"We can get them, can't we? We can get anything we need."

Joe had made up his mind not to speak unless he was asked a direct question. "Speak up," said the President. "I want to know what you think."

"Yes," said Joe, "you can get anything you want if you pay for it. But not in a day."

"Why not?"

"Because they don't know how."

"How long do you suppose it would take to set up an efficient Printing Office in Washington and do this work and other work of the sort under our own power?"

"I couldn't say," said Joe.

"But you must have an opinion."

"You mean on a business basis?"

"Yes."

"You could get a shop to turn out the blanks in three or four months, but maybe not before six months, I think, if you spent enough money on it," said Joe.

"I think you're wrong," said the President. "We could do it if we had to. Are you going to be able to get the blanks out on time?"

"Yes, sir," said Joe.

"You seem very certain of yourself," said the President.

Joe did not answer. "I say you seem very sure of yourself," said the President.

"Yes, sir," said Joe.

"You think you'll be able to have the orders out on time?"

"Yes, sir," said Joe.

"Well, see that you do."

"He will," said the Postmaster General smiling in his kindly manner.

"Well, Payne," said the President, "I suppose that settles it. Perhaps you've made a wise decision under the circumstances. Good day, Gentlemen." He held out his hand. Joe took it, famous flesh! and without smiling turned away.

"Oh Payne, I want to see you for a moment," said the President.

The Postmaster General didn't look well. "Better take care of yourself," said Joe to him before leaving.

"That's all right, Stecher. Glad you came, and best of luck. You're all right. Goodbye," and he held the door open for Joe to go out.

Joe went, as cold and collected as if he were going out to buy a paper. So cold he could see the very hairs on the doorman's eyebrows as he walked past him into the outer office.

And that's that, said he to himself. All there is to it. Just as simple as that. I wonder what he wanted to see me for. I suppose he just wanted to see me. Just to see what sort of a skunk I'd turn out to be. Pot bellied, weasel snouted, peanut browed. A regular crook. I suppose he had me all figured out in his mind.

A GREAT man. Poor fellow. Joe didn't like him. Too much noise, big ideas. Well, if you think that way then pretty soon you're going to begin to have to be successful whether you like it or not. Then you'll have to begin to make a few pretty excuses to yourself, just to make it work. Then you're going to have to invent a few convenient lies to cover up the failures.

I wouldn't want him in my shop. Not in my shop. He'd find all kinds of excuses for not doing what I told him to do. Good excuses too.

He sat down to put on his rubbers. He put his raincoat over his shoulders, took his hat in hand and went out. It was raining as hard as ever. Opening his umbrella he walked from the Executive Offices to the street down the splashed sidewalk. No use sending a wire this time. Pack and go home. That's over with.

And what of it? So that was the business of the United States. Pretty small business, but very different when you see it than when you read about it in the papers. What but some men, with women on their necks half the time, trying to find out what the other fellow's thinking. And what do they get when they get through? Anything accurate? Anything really thoughtful? Anything even just? Never. Just a vague approximation. My policy. The policy of the government. Yah! said Joe. Go lay an egg.

What does a policy do? What work does it do? It does plenty. It uproots everything in its path. You make up your mind you're going to plow through. Then you go ahead and plow. You don't care anything more about it. You don't even look. You plow straight ahead, flowers, birds' nests, men, lives, opportunities—oh well. No point to that. You have to plow.

But he came back to it. No, there's more to it than that. That's not all. You stop paying attention to the truth of the

detail. You don't look to see whether that man is an honest
man, whether he's doing the job well or ill. All you care
about is, My policy. Let the government do the public
printing, a "long range" policy. Hum! grunted Joe.

Up in the hotel room he looked at his right hand, opened
it and closed it a few times. Now you've got to pick up
your shaving things and your dirty underwear, he said to
it. Come on, get busy! You can't shake Presidents' hands all
day. Get to work.

Get to work. He breathed a sigh of relief. He walked to
the station through the rain to save the hack fare. He had
plenty of time though—with his small black satchel in his
hand.

He sat in the smoking car by the window and watched
the landscape all afternoon, drenched with rain, the trees in
and about Washington still in full leaf, thinner and thinner
as he rode northward and across New Jersey—still raining
—toward evening. A few desolate cows, the winter wheat
up here and there a green grain—but miles and miles of
useless land. He never could make that out. Why isn't it
cleared of brush and cultivated—as it would be in Germany?

My policy! what else? My policy. Nothing works effi-
ciently any more because of that idea. Church, government
—the only thing that works is one man that pays attention
to what he is doing and knows what to do about it. My
brother plays the violin in Prague. My sister shows her legs
on the stage—I'm a printer. I hope we do our jobs all right.
Because if we don't—It's because it's to the advantage of
someone or other, my policy!—or we'd plant as much as
we want and need and we'd have a world worth living in.

Waste, waste, waste. There's the solution to everything.
Just cultivate that land, just that little bit of acreage of New
Jersey, just as far as you can see on both sides of this train
window, that is going to waste. That's all you have to do.
But really use it. And there'd be no more poverty or mis-
ery in the entire world—Just put it to use.

They haven't the intelligence. And they're too lazy and

smug and—stupid. That's all that's the matter. Anybody could solve the troubles of the world in fifteen minutes—if people had good will—and somebody wasn't preventing it, for a profit: And for the satisfaction of establishing "my policies."

Nearly every barn had advertisements painted over it in big letters for tobacco money to some stupid farmer. Joe shook his head. He detested farmers. Horrible. And nobody can stop it. What's public opinion? Do you know what public opinion is? It's—why ain't I gettin' more of it? That's what public opinion is. I wonder how many million people a year look out of a window every year between New York and Philadelphia and not one, not a single one, sees for one split second what is right before them as plain as your nose on your face. Never. They never see anything simple. It's all right there—but they don't know it. They're too important. They know too much. They're legislators, statesmen, big business executives, women!—they don't know anything—except what they're told.

Am I any better? What do I do? I get all excited about printing a few blanks for postal money orders. What have I got to propose? Honesty. Do one little thing straight—like playing the violin. At least I know that. They go to a concert and hear a man play the violin well. Wonderful! Marvelous! They cry, they applaud, they feel good inside—and it costs like hell too and they can pay for it. But do they know what it means, that he plays well? Do they? Not one of them.

They don't know what excellence means. No, not one of them. They simply don't know that it means to do one thing well. The rest—? To do it well. Honestly. Every day. And never to lie. Never.

What good would it do for an artist to lie to a piano or to a violin? No good at all. But they want to play the violin by telling it that "my policy" is to play the violin standing on my head or sitting in a bathtub, or—while I'm eating. Or using a shovel instead of a bow.

Wonder if I'd better not eat here—before going home.

CHAPTER XVII. NIGHT

"WHAT'S THE MATTER with the baby?" said Joe after supper. "I never heard her cry like that."

"She's been crying all afternoon," said his wife.

"What've you done to her?"

"I don't know," said Gurlie glancing at him sharply. "I put her in our room tonight. Maybe it's strange to her."

"Why did you do that?"

"I don't want her back there any more."

"Why not?"

"She bothers my mother." Joe looked but was silent.

The baby behind the closed doors subsided for a moment and the family went on with the meal. Grandma hardly raised her head from the plate and as nobody seemed to have anything more to say, nobody said anything. They ate in silence.

But the child in the closed room had not gone to sleep. Lottie following the usual routine was far away snug in her own little bed, but not the baby. She lay with wide open eyes staring into the dark—expectantly. She felt completely off her base, not knowing what was going to happen. Something was going to happen. Someone was coming to take her. She knew that. And she'd be back, she knew that too—maybe. They were here now waiting for her—but she didn't want to go. Not yet.

She lay listening, a long time. Sometimes she heard talking in the next room. Sometimes she didn't hear it. There was a bar of light from the street below that lay diagonally across the ceiling above her. Then she fell asleep and slept —a long, long time.

It was late. Joe had gone out after supper and had not yet returned. Gurlie stretching herself in the big bed near the baby fell asleep too finally. Nothing of the day's events at home had as yet come to Joe's ears. The old lady had agreed to wait until Sunday when she would speak to her son Gunnar and ask him to take her away. She and her daughter were from now on through with each other. Definitely. A few nights more and that would be the end of it.

A new world filled the entire room when the baby wakened. Stumbling upon memory, the short but intense memory of an infant, she lay there again with wide open eyes staring into a blankness peopled vividly by what she had seen that day—the storm of the dark, the stress and rocking foundations, angry voices which had suddenly, out of nowhere, jangled upon her ears all afternoon.

Such a little-tin-cup what could it possibly mean to her? Something as natural, as simple and overwhelming as the dark itself had suddenly disrupted her life.

By a slight movement of the air in the room, barely stirring the window shade, there appeared on the ceiling once more the strip of narrow, flickering light from some street lamp outside. Flossie watched it until her eyes closed with the heaviness on them. Then she opened them again! but they *were* open! and there it was still, unmoving, where it had been before.

She wanted to cry only it wouldn't come, the light wouldn't let it. She had heard herself cry in the afternoon, she had felt it all over her driving her to greater and greater furies until she had sweat and fought to surround herself with its deafening protection—stopping occasionally now and then only to see what else might be going on. She had heard herself with astonishment and satisfaction. Out of desperation she had once bent herself backward on her head and her heels, yelling. Her mother had picked her up and she had stopped. She had been put down and she began again to yell.

The light flickered, flickered, flickered on the ceiling above her head and she watched it intently.

But she wanted to hear herself again—to know that she was there. It felt less lonely to yell—it was the night with its angry faces and loneliness that was terrifying, her own voice killed it but it came again when she stopped—so she took up courage and cried out aloud. She could have stopped if she wanted to, she knew that. But in the night when one is alone in a strange place distorted, familiar faces appear. Alone but for the light and her own voice, she cried out for relief.

"What in heaven's name are you yelling for now?" said Gurlie leaning over the crib. "Go to sleep. Are you sick? What is it?"

This startled the baby afresh, who didn't know what to believe seeing her mother appear over her that way out of the dark so suddenly. Gurlie felt her bottom. It was dry. She felt her head. She felt her belly. "There's nothing the matter with you. You're a bad girl. Go to sleep."

That's just exactly what she wanted to do, go to sleep. Go to sleep. She must go to sleep. No.

She could see her mother go out of the room and close the door behind her, muttering. She could see her mother's head and her back and her left hand on the doorknob. She saw the door closing and the arm get shorter and disappear. She didn't want her mother to leave her there alone. Then it was dark again. The light on the ceiling shone steadily.

Then, while she was looking at it, the light went out quickly and completely. It was gone. She waited—she waited, then slowly the ceiling of the room began to disappear, going up, up, up, up, up! and it was a pit! Down, down—as far as she could see and there she stood teetering all alone at the top—down, down, down.

As she began to fall, little Flossie cried out with all her might. She heard it and struggled out from her bed clothes and stood holding on the side of her crib. Then waited, alone in the dark.

No reply.

"Mammie! Mammie!" she cried. She was not used to crying this way so she stopped and looked around right and left but there was nobody near her, not even Lottie in the next crib.

Just behind her were streaks and billows of uninterpretable meaning to which she turned in terror. Was it a face with angry brows, that puffed and strained and bellowed? It approached and hovered in the room, contorted into namelessness, and exploded before her.

It wanted to smile, the baby could see that. But more powerful than itself, it took on a twisted shape, unwillingly —bulges and furrows that vanished and reformed.

Now it will come again. She saw it. It was her grand-mother, a big face that filled the whole room. Instead of getting larger as it approached, it grew smaller—until she reached for the familiar arms and hands to lift her. She pushed herself up on her toes to be taken and there was nothing there.

Now the face reappeared in furious agitation and it was her mother's face that came closer and closer and then, angry and distorted, burst suddenly and angrily over her.

She reached in the dark, tried to take a step and fell face down upon the crib.

Gurlie came into the room, took up the child, placed her under the covers. "Now close your eyes and go to sleep," she said. But she went out at once again and closed the door behind her.

Flossie tried to lie quiet but after a while she opened her eyes and looked up again into the dark. She knew perfectly well what she had been told to do. But she began to sob instead. She struggled against the covers but they were tucked in tight. At this she caught her breath once or twice but remained silent.

Finally the infant got control of herself and listened. "Mammie!" she cried. "Mammie!" Then she could hear voices in the other room. She waited for several long min-utes. She called again and waited and still nothing hap-pened.

At this she began to yell, dully, methodically, without rest just to hear herself yell. Unending misery of an unal-terable world. No beginning and no end. This is life and this is my reply to it. Sleep can bring no answer, sleep the interrupter that denies and defies the great law.

I will not sleep. I refuse, I refuse, I refuse. Assure me
that this is not true. That this is not the end. Assure me
that the world will go on as it did before this dreadful fall.
Something is lying on top of me. Something is carrying me
away. I want to come back to what I know, that held me
and did not drive me away, but I am falling.

I am being driven away into a place I never saw. The
darkness is falling and I am going up, rapidly, through it.
She was sobbing and screaming now, harder than ever. In
blank terror.

Why doesn't someone come to me? She reached up as if
expecting to be taken. The end is approached in darkness,
obliterating all that has been heretofore. Blackness, the
mother of sleep, the worst misfortune of all.

"The little brat!" said Gurlie to Joe when he came in
later and heard her. She had been shrieking and screaming
all evening.

"I told you it was her teeth."

"Nothing of the sort. No. I refuse to let you go in to her.
It's all she wants. She's going to do what I say or cry until
morning. I will not give in."

"And you want me to sleep in there with her?"

"She'll stop the minute we light the light."

"Got any beer on the ice?"

"Yes."

"Let's go in the kitchen. She'll quiet down. Where's
your mother?"

"She's asleep," said Gurlie. "She says she's leaving us on
Sunday." It was a relief to get that off her chest before the
old lady herself could say anything.

"What's happened?"

"We can't live in the same house. It's no use. I'm going to
get a good maid this time. I'll get some good-looking green
girl and train her. We'll have to have someone. I'll make a
good maid of her."

"Listen to that child yell," said Joe. "She must be sick.
What frightened her today?"

"Nothing that I know," said Gurlie.

"You can't tell me that," said her husband. "She wouldn't be like that for nothing."

"Maybe something happened this morning when I was downtown. She was crying when I came in."

"Did your mother say anything?"

"No. Just that she had been bad."

"Did she spank her or punish her?"

"Maybe. I can't think of everything."

"Did you ask her?"

"No. I can't talk to her any more."

"Listen to that," said Joe. "Isn't that bad for her?"

"Let her yell. Of course, pick her up, spoil her. She'll hate me—that's probably what you want."

"Well, don't start on me," said Joe. "I haven't done anything."

The insane night prodding the infant with its numb hands, revealed her father's voice to her but not her father. She had been at it for hours, anger, acceptance and loneliness. So that when Joe and Gurlie finally went in to her she didn't quiet as they expected she would but seemed in a dazed terror. She didn't know them.

Joe went to pick her up but she squirmed almost out of his arms. "Give her to me," said Gurlie. But the baby pushed her away, shaking and twisting her head.

"I think she's gone crazy," said Joe beginning to be frightened. "Shall I get a doctor?"

"I think she's got a fit," said his wife. Put some water in the tub—"

Night chortled in the corners of the room. "You did it. You did it. You'll never be able to undo this, never, never, never, never."

"Quick," said Gurlie. "Do what I tell you."

"No, don't be a fool," said Joe. "She hasn't got a fit. She's only frightened. She'll catch a cold."

"Here," he said. "Stop it. Look, look! the light!" And he took the baby to the light. "I'm going to take her out into the kitchen where we can quiet her. Wash her face with cold water."

The infant, unexpectedly, dropped her head forward as Joe held her and was really asleep at last. But when he had taken her back to the room and put her into the bed again, she awoke as suddenly with wide, unseeing eyes and began screaming once more.

"God, as if we didn't have enough," said Joe. "Now this. I think it's the vaccination. She's out of her mind. Give her an enema, it must be her stomach."

"No," said the night.

"What?" said Joe.

"I didn't say anything," said Gurlie. "I think we're going crazy ourselves. It's been too much. I wish you would get your business settled so this family can be normal again."

"I wish I'd never seen the God damned contract," said Joe. "I'll tear it up tomorrow and tell them all to go to hell. I'll move out to Cincinnati or St. Louis or anywhere away from New York. What did you give her to eat for supper?"

"What do you think I gave her? Caviar?"

"No, I thought you gave her pork tenderloin and horse radish and sauerkraut. What did your mother give her for lunch?"

The baby was quieting, quieting, quieting as they talked. Sobbing less and less—starting all over with a sudden jerk, opening her eyes a slit—as if it were there again, the terror, the loneliness and the endlessness of suffering. Then, right there under their eyes as they watched her, she was asleep.

"Thank the Lord for that," said Gurlie. "That was terrible. I can't understand what did it."

"You must have frightened her," said Joe.

"She'd better get over it then. Come on out of this room. I can't sleep now. Anything new to tell me today?"

"No," said Joe looking at his watch. "Two A.M. Nothing except that everything is settled. I'll get the presses on the floor tomorrow ready to set up. I've got a night watchman there tonight."

"What for?"

"Well, nothing is insured yet," said Joe, "for one thing. But everything else is settled or nearly so and the whole

lithographic department is coming over to me as soon as I
want them. Come on let's go to bed. I've got a big day
tomorrow." "Don't you want your beer?" "No. I suppose
we've got to go in there," he added.

The night stood outside the window this time and didn't
come in—but smiled. "See you later. But don't forget me.
She won't," he said pointing to the baby. "You'll see. You
did it. I touched her. There will always be night a little
written upon her brain. To some extent, my fine lady and
gentleman, who think you know so much, to some extent
she is mine. See that you take good care of her henceforth,
for me." And the thing was gone.

Joe dreamed that he had some sort of a frog-like beast in
his hand, only it wasn't a frog, it had a tail and he was holding its head under water, in a pail. "Don't do that," someone said, "that's cruel. You're drowning it." "That's what
I'm trying to do," said Joe. He didn't know why, he didn't
want to drown it but he had to. What else could he do with
it? It wasn't good for anything. Then the thing, which had
a big lizard's mouth, pulled its head to one side out of the
water and looked up at him. That was the last he remembered—for he woke suddenly.

"My God," he heard Gurlie saying. She was leaning over
the baby's crib looking down at it, its smeared little face, its
hair, the lace collar of its little nightdress—where it had
relieved itself—lying there in puddles and chunks.

"That explains it," said Joe.

"No," said his wife. "She had nothing different to eat
today than any other time. She just worked herself up into
it. It was the devil in her. The whole house has been upset
today."

"I suppose a troll spit in the milk this morning," said her
husband. And he rolled over on his side and was soon snor-
ing quietly. To which Gurlie added to herself, apropos of
nothing, as she was getting back into bed, "I'll be glad to
get rid of her. She's had her life, let me have mine."

IV

Drama

from **A Dream of Love**

The living room of the Thurbers' home, a rather old-fashioned house, built probably in the early 1900's, in a suburb near New York. It is evening—just after dark—in the early fall. The time is a few years previous to the Second World War. The fittings of the room are somewhat somber, with an appearance of settled home surroundings. In the middle of the room, at the back, is a large davenport couch with pillows at both ends; on the wall above this couch is a large modernist painting done in bold primary colors and with a white frame—the only object of the sort in the room. The entrance to the room is toward the rear on the right through a pair of double folding glass doors in front of which, forward along the wall, is an antique side-table with some books on it. In the middle of the left wall is a shallow bay window which looks out upon the street; in its embrasure there is a comfortable overstuffed chair. A floor-lamp, which gives off a rather dim light, stands to the left of the couch. The window shades are half drawn, but admitting the beams of a powerful street-lamp. The rattle of bus traffic is occasionally heard outside.

Mrs. Thurber is lying asleep on the couch. She has a blanket over her and the light from the floor-lamp catches her blond hair.

There is the noise of a door closing somewhere outside, followed by footsteps coming through the house. Suddenly the hall lights are snapped on, the light showing through the glass doors.

"Doc" Thurber comes in from the hallway and turns up the light of the floor-lamp. He takes off his overcoat and drops it carelessly on a chair, then stands looking down at his wife who does not immediately awaken.

261

DOC:

Hi. [*There is no response.*] Myra. Sweetheart. Myra.
Wake up.

MYRA [*waking*]:

What?

DOC:

Sleeping? So early?

MYRA [*sitting up, shading her eyes*]:

Oh, turn those lights down—a little. Please. [*He half dims
the lights.*] What time is it?

DOC:

About eight-thirty. Any calls?

MYRA:

I didn't hear anything. I was dog tired.

DOC:

You'll spoil your hair-do.

MYRA:

I didn't think you'd notice it. [*She sits up, arranging her
hair. Her skirts have caught about her hips as she does so.*]
Ooff!

DOC:

A damned good-looking woman. You always did have
beautiful legs. That's why I married you.

MYRA:

Yes, I know. [*She straightens her skirts.*] Where have you
been?

DOC:

Around. How about a little more light?

MYRA:

Sure, if you want to, go ahead. [*He turns up the light as
Myra picks up a book from the floor beside the couch.*]

DOC:

Don't read. Talk to me awhile, I'm restless. What have you been doing?

MYRA:

Reading—what else? Aren't you going into the office to write?

DOC:

Lay off, darling. I don't *always* go out there in the evening.

MYRA:

Pretty nearly always. Don't you—when you can?

DOC:

You know, you look tired. Why don't you take a vacation for yourself? You need it.

MYRA:

Not without you.

DOC:

That's ridiculous.

MYRA:

No. It's not ridiculous. I shouldn't enjoy myself without you. [*There is a pause.*] Perhaps you'd like to get rid of me, darling—for a week or so?

DOC:

That's an idea.

MYRA:

Then you'd be free. Free! To do as you please. Isn't that what you're living for?

DOC:

I'd still have my practice of medicine.

MYRA:

Give it up. You've always resented it.

DOC:

I have.

MYRA:

Because you've always resented me.

DOC:

You're wrong.

MYRA:

I'm right.

DOC:

You're wrong.

MYRA:

I interfere with you.

DOC:

That's right. How is anyone ever going to live with anyone else unless he interferes with him? So what? That has nothing to do with it.

MYRA:

Everything.

DOC:

You have to take it out of me, don't you. Don't I work hard enough for you?

MYRA:

For me?

DOC:

Who else?

MYRA:

Oh my dear husband, what a fool you are—and how lovable and transparent.

DOC:

That's bunk.

MYRA:

I'm not much use to you. I'm not much use to myself—and pretty much disgusted with myself most of the time. I don't know why. What do I do—now that the children are away? Almost nothing.

DOC:

Ain't it the truth.

MYRA:

What's the truth?

DOC:

Anything—that you say.

MYRA:

Walking out on me?

DOC:

Perhaps—when you least expect it.

MYRA:

Things go fast, remember, today.

DOC [*after a pause*]:

As far as medicine is concerned all I work for is your comfort and happiness. That's all I want—as far as I'm able to give it to you.

MYRA:

And I want only one thing—when I want anything.

DOC:

What's that?

MYRA:

You.

DOC:

You've got me—and how.

MYRA:

I've never had you. [*She yawns.*]

DOC:

No, you've never had me—in that way. I guess that's why you've kept on loving me—as I've wanted to be loved—by you.

MYRA [*looking up*]:

What's the matter with you? You certainly are off tonight.

DOC:

I love you!

MYRA:

My God! [*She smiles and shakes her head.*] Sweetheart. You're a nice boy and I'm stupid about you—but I don't want you now. You know you're itching to get away. Please go. Write me a beautiful poem. Go out in your office and work.

DOC:

Yeah—work.

MYRA:

Now look. You know I always like to have you close to me. Almost always. I love you. You don't love me—not in the same way. But that's my affair. I love you and believe in you. I tremendously admire you. But I don't trust you. Now yank up your pants—they're dragging at the back— and go out and enjoy yourself.

DOC:

O.K., puss. [*He leans over to kiss her.*]

MYRA:

You've had a drink.

DOC:

Just a short one.

MYRA [*putting down her book*]:

Say, where were you this evening?

DOC:

You gave me the call. Mrs. Tennant, our milkman's wife.
I got a queer hunch about that gal—I don't think she's going
to last very long.

MYRA:

Did you go anywhere else?

DOC:

Why?

MYRA:

Nothing. I guess I must have been dreaming. My head's
been heavy all afternoon. I wish you'd get out of here.

DOC [*picking up a book from the table*]:
Look at this. The Complete Collected Poems of Daniel T—
for Titcomb—Thurber. Complete all right—up to the time
of his death. How come?

MYRA [*changing the subject*]:
Would you care for anything as simple as a glass of iced
fruit juice? I'm awfully dry.

DOC:

No, thanks. How would you like to have me read some of
my poems to you?

MYRA:

I'd love it—if you can wait.

[*He is looking through the book. Myra goes out and
he sits down on the couch. Leafing through the book, he
comes to something that interests him and after a moment
begins to read aloud.*]

DOC:

    I lie here thinking of you—
        the stain of love
    is upon the world!
    Yellow, yellow, yellow

it eats into the leaves,
smears with saffron
the . . .
[*Myra returns with glasses of juice on a tray.*]

MYRA:

It sounds marvelous. Read it to me. Here take this first
[*She hands him a glass.*]—it'll do you good.

[*He sits with the book still in his hand and sips his drink.*]

DOC:

You know that was an interesting case I saw this evening.
There doesn't seem to be much the matter with the woman
—a little overweight . . . You know who I mean.

MYRA:

Yes, you told me. She hasn't been ill, has she?

DOC:

No. Just a hunch I have. I shouldn't be surprised they'd
find her dead in bed some morning.

MYRA:

So what? As far as I'm concerned, I'd love it if it happened
to me.

DOC:

That's putting it a little strong, isn't it, darling? [*He looks
hard at his wife.*]

MYRA:

No. How about reading?

DOC:

How about putting your head down in my lap?

MYRA:

All right.

[*The telephone rings in the hall.*]

DOC:

Shall I go?

MYRA:

No. Stay where you are. [*She goes to the phone—out of view—in the hall.*] Hello . . . Who is this calling? . . . No. I'm sorry, you'll have to give me your name . . . No . . . No . . . Is there anything I can do to help you? . . . Hm . . . [*She returns to the room.*] She hung up.

DOC:

Who was it?

MYRA:

I don't know. Some woman with a sick child. I don't pay any attention to them if they don't give me their names.

DOC:

That's a good example of the privacy we enjoy in our idle moments. [*He pauses.*] One thing I know, my dear: we've got to get the hell out of this kind of a life—if you call it that. It isn't good for either of us. Now that the kids are away it's getting terrific. And as far as I'm concerned—as far as money is concerned—as if we had any—they can have it!

MYRA:

It's up to you.

DOC:

You too.

MYRA:

All I want is a little place in the country—a place where flowers will *grow* and not choke to death with the oil and grease there is on the leaves here.

DOC:

And a private bath—your own—where nobody, not even I— especially I—could so much as peek inside the door. And hot and cold running water and electricity and gas—a modern heating and ventilating system. A simple little place where we should be happy and at peace together.

MYRA:

Happiness and peace!

DOC:

What little peace there is.

MYRA:

Hardly any.

DOC:

A hideout—for our old age. Perhaps in Vermont.

MYRA:

Where you, darling, could do what you've always wanted to do—quit the God-damned thankless practice of medicine and write, write, write to your heart's content.

DOC:

I'll bet I could make more money. I'll bet with a little luck I could make more money—as much as I make here now.

MYRA:

The way you practice medicine—or neglect your bills, I mean—you'd double your present earnings. But what would you do without all your women, darling?

DOC:

I'd find one up a tree somewhere.

MYRA:

You sure would. And drag her down by the hair—if she didn't drop on you first from a low branch. I don't care—so long as I have my garden. Really, Dan. I'm getting awfully fed up with this routine. The same thing, the same thing, over and over and over and over.

DOC:

Me too.

MYRA:

Why don't you really quit then?

DOC:

On what? I haven't got enough money to quit on—at my age.

MYRA:

Just quit.

DOC:

Just quit, huh? I'm going to quit—but I can't afford right now to do it.

MYRA:

Agh, you! Quit now, tonight. This minute.

DOC:

How?

MYRA:

Hang a sign up that you're not practicing medicine any more.

DOC:

You would!

MYRA:

I will!

DOC:

I think you took a swig of something out there in the kitchen.

MYRA:

You coward. You haven't got the nerve. Do you want me to do it? I'll do it. Why don't you give up being a half-time writer if you like to write that much? Why don't you make a decision one way or the other? I'll do it for you.

DOC:

Sure. If that's the way you feel about it, go ahead.

MYRA:

Well! Well! [*She looks at him and laughs.*] You poor baby. Come here and kiss me.

DOC:

Not tonight.

MYRA:

Look at you, pouting like an infant. So you don't want to quit your old practice of medicine? Believe me, if I felt the way you do about it I wouldn't for five minutes let anyone make me go on with it. And that's the way I feel about you. I wish I could quit this minute and leave you here—to go to hell any way you want to—you and your women. I wish I could do it.

DOC:

Why not?

MYRA:

Sure. Easy for you. Twenty women are just waiting to fling themselves at your feet. That's where a man has it easy—a man with an income. But what chance have I got? Who wants a woman like me?

DOC:

Don't kid yourself, you'd have some money.

MYRA:

You bet I'll have some money. I'll sell this house.

DOC [*startled*]:

This house?

MYRA:

Yes.

DOC:

Would you do that?

MYRA:

Would I do it? Huh!

DOC [*after a short pause*]:
At that, you'd be right. Maybe it's the writing that's at fault.

MYRA:
Deeper than that.

DOC:
I don't think so. It's the writing. Why do I write? Just about what you were saying a little while ago—I want to pass out. And I do pass out when I'm writing—forget everything except that. The works. Out the window.

MYRA:
Certainly it's not interesting to talk about.

DOC:
You got something there.

MYRA:
If only I could sleep better. You're asleep as soon as your head hits the pillow. But I stay awake half the night—listening to you snore. I really think we should have separate rooms.

DOC [*arranging himself on the couch*]:
Stretch out here and let me read to you for half an hour—that always puts you to sleep. Huh?

MYRA:
That isn't fair.

DOC:
Some of my own stuff. I haven't done it for years. Something about us, just us.

MYRA:
Read the one you were reading when I was in the kitchen—it sounded marvelous.

DOC:
Don't you want to put your head in my lap? I'll fix a pillow.

MYRA [*making herself comfortable on the couch*]:
Now read. This is heaven. What a marvelous way to spend my anniversary.

DOC:
Anniversary of what?

MYRA:
You wouldn't know . . . of the day you proposed to me.

DOC:
Is that right?

MYRA:
Do you remember what you said?

DOC:
Do *you?*

MYRA:
—when I asked you if you loved me?

DOC:
No. What did I say?

MYRA:
You said, "Love you? Hell no. I want to marry you."

DOC:
I don't believe I said that.

MYRA:
Then I asked you, "Why do you want to marry me?" And you said, "To love you, I suppose."

DOC:
Was I that intelligent—in those days? It must have been real passion.

MYRA:

I suppose I have never got over that first dazzlement.

DOC:

"When faith stood clear in your eyes." It was about all we had.

MYRA:

I had you—then.

DOC [*opening the book and reading*]:
          —a dream
  we dreamed
       each
  separately
      we two
  of love
      and of
  desire—

  that fused
  in the night—

       A dream
  a little false
  toward which
      now
  we stand
      and stare
  transfixed—

  All at once
       in the east
  rising!
       All white!

  a locust cluster
  a shad bush
      blossoming

And so
      we live
      looking—

a dream
      toward which
we love—
at night
      more
than a little
      false—

We have bred
we have dug
we have figured up
our costs
we have bought
an old rug—

We batter at our
unsatisfactory
      brilliance—

There is no end
      to desire—
[*He pauses.*]

MYRA:

You loved me, I think. But it's never been wholeheartedly
me. It's always been something else—someone else where I
was concerned.

DOC:

Give me time. I'm still young.

MYRA:

It's always been as though you were trying to escape.

DOC:

It can't be done. I've tested it.

MYRA:

You've succeeded pretty well in your day.

DOC:

You got to relax sometime.

MYRA:

I can't beat you at talking.

DOC:

Women usually do.

MYRA:

Not you. If only I were sure of your love.

DOC:

What for? There's no sense to it. Love is a matter of the will, pure and simple. I love you.

MYRA:

You force yourself to love. That's not it.

DOC:

You think it's something else? You *fall* in love, huh?

MYRA:

You do or you do not.

DOC:

Laughable. I love you, I tell you. But you drive me off.

MYRA:

Of course I drive you off—what do you think I am?

DOC:

I think you're an amazing woman whom I sometimes greatly admire, frequently count on in emergencies and always love —and protect.

MYRA:

You're a liar.

DOC:

You're a romanticist. What do you think a man is, a papaya? To digest your dinner? In pill form?

MYRA [*laughing*]:

You ass. But it's wonderful to be noticed—and talked to.

DOC:

Noticed! I make love to you day and night, year in, year out, and most of the time never even get a tumble.

MYRA:

Is this what you call making love to me? I'll bet there's a reason back of it and not a pretty one either—if I know you.

DOC:

After all, you can't walk if you don't move your legs.

MYRA:

You see. You're not coming clean.

DOC:

Listen, darling. I'm not a stone or a Diesel engine. I don't live on air.

MYRA:

Uh huh! Something's up. I knew it. Hurry and read to me, won't you? The one I asked you to read: "Yellow, yellow, yellow!"

DOC:

My dear wife, you make it almost impossible for me. [*He opens the book and begins to read.*] "Love Song." I wrote this when we were first married. You were away and I was thinking of you. It was just at sunset and I was looking toward the horizon where I knew you to be.

> I lie here thinking of you—
>
> the stain of love
> is upon the world!

Yellow, yellow, yellow
it eats into the leaves,
smears with saffron
the horned branches that lean
heavily
against a smooth purple sky!
There is no light
only a honey-thick stain
that drips from leaf to leaf
and limb to limb
spoiling the colors
of the whole world—

you, far off there under
the wine-red selvage of the west!

Have you ever seen the sky that way in the west just after
sunset? [*He looks at her.*] Myra darling? Christ! You're
not . . . crying, are you? God damn it, you mustn't do that.

MYRA [*with tears in her eyes*]:
It's so beautiful, my dear. I'm not sad, really. Happy. Really
happy. You're so lovely. I adore you.

DOC [*closing the book*]:
No more of that.

MYRA:
Go on, please. You don't understand. You can't. With all
your interests—how can you? I don't expect it. Really, I
don't expect it. I get angry at you. I feel lonely, neglected.
But I don't blame you. Ever. I love you. And that's my
life. That's all. I suppose you think it's stupid . . . I do,
myself, at times.

DOC:
No, I don't think it's stupid. But knowing myself—and the
way I live—doesn't it get awfully dull for you at times?

MYRA:

Never. I'm perfectly happy—though you may not think so. Perfectly happy—for me. I'm not an accomplished person, I'm sorry. I think perhaps we should never have married. [*She pauses.*] But you're marvelous. You're a wonderful person. And a great poet. When you die—I don't know . . .

DOC:

What don't you know?

MYRA:

I just don't know . . . that will be the end—as far as I'm concerned.

DOC [*after another pause*]:
One marriage! [*He kisses her hair.*]

MYRA:

Almost a miracle.

DOC:

Quite. [*A bus goes by in the street outside, rattling the windows.*] What in Christ's name is a man to do? I don't know. Is all poetry evil? I think so—since John Donne. [*He slings the book across the room.*]

MYRA:

What are you doing with my book? [*She gets up angrily and retrieves the book, straightening the pages.*] You have no right to do that.

DOC:

I'm sorry, dear—I'll get you another if it's torn.

MYRA:

That's not the point.

DOC:

Right here I'm happiest—if that's what we want. Here there is at least the possibility of contentment and peace.

MYRA:

What I don't understand is: you're an excellent physician and a good writer—sometimes I'm amazed how good you are—but what do you want? What do you want a woman to do—you're not subtle—blow her brains out for you? What in God's name is our relationship?

DOC:

Do you expect an answer?

MYRA:

Am I just a trough for you to feed out of?

DOC:

Our relationship? Something horrible, in all probability—if it isn't magnificent. Perverse. Insane—of which we shall never know anything. Murderous perhaps, but inevitable . . . I love you! —the second word being an eternal lie. And you can omit the "eternal" too . . . What does any man know? [*He is silent a moment.*] Suppose I were blocked out of existence—twenty-four hours from now. A plane crash or something like that. Don't you think you'd be happier?

MYRA:

Yes, in some ways.

DOC:

You would? Of course you would. [*He gets up and looks into the street.*]

MYRA:

Oh come on—forget it . . . I'm going up. I'm not angry, only a little surprised, that's all. I shouldn't be. It's been going on all my life, since we've been married. I should be used to it—but it still surprises me for some reason—and yet, what else better in life can I wish for? . . . I love you. I wouldn't give that up for anything else in the world. Good night, my dear. [*She starts out the door.*]

DOC [*near the window*]:
Oh, by the way, I'll be going to the city tomorrow. Want
to come along?

MYRA:
No. It's your afternoon off. Go ahead, enjoy yourself—but
it was nice of you to ask me. Good night. [*She goes out.*]

[*Doc stands looking out into the street for a moment.
Then he puts out the lights in the room, leaving those in the
hall burning. Taking up his overcoat, he hesitates, then puts
it on and goes into the hall. We hear the front door close as
he leaves the house.*]

CURTAIN

V

Autobiography

from *The Autobiography*

from CHAPTER 12.   EZRA POUND

EZRA POUND would come to my room to read me his poems, the very early ones, some of those in *A Lume Spento*. It was a painful experience. For it was often impossible to hear the lines the way he read them, and of all things in the world the last I should have wanted to do would have been to hurt him—no matter how empty I myself might have felt, and worthless, as a critic. But I listened; that's all he wanted, I imagine, from anyone. His voice would trail off in the final lines of many of the lyrics until they were inaudible—from his intensity. I seldom let on except, occasionally, to explode with the comment that unless I could *hear* the lines how could he expect me to have an opinion of them. What did he think I was, an apteryx?

Ezra was then learning to fence with Signor Terrone, the Penn coach. I had learned to fence in Paris in 1898, French style, which is somewhat different from the Italian. I went out for the team. Ez meanwhile had quit fencing and had joined the lacrosse squad. That didn't last long either.

He could never learn to play the piano, though his mother tried to teach him. But he "played" for all that. At home, I remember my mother's astonishment when he sat down at the keyboard and let fly for us—seriously. Everything, you might say, resulted except music. He took mastership at one leap; played Liszt, Chopin—or anyone else

285

you could name—up and down the scales, coherently to his own mind, any old sequence. It was part of his confidence in himself. My sister-in-law was a concert pianist. Ez never liked her.

Those were strange spring evenings when men would sit in groups on the grass in the Triangle and sing of Lydia Pinkham's Vegetable Compound, reputed to cure all the ills of the female race!

Once Ez asked me to go on a secret mission with him— to pick up one girl, yes, *one* girl, though why he wanted *me* along was more than I could figure. He had noted that a particularly lovely thing in her early teens, surely, would pass up Chestnut Street daily, at a certain hour, on her way home from school toward evening. I say school because her arms, when I saw her, were full of books. I acknowledged it, she was exceptional.

As she came along we drew beside her, one to the left, one to the right. I was not interested and found the goings on ridiculous. Ezra was Ronsard. The poor child was all but paralyzed with fear, panting to the point of speechlessness as she just managed to say in a husky voice, "Go away! Please go away! Please! Please!" I dropped back. Ezra continued for another twenty paces and then quit also—to bawl me out for not persisting. I told him what I thought of him. After all, what was there in it for me?

I remember, also, one moonlight adventure to meet two girls outside the grounds near some school at Chestnut Hill. Equally futile.

When the senior class at Penn, under Professor Clark, presented Euripides' *Iphigenia in Aulis*, in Greek, at the Philadelphia Academy of Music, Ezra was one of the women of the chorus. I was in the top balcony. The fellow who played the Messenger was superb that night and got an ovation for the impassioned delivery of his lines. But Ez was as much the focus of attention, at least for me. He was

dressed in a Grecian robe, as I remember it, a togalike
ensemble topped by a great blond wig at which he tore as
he waved his arms about and heaved his massive breasts in
ecstasies of extreme emotion.

Ezra never explained or joked about his writing as I
might have done, but was always cryptic, unwavering and
serious in his attitude toward it. He joked, crudely, about
anything but that. I was fascinated by the man. He was the
livest, most intelligent and unexplainable thing I'd ever
seen, and the most fun—except for his often painful self-
consciousness and his coughing laugh. As an occasional
companion over the years he was delightful, but one did
not want to see him often or for any length of time. Usually I got fed up to the gills with him after a few days. He,
too, with me, I have no doubt.

I could never take him as a steady diet. Never. He was
often brilliant but an ass. But I never (so long as I kept
away) got tired of him, or, for a fact, ceased to love him.
He had to be loved, even if he kicked you in the teeth for
it (but that he never did); he looked as if he might, but he
was, at heart, much too gentle, much too good a friend for
that. And he had, at bottom, an inexhaustible patience, an
infinite depth of human imagination and sympathy.
Vicious, catty at times, neglectful, if he trusted you not to
mind, but warm and devoted—funny too, as I have said.
We hunted, to some extent at least, together, and not each
other.

What I could never tolerate in Pound or seek for myself
was the "side" that went with all his posturings as the poet.
To me that was the emptiest sort of old hat. Any simpleton,
I believed, should see at once what that came from; the
conflict between an aristocracy of birth and that of mind
and spirit—a silly and unnecessary thing. The poet scorn-
ing the other made himself ridiculous by imitating that
which he despised. My upbringing assumed rather the
humility and caution of the scientist. One was or one was

not *there*. And if one was there, it behooved one to be at
one's superlative best, and, apart from the achievement, a
thing in itself, to live inconspicuously, as best it might be
possible, and to work single-mindedly for the task. Not so
sweet Ezra. . . .

CHAPTER 17. HELL'S KITCHEN

AT THE NURSERY and Child's Hospital, Sixty-first Street
and Tenth Avenue, where I interned next for almost a
year, the setup was entirely different from what I had
known at the French. Its situation, in the first place, was
different. It was still on the west side of the city, but somewhat further uptown in a notorious neighborhood called
San Juan Hill, from the site in Cuba made famous by a
colored regiment which had assaulted and captured the
place during the Spanish-American War. The old name had
been just plain Hell's Kitchen.

Pound had gone to London. Thence almost at once his
books began to arrive: *Personae* (his first success) and then
Exultations. "Come on over," he had written me, "and help
me chew off a chunk." But how could I leave? Then one
day Hilda Doolittle wrote saying that she also was off for
London. That was a surprise. I went down to the dock to
bid her good-bye and found her sitting on a trunk, her
father, the old astronomer, beside her, uncommunicative as
always. I doubt that he even saw me. It was a disconsolate
picture.

Sometime before Hilda's decision to go abroad, Ezra had
come back to this country because of an attack of jaundice
and stayed for a week at our house in Rutherford. One day
we went for a stroll around the old Kipp farm which then
occupied the center of Rutherford. Ezra was always afraid
of catching pneumonia and had borrowed a heavy white
sweater of Ed's, a regular football sweater, to protect him
from the cold wind. As we went along Union avenue, Ez

walking with his usual swagger, I said to him, "Look, Ez, there's the winter wheat (it was three or four inches high) coming up to greet you."

"It's the first intelligent wheat I've ever seen," was his reply. That's the way he felt. Such thoughts were always near the surface of his mind. It seemed to become him.

Ezra's insistence has always been that I never laid proper stress in my life upon the part played in it by my father rather than my mother. Oh, the woman of it is important, he would acknowledge, but the form of it, if not the drive, came unacknowledged by me from the old man, the Englishman. I'd question that sometimes, about his being English, in that Pop grew up in a Caribbean island surrounded by a semitropical sea rather than near the Baltic. Yet he was, one had to acknowledge, at heart a northerner. He was a stickler for fundamentals, I'll say that, and when he took hold of a thing insisted on going through with it to the bitter end to find out what it amounted to. If he couldn't understand a thing at last, he'd reject it, which was not Mother's saving way of facing the world.

When Ezra was staying with us once for a short time Pop looked at him with considerable doubt. He acknowledged that Ezra knew a good deal, though what he knew Pop was not by any means sure. He knew also that Ezra, being my friend, was welcome in our house. He was curious about Ezra: he wanted to hear this young man expound theories which, generally speaking, the older man rejected on general principle but, being both intelligent and generous-minded, he wanted to give my friend an opportunity to express himself. He wanted, in other words, to hear Ezra read his poems, to have him interpret them as he wished to, after which my father would make up his mind and that would be his judgment of their value.

So one evening Ezra read several poems. Pop listened. I listened also and so did Mother, who said nothing. The selection was from the early work, naturally, and I knew that it wasn't going across. But one poem especially Pop stuck on. Ezra had composed a short piece on the backs of certain books standing on the shelves of our bookcase or, if not our bookcase, though I think he composed it while he was with us, at least some bookcase. He spoke in the poem of certain jewels, red and blue and green. It wasn't a bad conceit and Ezra resolved it with considerable passion and ability. Pop couldn't get it.

"What are all the jewels you speak of?" he said. I must say I don't think I myself was entirely clear on the subject. "You make a good story of it," went on Pop, "but I don't know what you're talking about."

I don't remember precisely what went on after that nor Ezra's exact reply or how he approached it. But Pop and Ezra were on good terms, Ezra respected the older man, so that it must have ended in the direct and simple statement, "The jewels I speak of are the backs of the books in a bookcase."

"Oh," said Pop. "Of course," he went on, "being books and being precious to you as a student and a poet you treasure them, therefore you call them jewels. That I understand. But if that's what you wish the reader to understand, to make an intelligent impression on him, if it's books you're talking about, why don't you say so then?" Ezra appears never to have forgotten the lesson.

It was at this time that Ezra made the proposal, which, when I asked my father about it, caused him only to shake his head. It was as follows: That we get a big supply of "606," the new anti-syphilitic arsenical which Ehrlich had just announced to the world, and go at once with it to the north coast of Africa and there set up shop. Between us, I with my medical certificate and experience, he with his social proclivities, we might, he thought, clean up a million treating all the wealthy old nabobs there—presumably rotten with the disease—and retire to our literary enjoyments within, at most, a year. Maybe there was something in it, I don't know. But if I had ever spoken to Ez of a Herxheimer reaction he would have thought I was talking like a Penn-

sylvania Dutch farmer. Risks? The practical details meant
nothing to Ezra. It reminded me too much of a job I had
been offered—to take a wealthy but insane young man with
homicidal tendencies on a European tour. But Ezra couldn't
see my side of the argument. We didn't go.

How I ever got into the Nursery and Child's Hospital is
more than I know. I think I applied and they grabbed me,
that's all. I had hardly a week between quitting at the
French and beginning there. Doc Richardson was my Senior; there were only two of us. The man I wanted most to
work under there was Charles Gilmore Kerley, one of the
leading pediatricians of the day. I was extremely happy at
my good luck.

This was a very different setup from what I had been
experiencing at the French, as different as night and day, a
very much looser organization—and no Sisters of Charity.
The main building, just completed, was on the corner of
Sixty-first Street and Tenth Avenue, a six-story brick
structure just across Tenth from the most notorious block
in the New York criminal West Side, San Juan Hill or
Hell's Kitchen, as you preferred to call it. We didn't go out
much after dark unaccompanied, man or woman. There
were shootings and near riots and worse practically every
week-end. That block, the most heavily populated in the
city, was said to be honeycombed with interconnecting
tunnels from flat to flat so that a man who had taken it on
the lam, once he got inside an entry, was gone from the
police forever.

Our children's ward was back of the main building, the
maternity section. It was a two-floor brick cube consisting
of two small wards, holding eight beds each, right and left,
with a similar second floor.

The management of the place, aside from the nursing,
was riddled with corruption. There were a few nurses from
various outlying hospitals who had been sent there for their
pediatric and obstetric training, but there was no school.

Miss Cuthbertson, a large, straightforward Canadian woman, was in charge of the nursing program. Miss Malzacher, a dark, sweaty-looking creature with furtive, bulging eyes, was in charge of the office, and another mild plump little woman, whose name I have forgotten, was the over-all director in residence, a decorative fiftyish little figure, who kept a wonderful table for Richardson and me, but that was all. She had said, in fact, that that was the only way she could hold any resident physicians in the place: by feeding them well. Our sleeping quarters were nothing, worse than nothing, in fact on more than one occasion full of bedbugs. But the food was marvelous and we were interfered with in our work almost not at all. I can still remember those meals with the lady boss herself and Miss Cuthbertson—the four of us. The madam insisted that the Senior in charge carve the roasts, chickens and other meat she served. She felt it was part of her duty to teach us manners. We literally ate it up. Miss Cuthbertson was our pal. It worked out beautifully in that small intimate dining room on the back corridor of the old part of the original building.

There was plenty of work. That's what saved the place, medically speaking. During my time there I delivered three hundred babies and faced every complication that could be thought of. I learned to know and to admire women, of a sort, in that place. They led a tough life and still kept a sort of gentleness and kindness about them that could, I think, beat anything a man might offer under the same circumstances. I never saw one yet, white or black, that didn't give me a break if I treated her half-decently.

Miss Diamond, who wore a gold tooth in the front, was a first-rate Supervisor and head of the delivery room. Miss Becksted, Chief of Pediatric Service, a tough little English-woman, was another of my pals. At the beginning it seemed just what I wanted. Miss Diamond was the right woman for her situation. As she once said, "I'm going to run a three-foot streamer around this place below the sixth-floor windows and it's going to read: 'BABIES FRESH EVERY HOUR, ANY COLOR DESIRED, 100% ILLEGITIMATE!' "

She wasn't fooling, either. The women at the Nursery and Child's were the dregs of the city, a fine crew. Once I was called by Miss Diamond to help her separate five of them in a fight. They were lying, all approaching full term, on the stone floor of one of the upper hallways, snarling and spitting like cats. She told me that two or more were pregnant from the same man, and the others had joined in on one side or the other. She'd grab one by the foot and try to pull her out of the pile, but the floor was polished and Diamond was so strong she'd pull the whole sputtering mass in one direction or other. I stood looking at her, somewhat reluctant to join in.

"Grab a leg and pull against me," she yelled. So I did what she wanted but I couldn't hurt the things.

"Pull!" she said. But the women had their hands locked in each other's hair and we got no results.

"All *right*, you bitches," she told them, "I'll get the ether can!" And that she did. She got a towel, soaked it with ether, and waded in among them. They all let go all right and scrambled up without a word. It was the first time I had seen such a thing and told her so.

"Oh, that's nothing. We have it every once in a while around here. All we need is a ringleader and they're at it. I know who it is now, I got my eye on her. It won't happen again."

Miss Diamond—I don't think I ever knew her first name —was a big, sharp-chinned peroxide blond, the gold tooth right in front of her face, young and not at all bad-looking, somewhat of a Mae West type. When she set her jaw and her blue eyes began to snap, the women usually cowered; but she was a good nurse and a fast worker. In the end, the women knew she was for them. They respected her. So did I. She taught me a lot about obstetrics.

When I had come on duty during the first summer with the pediatric work—there had been nothing of that at the French—I was fascinated by it and knew at once that that was my field. We had 'em of all sorts, as you may imagine. We got most of the foundlings from all over the city when Bellevue didn't want them.

I'll never forget that summer. Some charitable-minded woman from the Riverside Drive section, fashionable at that time, offered us her apartment for a convalescent home on one condition, that we were not to put any sick children there, that is, very sick infants who might die on the premises.

It was agreed. She had removed the furniture from her parlor and dining room, covered the mirrors and carpets with proper drapes and runners. On each side we installed cribs and assigned certain nurses and attendants to care for a dozen or more infants who were to be kept there. It was a fine gesture on her part and we lived up to the agreement to the letter.

But something happened, as it usually does under such circumstances, to ruin all our plans. One of the children developed a severe case of infectious gastro-enteritis and before anyone knew it, had died, in three days! Something we were absolutely unprepared for. We couldn't let the lady find it out, but obviously we had to do something with the body. So that I, being on Pediatrics at the hospital, was assigned the job of covering up. I was dispatched by streetcar to the apartment with instructions to bring the dead infant to our morgue in a suitcase, which was provided for me. And I did it, by public conveyance, the suitcase under my knees as I sat there looking about me. I was not happy over it, all sorts of notions going through my head as I thought of what would happen if the rickety container should fly open and the body of the child fall out just at the wrong moment. I tell you I sweated over that job, plenty. When I got back I told them: No more!

In a day or two, the whole group at the residence was affected, we lost 90 per cent of them, but I never went back for another body. They had to close the place up.

It was when I was on duty with the infants and older children in the little building at the back of the Nursery and Child's that I was visited by Viola Baxter, one of Ezra's friends of the Utica days when he was at Hamilton College. She was beautiful and sympathetic, but when she saw what we had under our care, the very scum of the city streets, she was shocked—at our cruelty!

"Cruelty!" I said. "What do you mean? We can't dress them in pretty garments to make a show of them."

"But look at the poor miserable brats! Hear them cry. You're brutal, you're heartless—you're impossible."

"You don't know what you're talking about," I told her. "You ought to have seen this brat when we got him. He was the most bedraggled, neglected, dirty, emaciated piece of garbage—you couldn't possibly imagine what he looked like—sores, rickets, his legs out of shape, and look at him now—he's beautiful!"

"Beautiful? He needs his diaper changed this minute! Where are the nurses? You don't understand these things as a woman does. He smells."

"What do you want me to do?" I asked her. I could have kicked her out of the place. As a matter of fact, that particular infant was our special pride and joy, the most patient little beast I have ever witnessed—and one of the most understanding.

They weren't all like him. Some were enough to drive me half-insane with their screaming. I was, I must confess, to lose my temper one day, at a brat I had broken my heart over trying to recondition him. He'd yell at night, every night and only at night, right under my bedroom window across the alleyway, until one night I went to his crib—I could find nothing the matter with him to make him yell—and slapped a piece of three-inch adhesive over his mouth.

He could still breathe through his nose, but I thought better of it after a few minutes and took it off again.

That gave me an idea. One night I got hold of my nurse on duty—she used to wear long drawers—and told her I needed her assistance. We had a somewhat older boy than usual in one of the downstairs isolation rooms who had become particularly troublesome. Nothing we did seemed to make him comfortable. So that evening I primed her. We switched off all the lights, darkened the windows and went into the boy's room.

"Here's a flashlight," I said. "Stand there, right where I put you, and when I say go, you flash that light on the youngster where he lies." Oh, shades of old Krumwiede!

"O.K."

"Ready," I said.

"O.K."

"Go!" and I threw back the covers with one stroke leaving the child naked on the sheet!

About twenty enormous bedbugs darted in all directions from his carcass and disappeared into the corners of the bed. I had solved my problem!

Next day I got permission to buy half a barrel of bar-sulfur, big pieces round as my wrist. I got myself six old enameled basins, put them on bricks in the center of the wards and other rooms of the building, poured half a pint of alcohol into them and, having had the engineer seal up the cracks around the doors and windows, except those about the exit-door—leaving all used sheets, blankets, and clothing in the building—the weather being fine, I had the nurses deliver each child to me, naked, at the one door that remained accessible. There I wrapped each child in a fresh sterile blanket and carried it to a spot outside the building, in the sun, where I laid it on a board along the south wall. It was very amusing to see them lying there. We took pictures.

When this was finished and I had inspected the building to see that everything alive except the bugs was out of it in the fresh air, I set matches to the alcohol in the pans one by

one, beginning at the far end of the second floor. The stuff
went up like a flash. I had to run for it. Outside I sealed the
final door. We all for a while stood outside looking in as the
sulfur clouds in the room became denser and denser. I
could see the damned stuff in the nearest pan bubbling as it
burned.

When we opened the place up later in the day, you never
saw such heaps of insects on the floors and in the corners of
each bed! We swept them up dead into veritable pyramids.

I had turned out to be such a famous exterminator that I
got the nurses' dormitory as my next job—but the heavy
fumes trickled out under the main door there, cascaded
down the stair and damn near suffocated the private
patients in the rooms below.

Once later I did a job on the main business office where
an infant, critically ill with diphtheria, had been sitting for
two hours while we tried to find a place for it. There I
burned a formalin candle. Hours later when I opened the
door, one of our famous cats flew out from under Malzacher's desk coughing and spitting. I hope its fleas were
impressed.

Then one evening there was a terrific to-do on the avenue: screams and finally a pistol shot followed by the ringing of the out-patient bell. Hell's Kitchen or San Juan Hill
was merely living up to its reputation. I thought nothing
more of the affair but went about my business as usual until
the gossip as to what had happened reached through to me.

The police had brought in a young girl who had been
plenty roughed up. We didn't usually care for that sort of
case, but under the circumstances the nurses had to
straighten her out at least a little. They discovered that it
was not a girl at all, but a boy. He had apparently been
soliciting trade in doorways and the street entries to the
various houses on the block, the usual two-bit stand-up,
when one of his customers got wise to him. For the boy or
young man had an inflated rubber replica of the female
genitalia pulled up and strapped between his legs to make

him marketable. It must have gone fine for a while until this guy found himself cheated, got his hands on the thing and then hauled off and clipped the vendor on the jaw. And so the riot began!

A colored gal from the Bahamas at full term went in one of the back wards one day, sat on the toilet and had the child there, keeping the water running until it came out under the toilet door onto the tiles until the whole room was flooded. When we broke in, took her off the seat and cut the child's cord, it turned out to be as good as ever. We discharged them both a week later. It was midwinter, and the infant was found next morning wrapped in newspaper under a bench in Prospect Park. Automatically it was sent to us. One of the girls looked at it and immediately recognized it.

"Why, that's Joe we sent out of here yesterday! Look at him, isn't that Joe?"

Everyone clustered around. Sure enough, it was Joe.

One day I was examining a fifteen-year-old white girl—a cute kid who had been brought into the clinic for diagnosis by her mother who wanted to know what made her belly so big. The kid was not dumb and fought us every step of the way. Finally after threats by the mother and persuasion on my part, we got her dress off, but at that point she flew at us all and in her underwear dashed out the door and up the street like a young doe. That's the last I saw of her.

Another time I was delivering a case when they wheeled in a second. It was neck and neck. I stood between the tables, a glove on both hands and two nurses in attendance, when Miss Diamond brought in a third, dragged in a mattress, covered it with a sterile sheet and told the gal to go to it—on the floor. That was her style.

These were the ward cases. They'd come in around the sixth to the eighth month and work around the floors or just do nothing until they fell into labor, all sorts of women. One I remember was a morphine addict who begged me for a shot of the dope, three grams she wanted. I told her I'd give her a quarter of morphine but that was all. She begged and pleaded for more, but I had no instructions and didn't want to kill her. How did I know what she was up to? I guess I looked easy and they all tried to break me down. I got up to a half with her, then three-quarters of a grain every six to eight hours and kept her there until her time, she saying we were killing her.

We also had a few private rooms. Those women were of a different type. I remember my first twins were on that floor. Then one day I found myself taking the history of a young woman who quietly told me this story!

It was late in June, she had recently finished her year at a local college. The year before she had been seduced by her father's overseer at their farm in the Middle West. Finding herself pregnant, she induced her father to let her go east to college. She visited friends during the Christmas vacation, then at the end of the term, came here with us. It was a simple case. She gave the baby out for adoption and went home for the summer. I grew very fond of the woman.

The hospital backed up on some colored apartments. We would look into them idly sometimes going about our work. There were stray cats everywhere. At night, looking for food, I suppose, they'd climb the dumbwaiters making an awful racket so that someone offered a quarter a tail for any we could do away with. Occasionally we'd corner one in the pharmacy, catch it and give it the big Swede, and I mean big, who took care of the furnaces. We did it at least until we learned that with his enormous hands he'd avulse the poor beasts' tails, to claim the bounty, then throw the carcass in at the open furnace door—scratch him as the things might.

We often put up our own drugs at night in the pharmacy. One day the new night superintendent of nurses came there for something and before many minutes, I had her in my arms.

She wasn't as young as I, and had a sad story—the place was full of sad stories. Some one of the attending surgeons, a Dr. Tuttle, wanted her to take charge of his convalescent home somewhere in the mountains of Virginia. I never did find out where the girl came from—extremely pretty, unusually well-made, but hardly an intellectual—a futile, dispirited, lonely sort of woman, just the sort that would take the job of night superintendent in such an institution. Miss Cuthbertson seemed to think she was all right, but there certainly was a mystery about her. She seldom smiled. I suppose she had been married, or double-crossed in some way, or maybe her professional credits weren't up to the mark.

It became a bit serious in the pharmacy evenings after that. One day she asked me if I—or perhaps I asked her—if I might visit her in her room, on Twenty-third Street, that old row of houses that used to stand there between Eighth and Ninth Avenues.

"Yes," she said. She had full lips and big baby-doll eyes.

So I went. The room was on the fourth floor, right under the eaves, room for little more than the bed, the dresser and one chair. The poor child seemed really poor and humiliated in such surroundings. She had decorated the place with red candles and a fancy bedspread with roses. I wanted to lie on the bed with her. She shook her head.

"But you asked me to come and here we are."

She demurred. "Just say one word," she told me, "and you can have anything I've got."

So it hung, now, on one word. What word? I wondered, since I'd heard that before. Marriage, obviously. I still remember that little room under the eaves on West Twenty-third Street. It was so neat and futile.

By this time, Richardson had finished his term, the first half-year was ended and I was put in charge. I'd never had anything to do with Malzacher in the office, but we got along all right, so I was wholly unprepared for what was to follow. For at the end of the first month of the year 1909, I was handed the official forms from Albany to report the business of the hospital for that month: patients received, deaths, recoveries, patients discharged and so forth. It was an extensive and explicit sheet which I, as Resident Surgeon, had now to clear and sign.

The hospital, I thus discovered, was in part state-supported, though it had its separate Board of Governors, headed by one of the most distinguished figures in Wall Street banking circles. Each month we received funds from Albany commensurate with the admissions and discharges for that month. Miss Malzacher handed me a slip of paper giving the essential facts, which I was to fill in, in my own handwriting, sign and return the sheets to her to put with the other matters to be sent to the state capital.

"Fine," I said. "But how do you get these figures?"

"From the blue cards, you know," she said.

"Fine again," said I. "Show me the blue cards." The thing was we had blue and salmon cards, one for the outpatient department, which was large, and the others for the kids in the little back ward.

"I can't do that," she said. "This is a business matter, not a medical matter, and we can't release them."

"Is that so?" I said. "Then I can't sign the report."

"Why, no one has ever made such a fuss over so small a matter before. You'll have to sign them."

"Sure, after I see the cards." You see that's what I had been taught by my parents and I had no choice in the matter.

So the report went to Albany without my signature. Then all hell broke out.

They fired the report back at us and Malzacher began all over again on me.

But my back was up and there it was to stay.

After Malzacher, the doctors took their turn. They were some of the leading men in the East, though this was not one of their major appointments: Kerley, Davis, Mabbott

The William Carlos Williams Reader

and several others—"Maggoty" Mabbott the girls had nick-named him, because of the way he lingered over a vaginal examination. Kerley was one of the worst, all this at a bad time for me because Kerley had asked me what I intended to do after I had finished at Nursery and Child's. When I told him that I had no plans, he asked me if I would not come into his office for the first year. What an opportunity! A New York specialist. I was practically made, I thought.

Kerley came to me and said, "Look, Williams, why don't you sign that report? This is just a routine matter. It's been going on for years. There's no reason to suspect dishon-esty. You know who's at the head of the Board. Sign the damned thing and forget it."

"I'm sorry, Dr. Kerley," I said, "but unless I can verify what I'm signing, I can't put my name to it." He walked off disgusted.

Davis tried to laugh it off without success, and then Mab-bott, dear old Maggoty Mabbott, tried his hand at it. Mean-while our operating funds were being withheld.

"Williams, we all like you in this place. Your work has been excellent, outstanding. You have a brilliant future before you either in pediatrics or obstetrics. I know you're young and a stickler for your principles. But look, we doc-tors can't go against the business of an institution like this. Our business is to cure patients, not to worry over where the money comes from. You're actually doing everyone an injury by this eccentric conduct. Look, sign those papers and get the silly business over with." He stopped and smiled benignly at me.

I looked at him and said, "Dr. Mabbott, if someone handed you some scribbled figures on a piece of paper and told you to copy them into an official report, figures which you had no way of verifying, could you as a self-respect-ing person put your name to those figures, and would you do it?" I spoke straight to his face.

He looked hard at me and I could see the color rising. He

remained silent only a moment, then he said, "No, I'll be damned if I would," and turned and walked out.

Good old Maggoty Mabbott. But the Board would not release me. They said that they had arranged for the treasurer of the institution to sign the report and that I was suspended for two weeks for insubordination.

My head seethed, but before I left, Miss Cuthbertson, who had followed the proceedings with mounting excitement, begged me not to quit but to keep on, that she had some information that would be brought forward at the right time and place, please not to quit under attack, not to go back on her. I spent my two weeks at home. Pop had no suggestions other than to say that I was right in doing what I did. At the end of the two weeks, I returned to duty. Everything seemed fine.

But at the end of February, it began again. The previous month's report signed by the treasurer was not satisfactory to Albany. It had to have my signature and the office still refused to let me see and count the cards. Then Miss Cuthbertson played her card—but not officially, only to me where it did no good. She didn't come out publicly with the facts.

One day she had gone, not quite by chance, but knowing someone was in the Board Room, to see why they were so quiet there. Opening the door she discovered Miss M. on the end of the table, the President of the Board facing her, in a position that she, Miss Cuthbertson, would not describe to me. There it was, plain as daylight, the whole reason why the woman was being allowed to get away with her petty graft—that wealthy man.

If I could spill this in the papers, I thought. But Pop advised me against it.

A lawyer?

No. How can we afford to fight it? and with some of the leading specialists of New York too cowardly to back me, afraid of big money and what their stinking little hides might have to take for it. Sick, I had a horrible sore throat, in fact I could hardly talk above a whisper, I resigned. I didn't tell anyone about it, but I wrote a letter to the Board giving them a piece of my mind and started to close up shop.

The girls were marvelous to me. They were coming into my room with hot drinks, putting cold compresses on my throat, all but getting in bed with me to warm me when I had a chill, kissing me good night—but still I wrote the letter, went down and mailed it in the inside box at the door of the office.

Miss Cuthbertson had seen me go and, knowing my mood, rushed up to ask me what I had been up to.

"I've resigned," I said. "I wrote a letter to the Board of Governors telling them what I thought of them and mailed it."

"You fool. Where?"

"In the box at the office."

She ran out my door for it was not a U.S. Mailbox and could be opened with a key. But in a few moments she was back, licked.

"You've done it. That woman was too quick for me. She must have guessed what you were up to. She has taken your letter and has gone out and mailed it at the corner. I asked the officer at the door. He saw her do it. You fool—just when we could have beat them."

I didn't give a damn. I felt better in fact than I had felt in two months, unhappy as I must have been internally. I couldn't work with that gang any longer. My resignation was officially accepted. I packed and said good-bye and went home. My days of internship were over. Not a single doctor of the attending staff had stood by me. To hell with them all, I thought.

CHAPTER 43.   OF MEDICINE AND POETRY

WHEN they ask me, as of late they frequently do, how I have for so many years continued an equal interest in medicine and the poem, I reply that they amount for me to nearly the same thing. Any worth-his-salt physician knows that no one is "cured." We recover from some somatic, some bodily "fever" where as observers we have seen various engagements between our battalions of cells playing at this or that lethal maneuver with other natural elements. It has been interesting. Various sewers or feed-mains have given way here or there under pressure: various new patterns have been thrown up for us upon the screen of our knowledge. But a cure is absurd, as absurd as calling these deployments "diseases." Sometimes the home team wins, sometimes the visitors. Great excitement. It is noteworthy that the sulfonamids, penicillin, came in about simultaneously with Ted Williams, Ralph Kiner and the rubber ball. We want home runs, antibiotics to "cure" man with a single shot in the buttocks.

But after you've knocked the ball into the center-field bleachers and won the game, you still have to go home to supper. So what? The ball park lies empty-eyed until the next game, the next season, the next bomb. Peanuts.

Medicine, as an art, never had much attraction for me, though it fascinated me, especially the physiology of the nervous system. That's something. Surgery always seemed to me particularly unsatisfying. What is there to cut off or out that will "cure" us? And to stand there for a lifetime sawing away! You'd better be a chef, if not a butcher. There is a joy in it, I realize, to know that you've really cut the cancer out and that the guy will come in to score, but I never wanted to be a surgeon. Marvelous men—I take off my hat to them. I knew one once who whenever he'd get into a malignant growth would take a hunk of it and rub it into his armpit afterward. Never knew why. It never hurt him, and he lived to a great old age. He had imagination, curiosity and a sense of humor, I suppose.

The cured man, I want to say, is no different from any other. It is a trivial business unless you add the zest, whatever that is, to the picture. That's how I came to find writing such a necessity, to relieve me from such a dilemma. I found by practice, by trial and error, that to treat a man as something to which surgery, drugs and hoodoo applied was an indifferent matter; to treat him as material for a work of art made him somehow come alive to me.

What I wanted to do with him (or her, or it) fascinated me. And it didn't make any difference, apparently, that he was in himself distinguished or otherwise. It wasn't that I wanted to save him because he was a good and useful member of society. Death had no respect for him for that reason, neither does the artist, neither did I. As far as I can tell that kind of "use" doesn't enter into it; I am myself curious as to what I do find. The attraction is bizarre.

Thus I have said "the mind." And the mind? I can't say that I have ever been interested in a completely mindless person. But I have known one or two that are close to mindless, certainly useless, even fatal to their families, or what remains of their families, whom yet I find far more interesting than plenty of others whom I serve.

These are the matters which obsess me so that I cannot stop writing. I can recall many from the past, boys and girls, bad pupils, renegades, dirty-minded and -fisted, that I miss keenly. When some old woman tells me of her daughter now happily married to a handicapper at the Garden City track, that she has two fine sons, I want to sing and dance. I am happy. I am stimulated. She is still alive. Why should I feel that way? She almost caused me to flunk out of grammar school. I almost ruined my young days over her.

But I didn't. I love her, ignorant, fulsome bit of flesh that she was, and some other really vicious bits of childhood who ruined the record of the whole class—dead of their excesses, most of them. They flatter my memory. The thing, the thing, of which I am in chase. The thing I cannot quite name was there then. My writing, the necessity for a continued assertion, the need for me to go on will not let me stop. To this day I am in pursuit of it, actually—not there, in the academies, nor even in the pursuit of a remote and difficult knowledge or skill.

They had no knowledge and no skill at all. They flunked out, got jailed, got "Mamie" with child, and fell away, if they survived, from their perfections.

There again, a word: their perfections. They were perfect, they seem to have been born perfect, to need nothing else. They were there, living before me, and I lived beside them, associated with them. Their very presence denied the need of "study," that is study by degrees to elucidate them. They were, living, the theme that all my life I have labored to elucidate, and when I could not elucidate them I have tried to put them down, to lay them upon the paper to record them: for to do that is, after all, a sort of elucidation.

It isn't because they fascinated me by their evildoings that they were "bad" boys or girls. Not at all. It was because they were there full of a perfection of the longest leap, the most unmitigated daring, the longest chances.

This immediacy, the thing, as I went on writing, living as I could, thinking a secret life I wanted to tell openly—if only I could—how it lives, secretly about us as much now as ever. It is the history, the anatomy of this, not subject to surgery, plumbing or cures, that I wanted to tell. I don't know why. Why tell that which no one wants to hear? But I saw that when I was successful in portraying something, by accident, of that secret world of perfection, that they did want to listen. Definitely. And my "medicine" was the thing which gained me entrance to these secret gardens of the self. It lay there, another world, in the self. I was permitted by my medical badge to follow the poor, defeated body into those gulfs and grottos. And the astonishing thing is that at such times and in such places—foul as they may be with the stinking ischio-rectal abcesses of our comings and goings—just there, the thing, in all its greatest beauty, may for a moment be freed to fly for a moment guiltily about the room. In illness, in the permission I as a physician have had to be present at deaths and births, at the tormented battles between daughter and diabolic mother, shattered by a gone brain—just there—for a split second—

from one side or the other, it has fluttered before me for a moment, a phrase which I quickly write down on anything at hand, any piece of paper I can grab.

It is an identifiable thing, and its characteristic, its chief character is that it is sure, all of a piece and, as I have said, instant and perfect: it comes, it is there, and it vanishes. But I have seen it, clearly. I have seen it. I know it because there it is. I have been possessed by it just as I was in the fifth grade—when she leaned over the back of the seat before me and greeted me with some obscene remarks—which I cannot repeat even if made by a child forty years ago, because no one would or could understand what I am saying that then, there, it had appeared.

The great world never much interested me (except at the back of my head) since its effects, from what I observed, were so disastrously trivial—other than in their bulk; smelled the same as most public places. As Bob McAlmon said after the well-dressed Spanish woman passed us in Juarez (I had said, Wow! there's perfume for you!):

"You mean that?" he said. "That's not perfume, I just call that whores."

CHAPTER 51.

EZRA POUND AT ST. ELIZABETH'S

WHEN I go to see Ezra Pound today it is at St. Elizabeth's Hospital in Washington, the District of Columbia, where he has been confined since his arrest following the last war: a gray stone building, designed and constructed not more recently than before the turn of the century, I am sure, with high, barred windows and long, broad halls. At the end of one of these there is a table protected by a simple movable screen beyond which, in the corner, Ezra has his reclining chair and holds what state may be had. From one until four o'clock daily he may, if he wishes to, receive visitors. When I have been there his wife Dorothy has always been present. In fact, I believe she has not missed a single day to be at his side since the first day of his incarceration. On fine days in summer he is privileged to sit outdoors in the parklike grounds with her all during the afternoons. He has been an exemplary patient, according to the official directly responsible for his care. What will come of the situation only the future can tell.

But the first time I was a visitor at the place I was much more disturbed; the disturbed mind has always been a territory from which I shrank instinctively as before the unknown. Ezra's first weeks or months of close confinement among more or less desperate cases—his only exercise having been in a small concrete court surrounded by a high wall—had profoundly affected me, when I heard of it. I took a taxi out of Washington after a meeting of the Fellows of the Library of Congress, a twenty-minute ride, not knowing what I was going to find. We went in at one of the gates, apparently unguarded. It was a fine afternoon and I began to inquire where the building was that I had been told he was in. I don't know how many acres the institution occupies, but we must have covered them all when finally I got to the right one and, telling the taxi to wait, I went in for my visitor's permit.

"You'll find him sitting out there under the trees with his wife," said the man.

There he was, sure enough, in a brand-new beach chair, Dorothy before him reading aloud to him as I approached through a group of the other inmates who looked at me curiously. He didn't know I was coming, so that when I was almost up to him and he saw who I was, he leaped out of his chair and grabbed my outstretched hand—then embraced me.

"Well," said Dorothy, "it's Bill Williams. Isn't it?"

We talked at random for an hour that day. He looked much as I had always found him, the same beard and rest-

less twitching of the hands, shifting his shoulders about as
he lay back in the chair studying me, the same bantering
smile, screwing up his eyes, the half-coughing laugh and
short, swift words, no sentence structure worth mention-
ing. I was of course happy to find him looking so well.

We talked mostly of the situation of letters in our world
—not good; of personalities and the lack of initiative in
those who should be active—myself among the others,
implied.

Naturally we could not avoid the perennial subject, economics and the convictions shared by many with Ezra—that
it is international finance that brings us all at always shorter
and shorter periods to our ruin. That wars are made by the
international gang which runs Russia, England, France,
Germany, the United States and what others. They are
identifiable, have a known complexion—fool many but not
all—and that in the present instance F.D.R. was the prime
criminal. All I could do was to listen.

Dorothy listened too. This is her husband whose hard-
ship she devotedly shares: a tall, ascetic Englishwoman for
whom all who see and know her have a deep respect and
affection. The Pounds have no money. For the first winter
Dorothy lived in a third-floor unheated room adjacent to
the hospital. We invited her to come for a rest and visit at
our home near New York but she refused.

We talked that day under the trees of Nancy Cunard, I
remember, and of her experiences during the German
occupation in France and many other such things; of
Wyndham Lewis over whom both Dorothy and Ezra
laughed when I mentioned some of our experiences with
him at Buffalo the summer before. Ezra believes Lewis a
bit mad but thinks him one of the very few informed people of the world, quite excusably eccentric when you consider the blithering idiots who rule us from high places.

It is elementary to Pound that if anybody knew anything
at all that really goes on among governments, it would be
child's play to get on a solid basis of government and bring

about peace. But he thinks not more than five men in Washington know a single thing that is basically important—he considered Tinkham of Massachusetts one—so that if anything worthwhile gets done, it is by the purest accident.

For instance Ezra is convinced that after twenty minutes' instruction in the Georgian dialect, if at the beginning of our difficulties with Russia, Stalin would have given him a five-minute interview, he could have shown the man the error in his thinking, made him see, comprehend, and act on it, and all the subsequent confusion and disaster could have been avoided.

Marx never mentions in the *Kapital* one word of money, never knew anything of the true situation now governing the world. He was a product of the middle of the nineteenth century—all his libertarian dialectic goes back to that—and . . .

A dialectic, of whatever sort, is merely a premise, in this case false, logically followed to its verbal terminations, whereat we close our eyes and commit logical murder.

Why in a world dominated by such a theme look for love's subtleties or even its absence or presence.?

Do we have to be idiots dreaming in the semi-obscurities of a twilight mood to be poets? The culmination of our human achievement, all that we desire, can't be achieved by closing our eyes to a veritable wall barring our path. The theme of the poem must at such a point be the removal of the block to everything we might achieve once that barrier is removed. If we are to be taxed out of existence to feed private loans, the revenue from which is used by an international gang to perpetuate armed conflicts, at private profit—to further enrich the same gang—that, the inferno of the *Cantos*, must be one of the poet's nearest concern.

So we talked, of who is in the know, as against the self-interested mob of "legislators," the pitiful but grossly ignorant big-shots who play in with the criminals—in city, state and nations; of our first duty as artists, the only semi-informed men of the community, whose sweep is the whole field of knowledge. It is our duty at all costs to speak; at all costs, even imprisonment in such isolation, such quarantine, from the spread of information as a St. Elizabeth's affords.

I don't say that Ez *said* all this, but from his halting broken jabs and ripostes of conversation, it is what I inferred. On the way back to Washington this last time when he had stood up to bid me good-bye and I had got to the gate, thinking of many things, I hailed a taxi and when I got in found the driver was a colored man.

We started to talk, as I always do with these important messengers, saying something about the climate of the place and so forth and so forth. When I told him that I was a physician out to the hospital on a visit to an old friend who was confined there, he, as anyone might be, was interested mostly in himself.

"So you're a doctor. Look Doc, I got a bad back. As long as I'm sitting here driving, I do all right but as soon as I start to do any lifting, I'm no good."

"Sounds to me like you might have a dislocated intervertebral disc," I said. "How long has it been bothering you?"

"Oh, about two years."

"How did it come on? Suddenly after an accident or some heavy lifting?"

"It came on about a week after I was out with a woman friend of mine. We done about everything in the book. About a week later it began to bother me. I think it was that."

"Too much for you, huh?"

"Well, I think I strained myself."

"Perfectly possible. Have you done anything about it?"

"Oh yeah, I got a doctor, but he wants me to be operated on and I'm not hankering for it."

"How old are you?"

"Forty-eight years old. I knew a friend had it done, a woman, and she didn't come out so well. It's over a year now and she still can't do anything. Think I ought to go through with it?"

"It's just according to how much it bothers you," I said. "If it isn't bad, you might even get over it by leaving it alone, as long as you're symptom-free. But if it really bothers you, I think you ought to look into it. Surgery is the only sure cure—if you've got the right man."

"Oh he's a good man, all right. How long would it lay me up?"

"Well, they got to get the crushed pieces out of there, clean the edges up good and fuse the bones. I don't know too much about the technique but it'll be a minimum of six weeks, I'd think, before you're on your feet again, though it may be that they'll slap a plaster cast on you and get you going sooner."

We were silent awhile at one point at an intersection, then I went on—something about the present world situation on which he had some firm convictions: about what a fool Stalin would be to sit around the next two or three years until we had the mines all planted under him to blow him to kingdom come and not be readying himself to get the jump on us if he can.

I was a little surprised to hear such talk in Washington, D. C., from a man so *au courant* with public opinion.

"Maybe you're right," I said.

"Sure I'm right, wouldn't you do the same thing if you were in his position. We got to best him but it stands to reason that's what's in his mind."

"And what can we do about it?" I said.

"Not a thing, not a thing, except we can think—as long as we keep in line."

"That's what my friend is sitting out there in the hospital for, thinking things like that."

"Is that right. What did he do?"

"He broadcast against this country, from Italy, while we were at war."

"That's bad, you can't do that. What did he say?"

Then I went on to give a brief outline of Ezra's international opinions, the emphasis he lays on the exchange, the international gang, what Ezra calls F.D.R.'s failure to eradicate the basic evil at the critical point, his indictment of the international bankers, their history and their personnel in our day. My man listened closely as we drove through Washington traffic toward my hotel. As I got to the close of my little exposition, he stopped his taxi and turned to me.

"And that's what they got him locked up for," he said.

"Yes, substantially that's what it amounts to."

The man looked at me. "He ain't crazy," he said. "He just talk too much."

My occasions for visiting Ezra are not frequent. I go when I can as I did this last time in mid-winter when we cannot be outdoors but must remain by the big windows adjacent to the old round wooden table with the battered screen making a small room of it at the end of the corridor. I have never been in his cell where he is permitted to receive books and other small gifts of various sorts. The man is sixty-five now and has grown heavier during the past year. His reddish hair, beard and moustaches have been permitted to grow wildly at random—the long hairs framing his unchanged features half-ludicrously, half-frighteningly to resemble the face of the beast in Cocteau's well-known film—and as I speak of it, there is an even deeper resemblance there between the two creatures, Pound in actual life and the imaginative creature of the French film artist. Pound greatly admires Cocteau, and Dorothy during the last year sent me Cocteau's recent poems.

I had heard of a move that had been made to re-open the case, if the charge is still valid, in an attempt to have Pound removed from St. Elizabeth's for treatment under more favorable surroundings. But Pound had refused to entertain the idea, stating that he knew he would be shot by an agent of the "international crew" the moment he stood outside the hosptial gates. Maybe he's right, for one thing is certain: he'd never stop talking.

All my life has been one steady bawling out from this old intimate over my sluggishness in appreciating the gravity of the world situation in the terms of his dialectic. In many cases I can see the justice of his views, both in that particular, regarding the criminal abuse of the functions of money, as well as the place of the poem in our attack; it is a basic agent in putting pressure on the blackguards who compel servitude, abetted by the various English Departments of "the university" with their "sacred" regard for a debased precedent. Formally it plays right into the hands of the criminals in charge of government that alone can compel obedience.

"Attack at that level!" screams Pound.

But we do not see, as he points out, that in the formalisms of the poem itself the criminal sits secure, embedded there so that plaintive officialdom—with all their rewards and prizes, work for the very gang they would destroy. The poem (not "poetry," that sop) is the capsule where only, at times in the intelligence, the facts of the case may be made secure.

Hence the hatred of the poem, the vicious and violent attempt to suppress it—the shock that it at times occasions —and the constant attempt to defame any who is brushed by its flame—when it is a flame, which isn't, it must be said, often the case. The poem is the active agent, sometimes of a basic attack. In it the world may, and often has, to live in hiding.

They burn books, they suppress their freedom, incarcerate their perpetrators, even attempt to burn a picture, in the same mood, such as the "Guernica". This confirms Pound's reasons in using the poem as his take-off, as an oak uses an acorn for the same purpose, or mustard will cover a field with blossom.

A year ago, in the same month of February, when I quitted Ez and was walking toward the exit in the cold rain through the mud of the hospital grounds, I had to go past one of the old buildings. I felt now that I had begun to know the place, my first terror, physician though I am, at the total implications of the place having subsided. At first I had gone cold as I entered the narrow door in the tower which leads up by a winding stone stairway round and around to his floor. I had gone up two flights instead of one to the wrong level. I pressed the button of the bell and was admitted by a wary attendant. All about me were the inmates, lining the walls on both sides, some standing, some sitting, some lying on the stones. I followed the attendant who after identifying me by phone from the main office let me out again telling me to go a floor below and lean on the bell if no one answered the first time.

This I had grown used to. Some sense of humanity had returned to me as I walked along, taking a short cut to the exit which brought me within fifty feet of the building adjacent to the one Pound was occupying. A regularly spaced scream coming from somewhere in the building I was passing caught my ear, then as I came out beyond the edge of an angle in the wall, I saw a figure from which I could not remove my eyes. It is surprising how open and apparently unguarded the whole grounds of the institution present themselves to a visitor: you walk about, you go in and out apparently unobserved and certainly unobstructed, but as I looked up from the mud where I was somewhat carefully stepping, I saw this man, naked, full-on and immobile, his arms up as though climbing a wall, plastered against one of the high windows of the old building like a great sea slug against the inside of a glass aquarium, his belly as though stuck to the glass that looked dulled or splattered from the bad weather. I didn't stop, but kept looking up from time to time. I glanced around to see if there were any women about. There was no one on the grounds at that point but myself. The man's genitals were hard against the cold (it must have been cold) glass, plastered there in that posture of despair. When would they come and take him down? After all it was glass, window glass, bars though there were beyond it. The white flesh like a slug's white belly separated from the outside world, without frenzy, stuck silent on the glass.

I can't understand how Pound has been so apparently unmoved by his incarceration, guilty or essentially innocent as he may be. His mind has not budged a hair's breadth from his basic position, he has even entrenched himself more securely in it—recently finding precedents in the writings of a certain Controller of the Currency sixty or seventy-five years ago, who held similar views on our official perfidies. Pound has privileges, it must be acknowledged, and is kindly treated by the hospital personnel. But he does not waste them. He works constantly, reads interminably. The curator of the Oriental Library in Washington brings him the texts he is interested in when he wants them; he has the Greek of whoever it may be to decipher and understand. He may translate; he has his typewriter: his erudition is become more and more fearsome as time passes, whatever the outcome is to be.

And it must be said of a life of confinement, if he survives it, that much of the world's greatest writing has waited on a removal from the world of affairs for its doing. Concentration is what a man needs to bring his mind to harvest. We may and he will, whoever he may be, change ourselves by our contacts, but to drain off the good we must find quietude. The monk's cell is ideal for the purpose, though it has limitations in its narrowing orthodoxy or partisanship of outlook. Nevertheless it represents quiet, relief from economic pressures: one can write then. Prison, though, is better, or seems to have been so in the past. Aesop was a slave; many a Greek did his best work in exile to Sicily or even the next city. Sappho must have felt mightily confined by Lesbos; Raleigh wrote well in prison: *Pilgrim's Progress* came from confinement—as birth does also—but the best of all was *Don Quixote,* when Cervantes was put in jail. There are other examples.

The poem is a capsule where we wrap up our punishable secrets. And as they confine in themselves the only "life," the ability to sprout at a more favorable time, to come true in their secret structure to the very minutest details of our thoughts, so they get their specific virtue.

We write for this, that the seed come true, and it appears to be this which makes the poem the toughest certainty of continued life that experience acknowledges. Pound is writing and say what you will of government, our own in particular in this case, it is permitting him, to the limit of his ability, to avail himself of the stores of knowledge found in the national capital.

"Yes," I said to him as we were about to part again this last time, "what you say is quite true, but what you forget, Ez, is that logical as your elucidations may be, logic, mere logic, convinces no one."

For once he didn't reply, but Dorothy looked up suddenly and pointed a finger at him, opening her eyes and smiling, as much as to say, "there you are." He never said a word.

But when I reached home he sent me the usual semi-abusive letter—having regained his breath—followed by another letter a week or two later. He had smiled when I spoke of the autobiography, saying, "You can say anything you please about me with perfect safety, since I have no legal status in the country."

VI

Other Prose

from **Spring and All**

If anything of moment results—so much the better. And so much the more likely will it be that no one will want to see it.

There is a constant barrier between the reader and his consciousness of immediate contact with the world. If there is an ocean it is here. Or rather, the whole world is between: Yesterday, tomorrow, Europe, Asia, Africa—all things removed and impossible, the tower of the church at Seville, the Parthenon.

What do they mean when they say: "I do not like your poems; you have no faith whatever. You seem neither to have suffered nor, in fact, to have felt anything very deeply. There is nothing appealing in what you say but on the contrary the poems are positively repellent. They are heartless, cruel, they make fun of humanity. What in God's name do you mean? Are you a pagan? Have you no tolerance for human frailty? Rhyme you may perhaps take away but rhythm! why there is none in your work whatever. Is this what you call poetry? It is the very antithesis of poetry. It is antipoetry. It is the annihilation of life upon which you are bent. Poetry that used to go hand in hand with life, poetry that interpreted our deepest promptings, poetry that inspired, that led us forward to new discoveries, new depths of tolerance, new heights of exaltation. You moderns! it is the death of poetry that you are accomplishing. No. I cannot understand this work. You have not yet suffered a cruel blow from life. When you have suffered you will write differently?"

Perhaps this noble apostrophe means something terrible for me, I am not certain, but for the moment I interpret it to say: "You have robbed me. God, I am naked. What shall I do?"—By it they mean that when I have suffered (provided I have not done so as yet) I too shall run for cover; that I too shall seek refuge in fantasy. And mind you, I do not say that I will not. To decorate my age.

But today it is different.

The reader knows himself as he was twenty years ago and he has also in mind a vision of what he would be, some day. Oh, some day! But the thing he never knows and never dares to know is what he is at the exact moment that he is. And this moment is the only thing in which I am at all interested. Ergo, who cares for anything I do? And what do I care?

I love my fellow creature. Jesus, how I love him: endways, sideways, frontways and all the other ways—but he doesn't exist! Neither does she. I do, in a bastardly sort of way.

To whom then am I addressed? To the imagination.

In fact to return upon my theme for the time nearly all writing, up to the present, if not all art, has been especially designed to keep up the barrier between sense and the vaporous fringe which distracts the attention from its agonized approaches to the moment. It has been always a search for "the beautiful illusion." Very well. I am not in search of "the beautiful illusion."

And if when I pompously announce that I am addressed —To the imagination—you believe that I thus divorce myself from life and so defeat my own end, I reply: To refine, to clarify, to intensify that eternal moment in which we alone live there is but a single force—the imagination. This is its book. I myself invite you to read and to see.

In the imagination, we are from henceforth (so long as you read) locked in a fraternal embrace, the classic caress of author and reader. We are one. Whenever I say "I" I mean also "you." And so, together, as one, we shall begin.

CHAPTER 19.

o meager times, so fat in everything imaginable! imagine
the New World that rises to our windows from the sea on
Mondays and on Saturdays—and on every other day of the
week also. Imagine it in all its prismatic colorings, its counterpart in our souls—our souls that are great pianos whose
strings, of honey and of steel, the divisions of the rainbow
set twanging, loosing on the air great novels of adventure!
Imagine the monster project of the moment: Tomorrow
we the people of the United States are going to Europe
armed to kill every man, woman and child in the area west
of the Carpathian Mountains (also east) sparing none.
Imagine the sensation it will cause. First we shall kill them
and then they, us. But we are careful to spare the Spanish
bulls, the birds, rabbits, small deer and of course—the Russians. For the Russians we shall build a bridge from edge to
edge of the Atlantic—having first been at pains to slaughter all Canadians and Mexicans on this side. Then, oh then,
the great feature will take place.

Never mind; the great event may not exist, so there is no
need to speak further of it. Kill! Kill! the English, the
Irish, the French, the Germans, the Italians and the rest:
friends or enemies, it makes no difference, kill them all.
The bridge is to be blown up when all Russia is upon it.
And why?

Because we love them—all. That is the secret: a new
sort of murder. We make leberwurst of them. Bratwurst.
But why, since we are ourselves doomed to suffer the same
annihilation?

If I could say what is in my mind in Sanscrit or even
Latin I would do so. But I cannot. I speak for the integrity
of the soul and the greatness of life's inanity; the formality
of its boredom; the orthodoxy of its stupidity. Kill! kill!
let there be fresh meat . . .

The imagination, intoxicated by prohibitions, rises to drunken heights to destroy the world. Let it rage, let it kill. The imagination is supreme. To it all our works forever, from the remotest past to the farthest future, have been, are and will be dedicated. To it alone we show our wit by having raised in its honor as monument not the least pebble. To it now we come to dedicate our secret project: the annihilation of every human creature on the face of the earth. This is something never before attempted. None to remain; nothing but the lower vertebrates, the mollusks, insects and plants. Then at last will the world be made anew. Houses crumble to ruin, cities disappear giving place to mounds of soil blown thither by the winds, small bushes and grass give way to trees which grow old and are succeeded by other trees for countless generations. A marvellous serenity broken only by bird and wild beast calls reigns over the entire sphere. Order and peace abound.

This final and self inflicted holocaust has been all for love, for sweetest love, that together the human race, yellow, black, brown, red and white, agglutinated into one enormous soul may be gratified with the sight and retire to the heaven of heavens content to rest on its laurels. There, soul of souls, watching its own horrid unity, it boils and digests itself within the tissues of the great Being of Eternity that we shall then have become. With what magnificent explosions and odors will not the day be accomplished as we, the Great One among all creatures, shall go about contemplating our self-prohibited desires as we promenade them before the inward review of our own bowels—et cetera, et cetera, et cetera . . . and it is spring—both in Latin and Turkish, in English and Dutch, in Japanese and Italian; it is spring by Stinking River where a magnolia tree, without leaves, before what was once a farmhouse, now a ramshackle home for millworkers, raises its straggling branches of ivorywhite flowers.

CHAPTER I. SAMUEL BUTLER

The great English divine, Sam Butler, is shouting from a platform, warning us as we pass: There are two who can invent some extraordinary thing to one who can properly employ that which has been made use of before.

Enheartened by this thought THE TRADITIONAL-ISTS OF PLAGIARISM try to get hold of the mob. They seize those nearest them and shout into their ears: Tradition! The solidarity of life!

The fight is on: These men who have had the governing of the mob through all the repetitious years resent the new order. Who can answer them? One perhaps here and there but it is an impossible situation. If life were anything but a bird, if it were a man, a Greek or an Egyptian, but it is only a bird that has eyes and wings, a beak, talons and a cry that reaches to every rock's center, but without intelligence?—

The voice of the Delphic Oracle itself, what was it? A poisonous gas from a rock's cleft.

Those who led yesterday wish to hold their sway a while longer. It is not difficult to understand their mood. They have their great weapons to hand: "science," "philosophy" and most dangerous of all "art."

Meanwhile, SPRING, which has been approaching for several pages, is at last here.

—they ask us to return to the proven truths of tradition, even to the twice proven, the substantiality of which is known. Demuth and a few others do their best to point out the error, telling us that design is a function of the IMAGINATION, describing its movements, its colors— but it is a hard battle. I myself seek to enter the lists with these few notes jotted down in the midst of the action,

under distracting circumstances—to remind myself (see
p. 2, paragraph 4) of the truth. . . .

In works of the imagination that which is taken for great
good sense, so that it seems as if an accurate precept were
discovered, is in reality not so, but vigor and accuracy of
the imagination alone. In work such as Shakespeare's—

This leads to the discovery that has been made today—
old catalogues aside—full of meat—

"the divine illusion has about it that inaccuracy which
reveals that which I mean."

There is only "illusion" in art where ignorance of the
bystander confuses imagination and its works with cruder
processes. Truly men feel an enlargement before great or
good work, an expansion but this is not, as so many believe
today a "lie," a stupefaction, a kind of mesmerism, a thing
to block out "life," bitter to the individual, by a "vision of
beauty." It is a work of the imagination. It gives the feeling of completion by revealing the oneness of experience;
it rouses rather than stupefies the intelligence by demonstrating the importance of personality, by showing the
individual, depressed before it, that his life is valuable—
when completed by the imagination. And then only. Such
work elucidates—

Such a realization shows us the falseness of attempting to
"copy" nature. The thing is equally silly when we try to
"make" pictures—

But such a picture as that of Juan Gris, though I have not
seen it in color, is important as marking more clearly than
any I have seen what the modern trend is: the attempt is
being made to separate things of the imagination from life,
and obviously, by using the forms common to experience
so as not to frighten the onlooker away but to invite him.
. . . things with which he is familiar, simple things—at the
same time to detach them from ordinary experience to the
imagination. Thus they are still "real" they are the same
things they would be if photographed or painted by

Monet, they are recognizable as the things touched by the hands during the day, but in this painting they are seen to be in some peculiar way—detached

Here is a shutter, a bunch of grapes, a sheet of music, a picture of sea and mountains (particularly fine) which the onlooker is not for a moment permitted to witness as an "illusion." One thing laps over on the other, the cloud laps over on the shutter, the bunch of grapes is part of the handle of the guitar, the mountain and sea are obviously not "the mountain and sea," but a picture of the mountain and the sea. All drawn with admirable simplicity and excellent design—all a unity—

This was not necessary where the subject of art was not "reality" but related to the "gods"—by force or otherwise. There was no need of the "illusion" in such a case since there was none possible where a picture or a work represented simply the imaginative reality which existed in the mind of the onlooker. No special effort was necessary to cleave where the cleavage already existed.

I don't know what the Spanish see in their Velasquez and Goya but

Today where everything is being brought into sight the realism of art has bewildered us, confused us and forced us to re-invent in order to retain that which the older generations had without that effort.

Cezanne—

The only realism in art is of the imagination. It is only thus that the work escapes plagiarism after nature and becomes a creation

Invention of new forms to embody this reality of art, the one thing which art is, must occupy all serious minds concerned.

From the time of Poe in the U. S.—the first American poet had to be a man of great separation—with close identity with life. Poe could not have written a word without the violence of expulsive emotion combined with the

in-driving force of a crudely repressive environment.
Between the two his imagination was forced into being to
keep him to that reality, completeness, sense of escape
which is felt in his work—his topics. Typically American
—accurately, even inevitably set in his time. . . .

Whitman's proposals are of the same piece with the
modern trend toward imaginative understanding of life.
The largeness which he interprets as his identity with the
least and the greatest about him, his "democracy" represents the vigor of his imaginative life. . . .

The imagination uses the phraseology of science. It
attacks, stirs, animates, is radio-active in all that can be
touched by action. Words occur in liberation by virtue of
its processes.

In description words adhere to certain objects, and have
the effect on the sense of oysters, or barnacles.

But the imagination is wrongly understood when it is
supposed to be a removal from reality in the sense of John
of Gaunt's speech in Richard the Second: to imagine possession of that which is lost. It is rightly understood when
John of Gaunt's words are related not to their sense as
objects adherent to his son's welfare or otherwise but as a
dance over the body of his condition accurately accom-
panying it. By this means of the understanding, the play
written to be understood as a play, the author and reader
are liberated to pirouette with the words which have
sprung from the old facts of history, reunited in present
passion.

To understand the words as so liberated is to understand
poetry. That they move independently when set free is the
mark of their value

Imagination is not to avoid reality, nor is it description
nor an evocation of objects or situations, it is to say that
poetry does not tamper with the world but moves it—It
affirms reality most powerfully and therefore, since reality
needs no personal support but exists free from human

action, as proven by science in the indestructibility of matter and of force, it creates a new object, a play, a dance which is not a mirror up to nature but—

As birds' wings beat the solid air without which none could fly so words freed by the imagination affirm reality by their flight

Writing is likened to music. The object would be it seems to make poetry a pure art, like music. Painting too. Writing, as with certain of the modern Russians whose work I have seen, would use unoriented sounds in place of conventional words. The poem then would be completely liberated when there is identity of sound with something—perhaps the emotion.

I do not believe that writing is music. I do not believe writing would gain in quality or force by seeking to attain to the conditions of music.

I think the conditions of music are objects for the action of the writer's imagination just as a table or—

According to my present theme the writer of imagination would attain closest to the conditions of music not when his words are disassociated from natural objects and specified meanings but when they are liberated from the usual quality of that meaning by transposition into another medium, the imagination.

Sometimes I speak of imagination as a force, an electricity or a medium, a place. It is immaterial which: for whether it is the condition of a place or a dynamization its effect is the same: to free the world of fact from the impositions of "art" . . . and to liberate the man to act in whatever direction his disposition leads.

The word is not liberated, therefore able to communicate release from the fixities which destroy it until it is accurately tuned to the fact which giving it reality, by its own reality establishes its own freedom from the necessity of a word, thus freeing it and dynamizing it at the same time. . . .

from *In the American Grain*

The Fountain of Eternal Youth

HISTORY, history! We fools, what do we know or care?
History begins for us with murder and enslavement, not
with discovery. No, we are not Indians but we are men of
their world. The blood means nothing; the spirit, the ghost
of the land moves in the blood, moves the blood. It is we
who ran to the shore naked, we who cried, "Heavenly
Man!" These are the inhabitants of our souls, our murdered
souls that lie ... agh. Listen! I tell you it was lucky for
Spain the first ship put its men ashore where it did. If the
Italian had landed in Florida, one twist of the helm north,
or among the islands a hair more to the south; among the
Yamasses with their sharpened bones and fishspines, or
among the Caribs with their poisoned darts—it might have
begun differently.

When in the later years Ponce found his plantations
going under for lack of slaves—no more to be trapped in
Puerto Rico, *rico!* all ruined—he sought and obtained a
royal patent to find more in the surrounding islands. He
was granted the right to hunt out and to take the Caribs;
the Caribs whom The Great Maker had dropped through a
hole in the sky among their islands; they whose souls lived
in their bodies, many souls in one body; they who fought
their enemies, ate them; whose gods lived, Mabouya, in the
forest, Oumekon, by the sea—there were other gods—

His ship came into Guadeloupe—the great sulphur cone
back of the water. He had arrived straight from Spain, hot
foot after niggers. Having much soiled linen aboard from

the long trip, he ordered his laundresses ashore, with a body of troops to guard them, where a stream could be observed coming down to the sea.

It was a paradise. A stream of splashing water, the luxuriant foliage. A gorge, a veritable tunnel led upstream between cliffwalls covered by thick vines in flower attended by ensanguined hummingbirds which darted about from cup to cup in the green light. But the soul of the Carib was on the alert among the leaves. It was too late.

Fierce and implacable we kill them but their souls dominate us. Our men, our blood, but their spirit is master. It enters us, it defeats us, it imposes itself. We are moderns—madmen at Paris—all lacking in a ground sense of cleanliness. It is the Caribs leaping out, facing the arquebuses, thinking it thunder, looking up at the sky: No rain! No clouds! Then the second volley. Their comrades bleeding, dead. Kill! Not a Spaniard but they stretched out in the streambed. Hagh, I can hear the laundresses squeal on the shore—run hither and thither. The devils had them safe. Let old Ponce sit up in his hammock on the poop of his ship. Let him send other boats ashore. The Indians have grabbed up the women. Three naked savages shot through the chest from behind before they could gain the forest rolled over and gripped the females they had been carrying by the throat with their teeth. Worth being a laundress to be carried off that way, eh? Nice psychologic study, those women. And the damned bloodhound, Berrescien. Ponce had got his belly full. They outflanked him in canoes, ridiculed his strategy, took his chainshot in the chest and came back for more. They drove him off, so much so that they made him forget his dog, the precious Berrescien, of whom he thought more, that and his hidalgan pride, than—a population. The hound had been left behind in their scared flight. They saw him, they in the retreating boats, leap from the woods in pursuit of a flying Carib. Listen to this. The Indian swam out, the Spaniards in the boats

turned back for the beast. The dog was steadily gaining on
his victim. But, O Soul of the New World, the man had his
bow and arrow with him as he swam. Tell that to Wilson.
He stopped, turned, raised his body half out of the water,
treading it, and put a bolt into the damned hound's throat
—whom sharks swallowed. Then to shore, not forgetting—
leaping to safety—to turn and spit back the swallowed
chainshot, a derisive yell at the Christians.

They had the women and the dog. They left what they
had defeated, to—us.

If men inherit souls this is the color of mine. We are, too,
the others. Think of them! The main islands were thickly
populated with a peaceful folk when Christ-over found
them. But the orgy of blood which followed, no man has
written. We are the slaughterers. It is the tortured soul of
our world. Indians have no souls; that was it. That was
what they said. But they knew they lied—the blood-smell
proof. Ponce had been with the discoverer on his second
trip. He became a planter. Sugar cane was imported from
the Canaries, maize was adopted from the Indian souls. But
revenues dwindled where none would work save in the
traffic in girls: nine years old, reads the Italian's journal.
Slaves. The Indians having no souls knew what freedom
means. The Spaniards killed their kings, betrayed, raped,
murdered their women and children; hounded them into
the mountains. Ponce with wife and children in the *Casa
Blanca* was one of the bloodthirstiest. They took them in
droves, forced them to labor. It was impossible to them—
not having been born to baptism. How maddening it is to
the spirit to hear:—Bands of them went into the forests,
their forests, and hanged themselves to the trees. What else?
Islands—paradise. Surrounded by seas. On all sides "heavenly man" bent on murder. Self-privilege. Two women and
one man on a raft had gotten one hundred and fifty miles
out to sea—such seamen were they—then luck again went

against the Indian. Captured and back to slavery. Caravels
crept along the shore by night. Next morning when
women and children came down to the shore to fish—fine
figures, straight black hair, high cheekbones, a language—
they caught them, made them walk in bands, cut them
down if they fainted, slashed off breasts, arms—women,
children. Gut souls—

Thus the whole free population was brought into slavery
or killed off. Aboujoubo, greatest chief in the island of San
Ion, retreated in anguish to a rocky height. Ponce, now
Governor, since he dare not economically murder every
one, sallies out and is received by a native queen, girls dancing, gives one a gold crucifix, legend says. Two years later
finds her under a bush, both hands hacked off. Belly-hurt
he digs a shallow grave with his sword for her and shoves
the gold symbol into his wallet. He exchanges names with
a chief, sacred symbol of Indian faith and friendship.
Hounds him out later: I am Juan Ponce de Leon! says the
savage, standing before his followers—hanged nevertheless.
The hound, Berrescien, gone ahead into a rocky place,
comes spinning back, tumbling down, knocking against
rocks, a gash in his forehead. Ponce defeated, embittered
has the dog stretched upon a litter of leaves and branches
and carried to the ship.

Do these things die? Men who do not know what lives,
are themselves dead. In the heart there are living Indians
once slaughtered and defrauded—Indians that live also in
subtler ways: Ponce at fifty-two was rich, the murderous
campaigns of his youth had subjugated the island—allayed
his lust of common murder. The island was, in any case,
mostly conquered.

An old Indian woman among his slaves, began to tell
him of an island, Bimini, a paradise of fragrant groves, of
all fruits. And in the center of it a fountain of clearest
water of virtue to make old men young. Think of that!

Picture to yourself the significance of that—as revenge, as irony, as the trail of departing loveliness, *fata morgana*. Yet the real, the thing destroyed turning back with a smile. Think of the Spaniard listening. Gold. Gold. Riches. And figure to yourself the exquisite justice of it: an old woman, loose tongued—loose sword—the book, her soul already half out of her with sorrow: abandoned by a Carib who had fled back to his home having found Borequien greatly overrated. Her children enslaved—

The man, fifty-two, listened. Something has escaped him. At that moment rich, idle, he was relieved of his governorship. Vessels, three. He fitted them up at his own cost. Men enough, eager to serve the old master, rushed to his banner. Let the new governor complain that he was taking away too many able soldiers. Ponce smiled. Men whose terms of service had expired do as they please.

Por donde va la mar
Vayan las arenas—

They sailed north. It was March. In the wind, what? Beauty the eternal. White sands and fragrant woods, fruits, riches, truth! The sea, the home of permanence, drew them on into its endless distances. Again the new! Do you feel it? The murderer, the enslaver, the terror striker, the destroyer of beauty, drawn on by beauty across the glancing tropical seas—before Drake, before the galleons. The rhythm of the waves, birds, fish, seaweed as on the first voyage. They even put in at Guanahani for water—Columbus' first landfall; then populous, inviting; now desolate, defeated, murdered—unpeopled.

March! Spring! to the north. The argosy of the New World! In search of eternal youth. In search of the island of Bimini—an old woman's tale. The destroyer. Admonished that he had done enough, still there floated a third world to discover: no end—away from the beginning—tail chaser.

A Carne de lobo
Diente de perro

he could not halt—no end. Curious that Amino—the boy of Palos who watched Columbus prepare his vessels for the first voyage and went on the second—should be his pilot. Sea scud. The same piloted Cortez to Mexico.

Let them go. They found nothing but a row of white islands called "The Martyrs," a catch of turtles, Las Tortugas, a sandy coastline, a devil of a current that shoved them about and devilish Indians who drove them back from the watering places—flamingoes, pelicans, egrets, herons—Rousseau has it. Thickets with striped leaves, ferns emerging from the dark, palms, the heat, the moon, the stars, the sun in a pool of swampwater. Fish fly. In the water seals—back to Cuba.

Old now, heavy at heart over the death of his bloody pet, Ponce retired to his Casa Blanca and sulked for three years. Then came the news of Cortez' triumph and the wealth of Montezuma.

Ponce—

de Leon
en nombre y podesta

—the victor,
now defeated, must stir again. Back to Florida thinking to find on the continent, he only then found that he had discovered, another Tehuantepec.

But this time the Yamasses put an arrow into his thigh at the first landing—and let out his fountain. They flocked to the beach, jeered him as he was lifted to the shoulders of his men and carried away. Dead.

Sir Walter Raleigh

OF THE PURSUIT of beauty and the husk that remains, perversions and mistakes, while the true form escapes in the
wind, sing O Muse; of Raleigh, beloved by majesty, plung-
ing his lust into the body of a new world—and the deaths,
misfortunes, counter coups, which swelled back to certify
that ardor with defeat. Sing! and let the rumor of these
things make the timid more timid and the brave desperate,
careless of monuments which celebrate the subtle conver-
sions of sense and let truth go unrecognized. Sing! and
make known Raleigh, who would found colonies; his England became a mouthful of smoke sucked from the embers
of a burnt weed. And if the nations, well founded on a
million hindrances, taxes, laws and laws tò annul laws must
have a monument, let it be here implied: this undersong,
this worm armed to gnaw away lies and to release—
Raleigh: if it so please the immortal gods.

Sing of his wisdom, O Muse: The truth is that all nations,
how remote soever, being all reasonable creatures, and
enjoying one and the same imagination and fantasy, have
devised, according to their means and materials, the same
things.

They all have lighted on the invention of bows and
arrows; all have targets and wooden swords, all have instru-
ments to encourage them to fight, all that have corn beat it
in mortars and make cakes, baking them upon slate stones;
all devised laws without any grounds had from the scrip-
tures or from Aristotle's Politick, whereby they are governed; all that dwell near their enemies impale their
villages, to save themselves from surprise. Yea, besides the

same inventions, all have the same natural impulsions; they follow nature in the choice of many wives; and there are among them which, out of a kind of wolfish ferocity, eat man's flesh; yea, most of them believe in a second life, and they are all of them idolators in one kind or another—

These things, still chewing, he chewed out. And as an atheist, with Marlow, they would have burned him. It was his style! To the sea, then! mixed with soundest sense—on selling cannon to one's enemies.

But through all else, O Muse, say that he penetrated to the Queen!

Sing! O Muse and say, he was too mad in love, too clear, too desperate for her to trust upon great councils. He was not England, as she was. She held him, but she was too shrewd a woman not to know she held him as a woman, she, the Queen; which left an element. Say that he was made and cracked by majesty, knew that devotion, tasted that wisdom and became too wise—and she all eyes and wit looking through until her man, her Raleigh became thin, light, a spirit. He was the whetter, the life giver through the Queen—but wounded cruelly. In this desperate condition, will-less, inspired, the tool of a woman, flaming, falling, being lifted up, robbed of himself to feed her, caught, dispatched, starting, held again, giving yet seeking round the circle for an outlet: this was, herself; but what, O Muse, of Raleigh, that proud man?

Say, first, he was the breath of the Queen—for a few years; say, too, that he had traveled much before he knew her, that he had seen the tropics and explored the Orinoco River for a hundred miles. Then say, O Muse, that now he saw himself afar, that he became—America! that he conceived a voyage from perfection to find—an England new again; to found a colony; the outward thrust, to seek. But it turned out to be a voyage on the body of his Queen: England, Elizabeth—Virginia!

He sent out colonists, she would not let him go himself; nothing succeeded. It was a venture in the crook of a lady's finger, pointing, then curving in. Virginia? It was the nail upon that finger. O Raleigh! nowhere, everywhere—and nothing. Declare, O Muse, impartially, how he had gone with the English fleet to strike at Spain and how she called him back—Sire, do you not know, you!? These women are my person. What have you dared to do? How have you dared, without my order, to possess yourself of what is mine? Marry this woman!

Sing, O Muse, with an easy voice, how she, Elizabeth, she England, she the Queen—deserted him; Raleigh for Leicester, Essex now for Raleigh; she Spencer whom he friended, she "The Faery Queen," she Guiana, she Virginia, she atheist, she "my dear friend Marlow," she rents, rewards, honors, influence, reputation, she "the fundamental laws of human knowledge," she prison, she tobacco, the introduction of potatoes to the Irish soil: It is the body of the Queen stirred by that plough—now all withdrawn.

O Muse, in that still pasture where you dwell amid the hardly noticed sounds of water falling and the little cries of crickets and small birds, sing of Virginia floating off: the broken chips of Raleigh: the Queen is dead.

O Virginia! who will gather you again as Raleigh had you gathered? science, wisdom, love, despair. O America, the deathplace of his son! It is Raleigh, anti-tropical. It is the cold north, flaring up in ice again.

What might he have known, what seen, O Muse?—Shoal water where we smelt so sweet and so strong a smell, as if we had been in the midst of some delicate garden; and keeping good watch and keeping but slack sail—we arrived upon the coast; a land so full of grapes as the very beating and surge of the sea overflow them, such plenty, as well there as in all places else, on the sand and on the green soil on the hills, as well as every little shrub, as also climbing towards the tops of high cedars, that in all the world I think a like abundance is not to be found. And from below the hill such a flock of cranes, mostly white, arose with such a cry as if an army of men had shouted all together.— He might have seen the brother of the king, Granganimo, with copper cap, whose wife, comely and bashful, might have come aboard the ship, her brows bound with white coral; or running out to meet them very cheerfully, at Roanoak, plucked off his socks and washed his feet in warm water. A people gentle, loving, faithful, void of all guile and treason. Earthen pots, large, white and sweet and wooden platters of sweet timber.

Sing, O Muse and say, there is a spirit that is seeking through America for Raleigh: in the earth, the air, the waters, up and down, for Raleigh, that lost man: seer who failed, planter who never planted, poet whose works are questioned, leader without command, favorite deposed—but one who yet gave title for his Queen, his England, to a coast he never saw but grazed alone with genius.

Question him in hell, O Muse, where he has gone, and when there is an answer, sing and make clear the reasons that he gave for that last blow. Why did he send his son into that tropic jungle and not go himself, upon so dangerous an errand? And when the boy had died why not die too? Why England again and force the new King to keep his promise and behead him?

Voyage of the Mayflower

THE PILGRIMS were seed of Tudor England's lusty blossoming. The flamboyant force of that zenith, spent, became in them hard and little. Among such as they its precarious wealth of petals sank safely within bounds to lie dreaming or floating off while the Restoration throve, a sweltering seclusion of the hothouse, surrounded by winter's cold.

In those little pips a nadir, sure as the sun, was reached, in which lay the character of beginnings in North America. As particles stripped of wealth, mortifying as they were mortified, "*predicateurs*," greatly suffering, greatly prepared to suffer, they were the perfect sprout for the savage continent God had driven them to. But Puritans, as they were called, if they were pure it was more since they had nothing in them of fulfillment than because of positive virtues.

By their very emptiness they were the fiercest element in the battle to establish a European life on the New World. The first to come as a group, of a desire sprung within themselves, they were the first American democracy—and it was they, in the end, who would succeed in making everything like themselves. No man led them; there was none. The leaders had failed long since for them at home— if there ever had been any—and those still at home were still more removed from them than ever. Stripped and little they came resting on no authority but the secret warmth of their tight-locked hearts. But, unhappily, never had they themselves nor has any one penetrated there to see what was contained. The emptiness about them was sufficient

terror for them not to look further. The jargon of God,
which they used, was their dialect by which they kept
themselves surrounded as with a palisade. They pleaded
weakness, they called continually for help (while working
shrewdly with their own hands all the while), they asked
protection—but the real help had been to make them small,
small and several, several and each as a shell for his own
"soul." And the soul? a memory (or a promise), a flower
sheared away—nothing.

Theirs is the secret of fairy tales, the descent of the
"soul" into picturesque smallness: children, dwarfs, elves;
the diminutive desires of the lowly for—they scarcely
know what. The "God" of the Pilgrims is redolent of these
mysteries. All their fears, their helplessness, the uncer-
tainty of their force—have the quality of such lore. The
pathetic detail of the rough sailor who cursed the poor people and what happened to him is strongly in this mood. It
shows also the collective sense of the destiny common to
lowly people.

From the outset they had had trouble, then the account
goes on:—"These troubles being blowne over, and now all
being compacte together in one shipe, they put to sea again
with a prosperous winde, which continued diverce days
together, which was some incouragement unto them; yet
according to ye usuall maner many were afflicted with sea
sickness. And I may not omit here a spetial worke of God's
providence. Ther was a proud and very profane younge
man, one of ye seamen, of a lustie body, which made him
the more hauty; he would allway be contemning ye poore
people in their sickness, and cursing them dayly with gree-
ous execrations, and did not let to tell them, that he hoped
to cast halfe of them over board before they came to their
journey's end, and to make merry with what they had; and
if he were by any gently reproved he would curse and
swear most bitterly. But it pleased God before they came
halfe seas over, to smite this yong man with a greeveous

disease, of which he dyed in a desperate maner, and so was himself ye first yt was throwne overboard. Thus his curses light on his owne head; and it was an astonishment to all his fellows for they noted it to be ye just hand of God upon him."

The dreadful and curious thing is that men, despoiled and having nothing, must long most for that which they have not and so, out of the intensity of their emptiness imagining they are full, deceive themselves and all the despoiled of the world into their sorry beliefs. It is the spirit that existing nowhere in them is forced into their dreams. The Pilgrims, they, the seed, instead of growing, looked black at the world and damning its perfections praised a zero in themselves. The inversion of a Gothic Calvin.

For the Puritans there had been a decline of which it was their miserable fate never to know, while they raised their holy incantations. These are not the great flower of the spirit. Purged by hard experience (worn bodies from which a white dove springs), they are not all soul as they and we have imagined. Bodily suffering was more an alleviation than otherwise, a distraction that kept them mercifully blinded. They were condemned to be without flower, to sow themselves basely that after them others might know the end. Each shrank from an imagination that would sever him from the rest.

And so they stressed the "spirit"—for what else could they do?—and this spirit *is* an earthly pride which they, prideless, referred to heaven and the next world. And for *this* we praise them, instead of for the one thing in them that was valuable: their tough littleness and weight of many to carry through the cold; not their brokenness but their projection of the great flower of which they were the seed.

The Pilgrims were mistaken not in what they did, because they went hard to work with their hands and heads, but in what they imagined for their warmth. It could

not have been otherwise. But it is sordid that a rich world
should follow apathetically after. Their misfortune has
become a malfeasant ghost that dominates us all. It is they
who must have invented the "soul," but the perversion is
for this emptiness, this dream, this pale negative to usurp
the place of that which really they were destined to
continue.

This stress of the spirit against the flesh has produced a
race incapable of flower. Upon that part of the earth they
occupied true spirit dies because of the Puritans, except
through vigorous revolt. They are the bane, not the staff.
Their religious zeal, mistaken for a thrust up toward the
sun, was a stroke in, in, in—not toward germination but the
confinements of a tomb.

Everything attests their despoiled condition: the pitiful
care for each one, the talk of the common wealth (common
to all alike, so never the proud possession of any one) and
the church—that secret inversion of loveliness; their lost
position, itself, in the new land, the cold, disease, starvation
—inexplicable, unavoided troubles; their committing themselves not to any plan but floating on the ocean as a seed to
God—to the sea and the winds—trustful, in a leaky boat. It
is the weakling in us all that finds this beautiful. So with the
low condition of their words themselves, the bad spelling
of their journal; treated with contempt by the least of those
they had to do with, so contemned that no one would lend
them money "so they were forst to selle of some provisions
to stop this gape"; their continually expressed love of each
other, "Beloved friends, sory we are that there should be
occasion of writing at all unto you," etc.

"So they comited them selves to ye will of God and
resolved to proceed. In sundrie of these storms the winds
were so feirce and ye seas so high, as they could not beare
a knote of saile, but were forced to hull, for diverce days
together. And in one of them, as they thus lay at hull in a
mighty storm, a lustie young man (called John Howland)

coming upon some occasion above ye gratings, was, with a seel of ye shipe thrown into ye sea: but it pleased God yt he caught hold of ye topesaile halliards, which hung over board, and ran out at great length: yet he held his hould (though he was sundrie fadomes under water) till he was hold up by ye same rope to ye brim of ye water, and then with a boat hooke and other means got into ye shipe again, and his life saved; and though he was something ill with it, yet he lived many years after, and became a profitable member both in church and comone wealth."

This passage is perfect: the one man of it, at sea, in the merciful guardianship of God, (washed away, howbeit), relying on his own hands and feet saves himself by force of himself, is hauled back by others like himself; the minute care for detail, the note of his subsequent illness, and yet, the moral at the end.

And this moral? As with the deformed Aesop, morals are the memory of success that no longer succeeds.

But the enjoyment of the lust, the hidden flower, they martyrized as the spirit or the soul, has curious turns. Primarily despoiled by providence; clinging with the doggedness of a northern race, cold, close and slow to that; they become unfit, except where there exists the same sort of stress which brought them into being; the hard, repressive pioneer soil of the mind. They must have relied on vigorous hypocrisy to save them—which they did. But this they could not revere.

If the "puritan" in them could have ended with their entry into the New World and the subtle changes of growth at once have started (See Cotton Mather's "Wonders of the Invisible World," the prefatory remarks), everything would have been different, but the character of the land was not favorable. They did try to land further south.

In fear and without guidance, really lost in the world, it is they alone who would later, at Salem, have strayed so far —morbidly seeking the flame,—that terrifying unknown image to which, like savages, they too offered sacrifices of human flesh. It is just such emptiness, revulsion, terror in all ages, which in fire—a projection still of the truth—finds that which lost and desperate men have worshiped. And it is still to-day the Puritan who keeps his frightened grip upon the throat of the world lest it should prove him—empty.

Such would the New World become. Their strength made it, but why, why the perpetual error of remaining at that low point? It is that at which the soul, dying in them, not liberated by death, but dead—is sad.

The result of that brave setting out of the Pilgrims has been an atavism that thwarts and destroys. The agonized spirit, that has followed like an idiot with undeveloped brain, governs with its great muscles, babbling in a text of the dead years. Here souls perish miserably, or, escaping, are bent into grotesque designs of violence and despair. It is an added strength thrown to a continent already too powerful for men. One had not expected that this seed of England would come to impersonate, and to marry, the very primitive itself; to creep into the very intestines of the settlers and turn them against themselves, to befoul the New World.

It has become "the most lawless country in the civilized world," a panorama of murders, perversions, a terrific ungoverned strength, excusable only because of the horrid beauty of its great machines. To-day it is a generation of gross know-nothingism, of blackened churches where hymns groan like chants from stupefied jungles, a generation universally eager to barter permanent values (the hope of an aristocracy) in return for opportunist material advantages, a generation hating those whom it obeys.

What prevented the normal growth? Was it England, the northern strain, the soil they landed on? It was, of course, the whole weight of the wild continent that made their condition of mind advantageous, forcing it to reproduce its own likeness, and no more.

Jacataqua

TERROR enlarges the object, as does joy. "The whole forest seemed to open," says the hunter of his first tiger, "I don't know what its exact size may have been; but, to me, it seemed thirty feet high." So, by emotional grandeur, were the heroes of antiquity conceived; and so, to the joyful eye of the lover seems the object of his delight, bringing such wonder and awe, that each motion—each look—is exaggerated, filled with power and significance, intensified to a degree that puts colder measurements aside. From this, the lore of romance has grown. In America, the legend of a horror before the war-whoops of the Indians gives some inkling of a great dread the colonists experienced—but there is rarely a countering legend of joy.

We believe that life in America is compact of violence and the shock of immediacy. This is not so. Were it so, there would be a corresponding beauty of the spirit—to bear it witness; a great flowering, simple and ungovernable as the configuration of a rose—that should stand with the gifts of the spirit of other times and other nations as a standard to humanity. There is none.

"The United States, without self-seeking, has given more of material help to Europe and to the world in the last ten years in time of need, than have all other nations of the world put together in the entire history of mankind. It has stamped out yellow fever from the coasts of South America, etc."

It is our need that is crying out, that and our immense wealth, the product of fear,—a torment to the spirit; we sell—but carefully—to seek blessings abroad. And this wealth, all that is not pure accident—is the growth of fear.

It is this which makes us the flaming terror of the world, a Titan, stupid (as were all the giants), great, to be tricked or tripped (from terror of us) with hatred barking at us by every sea—and by those most to whom we give the most. In the midst of wealth, riches, we have the inevitable Coolidge platform: "poorstateish"—meek. THIS is his cure before the world: our goodness and industry. THIS will convince the world that we are RIGHT. It will not. Make a small mouth. It is the acme of shrewdness, of policy. It will work. We shall have more to give. Logical reasoning it is: generous to save and give. It is bred of fear. It is as impossible for a rich nation to convince any one of its generosity as for a camel to pass through the eye of a needle. Puritanical; pioneer; "out of the small white farm-house"—the product of delay. The characteristic of American life is that it holds off from embraces, from impacts, gaining, by fear, safety and time in which to fortify its prolific carcass —while the spirit, with tongue hanging out, bites at its bars —its object just out of reach. Wilson grazed heaven by his lewdness; the door stood open till it was slammed closed. I relish the back door gossip that made him impossible.

Delay, all through youth, halt and cessation, not of effort, but of touch, all through life as it is learned: no end save accumulation, always upon the way to BIGGER opportunity; we keep realization from the mind with a purpose till men are trained never to possess fully but just to SEE. This makes scientists and it makes the masochist. Keep it cold and small and under the cold lens. It is bastardization as of astronomy that has no counterpart with us in the aspirations or the conceits of the flesh; a passion equal to the straining of a telescope. Digressions—The American character is acquisitive, but mediate, like the Morgan interests, Mr. Franklin at the helm, the International Mercantile Marine that owns, as mortgager, the White Star, the Red Star, the Atlantic Transport lines, etc. American lines but English ships. We own them. But who HAS them? A more practical race used to holding India. Crude as iron.

What would be better to-night than a long hour of
music, at ease and away from disturbance, a friend or two
of the same humor with a little talk now and again when
the musician, since it should be a woman, rested,—the
pause before the sexual act, that interruption from desire
that piles up a weight of energy behind it like stones do a
river. The impossibility to attain is the source of all good in
the world, the real reason for the Puritan. No, not *all good*,
though so it seems to Americans. There is a kind of piling
of experience upon experience that is not bound to satiety,
but to wisdom, the highest knowledge of all, to Buddha, if
one likes, to release, to relief, to the dangerous ground of
pleasure: *Jenseits des lust princip*, Freud sees it, beyond
the charmed circle. It is no matter, since it is unknown in
the province I am discussing. Here, through terror, there is
no direct touch; all is cold, little and discreet:—save just
under the hide.

There are no American servitors. An American will not
serve another man. This is a fear. Nothing is so delightful
as to serve another. Instead of that, we have "service," the
thing that Rabindranath Tagore so admired, telling us we
did not know we had it: Sending supplies to relieve the
cyclone sufferers in Indiana. It is a passion. But to serve
another, with a harder personal devotion is foreign to us: a
trick for foreigners, a servant's trick. We are afraid that we
couldn't do it and retain our self-esteem. We couldn't.
Thus we see of what our self-esteem is made.

"Don't let's have any poor," is our slogan. And we do
not notice that the chief reason for this is that it offends us
to believe that there are the essentially poor who are far
richer than we are who give. The poor are ostracized. Cults
are built to abolish them, as if they were cockroaches, and
not human beings who may not want what we have in such
abundance. THAT would be an offense an American could
not stomach. So down with them. Let everybody be rich
and so EQUAL. What a farce! But what a tragedy! It rests

upon false values and fear to discover them. Do not serve another for you might have to TOUCH him and he might be a JEW or a NIGGER.

Do you realize the fascination the story of the white woman who had twin nigger babies has for us? They accused the woman of having had intercourse with the apartment's colored elevator boy. Her husband abandoned her at once, of course,—charming man. But you know Mendel's law; they discovered there had been a darky in *his* family six generations before! There's the dénouement for every good American. Be careful whom you marry! Be careful for you can NEVER know. Watch, wait, study.

Deanimated, that's the word; something the sound of "metronome," a mechanical means; Yankee inventions. Machines were not so much to save time as to save dignity that fears the animate touch. It is miraculous the energy that goes into inventions here. Do you know that it now takes just ten minutes to put a bushel of wheat on the market from planting to selling, whereas it took three hours in our colonial days? That's striking. It must have been a tremendous force that would do that. That force is fear that robs the emotions; a mechanism to increase the gap between touch and thing, *not* to have a contact.

America adores violence, yes. It thrills at big fires and explosions. This approaches magnificence! The finest fire-fighters in the world. We live not by having less fires but more, by the excitement of seeing torturing things done well, with light ease even. But we have violence *for service*, mark it. Battleships *for peace*. The force of enterprise *for bringing bananas* to the breakfast table. Massive mining operations to transport us—whither? Bathrooms, kitchens, hospitals with a maximum of physical convenience and a minimum of waste to spare us—for what? We never ask. It is all a bar to more intimate shocks. Everything is for "generosity" and "honor." *It has to be* for us to get away with it. Therefore, we cannot acknowledge, really, downright, thievery in our friends. We can't get to it. Did we do so, we should know many things most disturbing to our peace of mind.

Atlanta, Georgia, is far worse than Paris for girls on the streets soliciting, but there is no good in it,—I don't suppose there has ever been an American woman like Kiki or that delightful Baroness who paraded Fifth Avenue one day with a coal-scuttle for a chapeau. Naturally they arrested her. Naturally. She would have been arrested in any city, but not, I imagine, with quite such a sense of duty as in America. To permit such a thing would cast a very awkward light on us all.

The impact of the bare soul upon the very twist of the fact which is our world about us, is un-American. *That* we shun and rush off to the laboratory, the wheatfield (hiding our indecent passion in meddling, playing) in a spirit of service—our chemistry is all that—salt away the profits, and boast of our saving, stabilizing *Constitution* in dread, as of a glass heart, fiercely aligning ourselves in its defense as if it were something else than a mechanical shift.

Men weaving women, women spouting men—colleges and streets torturing and annealing the machinery to cure cancer and kill mosquitoes, to carry fish in proper cars and fruit in others, to kill the *Aedes Egyptus* in the domestic water supply of Quito by the use of minnows in the house tanks—Our life is tortuous and grotesque, huge fetishes by which we are ruled in utter darkness—or we fly abroad for sensation: Anything to escape—we fear simplicity as the plague. Never to allow touch. What are we but poor doomed carcasses, any one of us? Why then all this fury, this multiplicity we push between ourselves and our desires? Twisting and bending; that nervous habit of wanting to be thought pleasant—tortuous and grotesque.

It is the women above all—there never have been women, save pioneer Katies; not one in flower save some moonflower Poe may have seen, or an unripe child. Poets?

Where? They are the test. But a true woman in flower, never. Emily Dickinson, starving of passion in her father's garden, is the very nearest we have ever been—starving.

Never a woman: never a poet. That's an axiom. Never a poet saw sun here.

Oh, men have had women, millions of them, of course: good, firm Janes. But one that spouted any comprehensive joy? Never. Dolly Madison was a bright doll. At best they want to be men, sit and be a pal. It's all right. How could they do anything else with the men brutally beaten by the life—

Do you know that the old town-records in Massachusetts show few men without two and many with as many as seven wives? Not at all uncommon to have had five. How? The first ones died shooting children against the wilderness like cannon balls. There's a reason for traditional cleverness! And we talk about the wilderness with affection. We are blind asses, with our whole history unread before us and helpless if we read it. Nothing noticed. Nothing taught in the academies. You'd think that THAT would force us into some immediacy. NEVER. We write books deploring the post-war hilarity of our present-day girls. Mr. Hungerford assures me the girls are no different now than they were before the Rebellion. But shh! Ben Franklin, who started black with an illegitimate son, was forced to turn white, poor Richard, to save himself later. He saw the hell and warned us, warned us to save our pennies. So, too, spendthrift Cleveland who became economist.

Our life drives us apart and forces us upon science and invention—away from touch. Or if we do touch, our breed knows no better than the coarse fiber of football. Though Bill Bird says that American men are the greatest business men in the world: the only ones who understand the passion of making money: absorbed, enthralled in it. It's a game. To me, it is because we fear to wake up that we play so well. Imagine stopping money making. Our whole con-

ception of reality would have to be altered. But to keep a
just balance between business and another object is to spoil
the intoxication, the illusion, the unity even. It's very hard
on the poet who must be something or other in order to
live. To live against the stream, Emily Dickinson, about
the only woman one can respect for her clarity, lived in
her father's back yard.

Our breed knows no better than the coarse fibre of football, the despair we have for touching, the cheek, the breast
—drives us to scream in beaten frenzy at the great spectacle of violence—or to applaud coldness and skill.

Who is open to injuries? Not Americans. Get hurt;
you're a fool. The only hero is he who is not hurt. We have
no feeling for the tragic. Let the sucker who fails get his.
What's tragic in that? That's funny! To hell with him. He
didn't make good, that's all.

It's a kind of celluloid of gayety (I am speaking of the
theaters), a numbing coat that cuts us off from touch. Did
you see the expression on Coolidge's face when Al Jolson
did his stuff before him on the White House lawn? embarrassment, shame, fear to seem not to be amused, desire to
get away—very bad taste on everybody's part. But it was
really funny to see. That jazz dose and the Puritan: something akin: both removed from simplicity, really, and
touch: each his own way, that shaky shimmy and the—
shame.

What is the result? The result is the thing that results, of
course.

Anyhow, it's curious to pick up results, you'll find tail
ends of New England families—all burnt out; charming
people: an old man marries a girl: male sons aplenty who
sew and wash and make pies; embroider, select their mother's hats and dress fabrics—and paint pictures: long skinny
men with emotional wits who have smelt losses. A bastard
aristocracy. Men who, when their friends disappoint them,
grow nervous and cry all night. It is because there are no

women. These men are more out of place in pushing young America than a Chinaman—or a Tibetan.

Women—givers (but they have been, as reservoirs, empty) perhaps they are being filled now. Hard to deal with in business, more conservative, closer to earth—the only earth. They are our cattle, cattle of the spirit—not yet come in. None yet has raised benevolence to distinction. Not one to "wield her beauty as a scepter." It is a brilliant opportunity.—But the aesthetic shown by American artists (the test of the women) is discouraging: the New England eunuchs,—"no more sex than a tapeworm"—faint echoes of England, perhaps of France, of Rousseau, as Valéry Larbaud insists,—Ryder: no detail in his foregrounds just remote lusts, fiery but "gone,"—Poe: moonlight. It is the annunciation of the spiritual barrenness of the American woman.

Violence—the newspapers are full of murder, but it is for the papers: that's not immediacy but FEAR. It is the hysteria of cheated folk, similar to the outbreaks of murder and suicide in the Germanic countries after the war—The old man that murdered the woman with a Polish name in Perth Amboy. It is so clear: A man without a woman finds one. She immediately starts to torture him. It's all they can do. "Take it out of the son of a bitch"—he's put himself in a compromising position and deserves to be castrated. Every force is piled against him. So he murders her. But is THAT a deed of passion? Surely not. Or the motion picture murders. It's the shriek of starvation. As Charlot said after his first abortive attempt to get a wife: "Such is life in the Great West," that land of wealth and promise. As Roosevelt said of Roosevelt after this last gubernatorial campaign in New York: "He's a *promising* young man." Yes, it's a promising country. It's what the French say of our women in Paris: *promising* young women.

Dr. Gaskins sensed it cynically: The ideal woman should end at the eyebrows and have the rest filled in with hair. It is the practical answer to the immediate American need. Pragmatism. It's inevitable that men shall go down the scale until they strike what they want—or can get. There was the young medical fellow, a New Englander, in the State Asylum at Worcester, a periodic maniac; his history fascinated me. He is a clever physician, and a man of excellent antecedents. Shortly after college (and a medical education takes so long that a man is in his late twenties before he can afford to marry) he married a woman far below his class,—he had to to get her. Shortly realizing his fatal error, he promptly, being a sensitive man, went insane,—and was as promptly divorced and committed to the asylum by his wife, proving the soundness of his mind—fundamentally. He has married three times since and has always gone mad: a little like Strindberg. But the reasoning here is truly American. Trained a Puritan, he was bursting for lack of sexual satisfaction. Unwilling to commit the sin of fornication and being unable to get a wife of his own class, due to poverty, or what not—he married someone below his scale of aesthetic or emotional relief. Thus the greater was sacrificed to the lesser. Now he was overcome with anguish. His life was ruined. He bitterly assailed himself for his folly and lost all control. In the hospital, he worked well in the laboratory—but he was truly insane. There is no class to absorb this stress.

There is a story told of George Moore the last time he was in New York. Meeting at a tea some well shaped American woman, who was apparently intent upon showing herself to the world (though the poor thing probably didn't mean it), Moore asked her to go upstairs and undress for him that he might see her naked. She indignantly refused of course. But I like his gesture. Naturally she didn't HAVE to do as he wanted her to; yet he nailed her. And he nailed us. I think he was sufficiently distinguished for her to have satisfied him.

Or, if a girl is—(not generous, bah!) but discerning with her whole body—that's it, a woman must see with her

whole body to be benevolent.—If in the eighth grade she
begins to discern the depth of her necessity—she is made
to feel that there is something *wrong* about her, not reckless but fundamentally *wrong*. In contradistinction, a
woman from Adrianople might be taught not that it is
wrong to give herself but that murder will follow it, or
that it is a dangerous gift to be given *rarely*, but a GIFT.
So she is shut up, like a French girl of better family, say;
as we do wheat or a case of fine fruit. But the American
girl who can run free must be protected in some other way
so she is *frightened*—if possible. She is a low thing (they
tell her), she is made to feel that she is vicious, evil—It
really doesn't do anything save alter the *color* of her deed,
make it unprofitable, it scrapes off the *bloom* of the gift—
it is puritanical envy. When she gives, it will be probably
to the butcher boy—since she has been an apt pupil and
believes that she is *evil*, believes even that her pleasure is
evil.

It's the central lie! but she is sure of it and gives her virginity to the butcher boy instead of having at least a decent
romance. As Ken. says: we get (that is, presuming we are
poets) the daughters of the butcher. In the boarding school
at Burlington, my friend, a teacher, was on the alert. The
tension was horrible in this fashionable school. Several of
the women were watching at points of vantage—with what
feelings in their own hearts it would be easy to say. Soon a
soft whistle, then the window opened and the conventional
knotted sheet ladder dropped out. There was a buggy
down the road. Just as the second of the two girls reached
the ground, they were both seized. In a wild scramble the
young fellows escaped. Yes, the butcher boy and his pal.
Of course, these things cannot be permitted.

Our girls have excellent physiques, really superb. I have
often watched, as who has not—for they are coming out—
some bather in the little stuff they wear to-day with acid
passion. And there you are. They are fit only to be seen in
shows, or, in the train of a launch, on aquaplanes, six at a

time, the swift motion only serving to give the authentic sense of slipperiness, pseudo-naiads without the necessary wildness and the chill—fit only to be seen by the box, like Oregon apples, bright and round but tasteless—wineless, wholesale.

Why one of the hottest women that I know, lascivious in what might have been the sense in which I speak of it, but too timid, unable to stem the great American tide inimical to women, spent almost the whole war period in Washington. She was a yeomanette but employed her spare time spying on middle-aged men, Majors with wives in Omaha, who were giving the nights to their stenographers—as it was done during the war. This girl's passion was horrible to behold. It turned slightly later, though she didn't perhaps perceive it, to other women. She wrote to me from time to time of her experiences. I liked her and enjoyed her letters. In one letter, among other things, she said that no one could *imagine* what it meant to a girl to lose her virginity. But yes, I could imagine it, better than she. It means *everything* in America. Well, of course, it has meant more than it does today but I am tracing the tendency. It means that she gets such a violent jolt from her past teaching and such a sense of the hatred of the world (as she conceives it must be) against her that she is ready to commit suicide. Or "go to the dogs." That it might be the opening of wonders, of freedom to "save the nation," that it might at least be an opportunity for practical use to the half of humanity that needs just that, never occurs to her. She is crushed. Or one imagines she is. As a matter of fact, Wally Gould tells of the two Lewiston girls who were coming home by moonlight from a rendezvous in the woods with two boy friends; one was crying, but the other sighed, and said, "Well, *that's* over with"—and next day when the old fool of a neighbor was sending a box of candy to the widow, she dumped the sweets out and filled the box with horse manure.

Intelligent, our girls are, their minds are whip-like, if they don't rot, as did Martha's, she who beat the record of all years at Cornell; was secretary to Altman; was graduated as a trained nurse and, what a volcano of energy!— taught Greek in a school till she went mad at the slowness of the pupils—and married that marvelous little lame Irishman, Darby—who has the moods of a rose. What a woman! spending her life now as servitor to women in the Insane Hospital on Ward's Island—after being an inmate for years there herself—and recovering. What an energy wasted there! No place for it in the world save among the insane. Especially no place for it in the United States.

Whip-like intelligences, lost after a few years. Perverse, they "*deraille*," as Brancusi says, too easily. To them, Paris is bizarre, a "place to spill the nerves," a bewildering surprise. They cannot carry a weight, as French women do their men; under the release of Paris, they are just useless, often coarse, lewd, drunk. What's that but unsatisfying. I salute them, because only for American women, have I any deep fellow feeling, or at least they are the only ones that seem to me satisfying. Great experimenters with the emotions, "Paris" appears in so many literatures and there are so many appearances that are "Paris," heaven knows whom they are influencing. I wish they could live at home. Imagine fleeing from the world to a woman—and leaving her—strengthened, fortified, above all *free* to GO! That costs money here! Of course men should spend money upon women, especially American men.

Of course, our history has been short and comparatively obscure, for the most part. There must be character in out-of-the-way places, naturally, but none has raised the point of which I speak, to distinction. They existed, we know, degraded and demeaned in the pioneer camps, as in Maine —discredited save in a few bad narrative verses and short stories—oh, any number of stories: drunk and waking up in a whore's bed, etc. Many men tell of that primitive kindness and *savoir faire* in the frontier camps, the purse returned with money intact. To that understanding one must bow. But there has been no genius in a women, to see a man's talent and coax it up, as did Miss Li, let us say, in the Chinese legend. Never a character to raise into story.

The incidents of our lives are too completely surrounded by delays—the violence of our athletic games is mostly a delay. Of course, it is fortunate that we are so active and fearless. The youth must be "taken up" somehow. It is taken up *completely* in a great many cases, though. A good many college athletes are "burnt out" in their three years of competition; it is too much. They frequently find it impossible to breed, if that were all.

Poets, through their energy, receive such a stamp of the age upon their work, that they are marked, in fact, even in the necessities of their defeat, as having lived well in their time. Poets are defeated but in an essential and total defeat at any time, that time is stamped in character upon their work, they give shape to the formless age as by a curious die,—and so other times recognize them, the positives that created the forms which give character and dignity to the damp mass of the overpowering but characterless resistance. So Jacataqua gave to womanhood in her time, the form which bitterness of pioneer character had denied it.

At the left, with the company but not of it, silent in the midst of noise and laughter, one group accorded well with the wooded hill and quiet river, twenty or more Abenaki braves from Swan Island, picturesque in hunting garb. Perhaps none of all the company felt more interest and curiosity than did those dusky warriors, but their stolid faces and occasional guttural ejaculations gave no sign of the fire within.

Three paces in front of these silent braves stood their Sachem, Jacataqua, a girl scarce eighteen, in whom showed the best traits of her mixed French and Indian blood.

"These Anglese for whom we watch, who are they?" she asked Squire Holworth, near her.

"Soldiers who go to fight the English at Quebec under Arnold."

As the transports began to arrive and the eleven hundred disembarked, Captain Howard, commandant of Fort Westward, came up from the landing with the most notable of the guests. It was upon the reckless, dashing Arnold that all eyes were turned. Jacataqua's Abenakis stood in the same stolid silence, still a group apart, but the maiden herself, for once yielding to the wild pulses of her heart, stepped between the sturdy squires to a point of vantage whence she might gaze upon the warrior whom all men seemed to honor.

One swift glance she gave the hero, then her black eyes met a pair as dark and flashing as her own, met and were held. She turned to the man at her side.

"That, that Anglese! Who?"

"Thet? Thet's young Burr, the one Cushing said got off a sick bed to come."

Startled, she stepped back among her people.

Young Burr but waited to gain his genial host's attention to ask, excitedly:

"Who is that beauty?"

"Jacataqua, Sachem of the Indians of Swan Island; you passed the wigwams of her people on the way up the river."

In a moment, Burr was standing before the Indian princess, for the first and last time at a loss before a woman. Primitive and direct, it was she who opened the conversation and opened it with a challenge:

"These," with a wave of her brown hand toward Howard and the group of officers, "these want meat. You hunt with me? I win."

from *Edgar Allan Poe*

POE was not "a fault of nature," "a find for French eyes," ripe but unaccountable, as through our woollyheadedness we've sought to designate him, but a genius intimately shaped by his locality and time. It is to save our faces that we've given him a crazy reputation, a writer from whose classic accuracies we have not known how else to escape.

The false emphasis was helped by his Parisian vogue and tonal influence on Baudelaire, but the French mind was deeper hit than that. Poe's work strikes by its scrupulous originality, *not* "originality" in the bastard sense, but in its legitimate sense of solidity which goes back to the ground, a conviction that he *can* judge within himself. These things the French were *ready* to perceive and quick to use to their advantage: a new point from which to readjust the trigonometric measurements of literary form.

It is the New World, or to leave that for the better term, it is a *new locality* that is in Poe assertive; it is America, the first great burst through to expression of a re-awakened genius of *place*.

Poe gives the sense for the first time in America, that literature is *serious*, not a matter of courtesy but of truth.

The aspect of his critical statements as a whole, from their hundred American titles to the inmost structure of his sentences, is that of a single gesture, not avoiding the trivial, to sweep all worthless chaff aside. It is a movement, first and last to clear the GROUND.

There is a flavor of provincialism that IS provincialism in the plainness of his reasoning upon elementary grammatical, syntactical and prosodic grounds which awakened

Lowell's derision. But insistence upon primary distinctions, that seems coldly academic, was in this case no more than evidence of a strong impulse to begin at the beginning. Poe was unsophisticated, when contrasted with the puerile sophistications of a Lowell. It is a *beginning* he has in mind, a juvenescent *local* literature. By this he avoids the clownish turn of trying to join, contrary to every reasonable impulsion, a literature (the English) with which he had no actual connection and which might be presumed, long since, to have passed that beginning which to the *new* condition was requisite.

But Mr. Lowell's comment had to be answered:

"Here comes Poe with his Raven, like Barnaby Rudge—
Three fifths of him genius, and two fifths sheer fudge;
Who talks like a book of iambs and pentameters
In a way to make all men of common sense damn meters
Who has written some things far the best of their kind;
But somehow the heart seems squeezed out by the mind."

It brings a technical retort from Poe upon the grounds that, "We may observe here that *profound* ignorance on any particular topic is always sure to manifest itself by some allusion to 'common sense' as an all-sufficient instructor." Then he tears L.'s versification to pieces, adding, "Mr. L. should not have meddled with the anapestic rhythm: it is exceedingly awkward in the hands of one who knows nothing about it and who *will* persist in fancying that he can write it by ear." But, previously, he had nailed the matter in a different vein. Lowell "could not do a better thing than to take the advice of those who mean him well, and leave prose, with satiric verse, to those who are better able to manage them; while he contents himself with that class of poetry for which, and for which alone, he seems to have an especial vocation—the poetry of *sentiment*." But Poe might have added finally, in his own defense, what he says elsewhere, concerning the accusation in L.'s last two lines: "The *highest* order of the imaginative intellect is always preeminently mathematical—" . . .

Poe was NOT, it must be repeated, a Macabre genius, *essentially* lost upon the grotesque and arabesque. If we have appraised him a morass of "lolling lilies," *that* is surface only.

The local causes shaping Poe's genius were two in character: the necessity for a fresh beginning, backed by a native vigor of extraordinary proportions,—with the corollary, that all "colonial imitation" must be swept aside. This was the conscious force which rose in Poe as innumerable timeless insights resulting, by his genius, in firm statements on the character of form, profusely illustrated by his practices; and, *second* the immediate effect of the locality upon the first, upon his nascent impulses, upon his original thrusts; tormenting the depths into a surface of bizarre designs by which he's known and which are *not at all* the major point in question.

Yet BOTH influences were determined by the locality, which, in the usual fashion, finds its mind swayed by the results of its stupidity rather than by a self-interest bred of greater wisdom. As with all else in America, the value of Poe's genius TO OURSELVES must be *uncovered* from our droppings, or at least uncovered from the "protection" which it must have raised about itself to have survived in any form among us—where everything is quickly trampled.

Poe "saw the end"; unhappily he saw his own despair at the same time, yet he continued to attack, with amazing genius seeking to discover, and discovering, points of firmness by which to STAND and grasp, against the slipping way they had of holding on in his locality. Either the New World must be mine as I will have it, or it is a worthless bog. There can be no concession. His attack was *from the center out*. Either I exist or I do not exist and no amount of pap which I happen to be lapping can dull me to the loss. It was a doctrine, anti-American. Here everything was makeshift, everything was colossal, in profusion. The frightened hogs or scared birds feeding on the corn— It left, in 1840, the same mood as ever dominant among us.

Take what you can get. What you lack, copy. It was a population puffed with braggadocio, whom Poe so beautifully summarizes in many of his prose tales. To such men, all of them, the most terrible experience in the world is to be shown up. This Poe did, in his criticisms, with venomous accuracy. It was a gesture to BE CLEAN. It was a wish to HAVE the world or leave it. It was the truest instinct in America demanding to be satisfied, and an end to makeshifts, self deceptions and grotesque excuses. And yet the grotesque inappropriateness of the life about him forced itself in among his words.

One is forced on the conception of the New World as a woman. Poe was a new De Soto. The rest might be content with little things, not he.

"Rather the ice than their way."

His attack upon the difficulty which faced him was brilliantly conceived, faultlessly maintained and successful. The best term is perhaps: immaculate.

What he wanted was connected with no particular place; therefore it *must* be where he *was*. . . .

Lowell, Bryant, etc., concerned poetry with literature, Poe concerned it with the soul; hence their differing conceptions of the use of language. With Poe, words were not hung by usage with associations, the pleasing wraiths of former masteries, this is the sentimental trap-door to beginnings. With Poe words were figures; an old language truly, but one from which he carried over only the most elemental qualities to his new purpose; which was, to find a way to tell his soul. Sometimes he used words so playfully his sentences seem to fly away from sense, the destructive! with the conserving abandon, foreshadowed, of a Gertrude Stein. The particles of language must be clear as sand.

This was an impossible conception for the gluey imagination of his day. Constantly he labored to detach SOMETHING from the inchoate mass—That's it:

His concern, the apex of his immaculate attack, was to detach a "method" from the smear of common usage—it is the work of nine tenths of his criticism. He struck to lay low the "*niaiseries*" of form and content with which his world abounded. It was a machine-gun fire; even in the slaughter of banality he rises to a merciless distinction. He sought by stress upon construction to hold the loose-strung mass off even at the cost of an icy coldness of appearance; it was the first need of his time, an escape from the form-less mass he hated. It is the very sense of a beginning, as *it is the impulse which drove him to the character of all his tales*; to get from sentiment to form, a backstroke from the swarming "population."

He has a habit, borrowed perhaps from algebra, of bal-ancing his sentences in the middle, or of reversing them in the later clauses, a sense of play, as with objects, or numer-als which he *has* in the original, disassociated, that is, from other literary habit; separate words which he feels and turns about as if he fitted them to his design with *some* sense of their individual quality: "those who belong prop-erly to books, and to whom books, perhaps, do not quite so properly belong."

The strong sense of a beginning in Poe is in *no one* else before him. What he says, being thoroughly local in origin, has some chance of being universal in application, a thing they never dared conceive. Made to fit a *place* it will have that actual quality of *things* anti-metaphysical—

About Poe there is—

No supernatural mystery—

No extraordinary eccentricity of fate—

He is American, understandable by a simple exercise of reason; a light in the morass—which *must* appear eerie, even to himself, by force of terrific contrast, an isolation that would naturally lead to drunkenness and death, logi-cally and simply—by despair, as the very final evidence of a too fine seriousness and devotion.

It is natural that the French (foreigners, unacquainted with American conditions) should be attracted by the sur-face of his genius and copy the wrong thing, (but the expressive thing), the strange, the bizarre (the recoil) without sensing the actuality, of which that is the complement,—and we get for Poe a REPUTATION for eccentric genius, maimed, the curious, the sick—at least the unexplainable crop-up, unrelated to his ground—which has become his inheritance. . . .

On him is FOUNDED A LITERATURE—typical; an anger to sweep out the unoriginal, that became ill-tempered, a mono-maniacal driving to destroy, to annihilate the copied, the slavish, the FALSE literature about him: this is the major impulse in his notes—darkening as he goes, losing the battle, as he feels himself going under—he emerges as the ghoulish, the driven back. It is the crudeness with which he was attacked in his own person, scoffed at—

He declares, maintains himself, pre-supposes himself and IS first rate. FIRST!—madly, valiantly battling for the right to BE first—to hold up his ORIGINALITY—

"If a man—if an Orphicist—or SEER—or whatever else he may choose to call himself, while the rest of the world calls him an ass—if this gentleman have an idea which he does not understand himself, the best thing he can do is to say nothing about it; . . . but if he have any idea which is actually intelligible to himself, and if he sincerely wishes to render it intelligible to others, we then hold it as indisputable that he should employ those forms of speech which are the best adapted to further his object. He should speak to the people in that people's ordinary tongue. He should arrange words such as are habitually employed for the preliminary and introductory ideas to be conveyed—he should arrange them in collocations such as those in which we are accustomed to see those words arranged." "Meantime we earnestly ask if *bread-and-butter* be the vast IDEA in question—if *bread-and-butter* be any portion of this vast IDEA? for we have often observed that when a SEER has to speak of even so usual a thing as bread-and-butter, he can never be induced to mention it outright . . ."

The language of his essays is a remarkable HISTORY of the locality he springs from. There is no aroma to his words, rather a luminosity, that comes of a disassociation from anything else than thought and ideals; a coldly nebulous, side to side juxtaposition of the words as the ideas—It seems to fall back continuously to a bare surface exhausted by having reached no perch in tradition. Seldom a long or sensuous sentence, but with frequent reduplication upon itself as if holding itself up by itself.

Thought, thought, mass—and the sense of SOMETHING over the heads of the composite particles of the logic, the insignificance of the details, WHICH HE DID ACTUALLY achieve. A "childlike," simple, deductive reasoning IS his criticism—a sense of BEGINNING—of originality that presupposes an intrinsic WORTH in the reasoner—a sense of *stripped*, being clothed, nevertheless.

Unwilling to concede the necessity for any prop to his logical constructions, save the locality upon which originality is rested, he is the diametric opposite of Longfellow —to say the least. But Longfellow was the apotheosis of all that had preceded him in America, to this extent, that he brought over the *most* from "the other side." In "*Longfellow and Other Plagiarists*," Poe looses himself to the full upon them. But what had they done? No more surely than five hundred architects are constantly practicing. Longfellow did it without genius, perhaps, but he did no more and no less than to bring the tower of the Seville Cathedral to Madison Square.

This is the expression of a "good" spirit. It is the desire to have "culture" for America by "finding" it, full blown —somewhere. But we had wandered too far, suffered too many losses for that. Such a conception could be no more than a pathetic reminiscence. It had NOTHING of the New World in it. Yet, it was bred of the wish to bring to the locality what it lacked.

What it lacked, really, was to be cultivated. So they build an unrelated copy upon it; this, as a sign of intelligence,— vigor. That is, to bring out its qualities, they cover them. Culture is still the effect of cultivation, to work with a thing until it be rare; as a golden dome among the mustard fields. It implies a solidity capable of cultivation. Its effects are marble blocks that lie perfectly fitted and aligned to express by isolate distinction the rising lusts which threw them off, regulated, in moving through the mass of impedimenta which is the world.

This is culture; in mastering them, to burst through the peculiarities of an environment. It is NOT culture to *oppress* a novel environment with the stale, if symmetrical, castoffs of another battle. They are nearly right when they say: Destroy the museums! But that is only the reflection, after all, of minds that fear to be slavish. Poe could look at France, Spain, Greece, and NOT be impelled to copy. He could do this BECAUSE he had the sense within him of a locality of his own, capable of cultivation.

Poe's use of the tags of other cultures than his own manages to be novel, interesting, useful, *unaffected*, since it succeeds in giving the impression of being not in the least dragged in by rule or pretence but of a fresh purpose such as I have indicated. There is nothing offensively "learned" there, nothing contemptuous, even in the witty tricks with bogus Latin which he plays on his illiterate public, which by *its* power, in turn, *permits* him an originality, *allows him*, even when he is satiric, an authenticity—since he is not seeking to destroy but to assert, candidly, and to defend *his own*.

He was the first to realize that the hard, sardonic, truculent mass of the New World, hot, angry—was, in fact, not a thing to paint over, to smear, to destroy—for it WOULD not be destroyed, it was too powerful,—it smiled! That it is NOT a thing to be slighted by men. Difficult, its very difficulty was their strength. It was in the generous bulk of its animal crudity that their every fineness would be found safely imbedded.

Poe conceived the possibility, the sullen, volcanic inevitability of the *place*. He was willing to go down and wrestle with its conditions, using every tool France, England, Greece could give him,—but to use them to original purpose.

This is his anger against Longfellow.

The difficulty is in holding the mind down to the point of seeing the *beginning* difference between Poe and the rest. One cannot expect to see as wide a gap between him and the others as exists between the Greek and the Chinese. It is only in the conception of a *possibility* that he is most distinguished. His greatness is in that he turned his back and faced inland, to originality, with the identical gesture of a Boone.

And for *that* reason he is unrecognized. Americans have never recognized themselves. How can they? It is impossible until someone invent the ORIGINAL terms. As long as we are content to be called by somebody's else terms, we are incapable of being anything but our own dupes.

Thus Poe must suffer by his originality. Invent that which is new, even if it be made of pine from your own yard, and there's none to know what you have done. It is because there's no *name*. This is the cause of Poe's lack of recognition. He was American. He was the astounding, inconceivable growth of his locality. Gape at him they did, and he at them in amazement. Afterward with mutual hatred; he in disgust, they in mistrust. It is only that which is under your nose which seems inexplicable.

Here Poe emerges—in no sense the bizarre, isolate writer, the curious literary figure. On the contrary, in him American literature is anchored, in him alone, on solid ground.

In all he says there is a sense of him *surrounded* by his time, tearing at it, ever with more rancor, but always at battle, taking hold.

But Poe—differing from pioneers in other literatures, the great beginners—due to the nature of the people, *had first to lift his head through* a successful banality. This was a double impost. But he did it, NOT by despising, ignoring, slighting the work that preceded him but by attacking it. "Among all the pioneers of American literature, whether prose or poetical, there is *not one* (Note: In his own estimate even, he begins.) whose productions have not been much overrated by his countrymen.

"But originality, as it is one of the highest, is also one of the rarest of merits. In America it is especially, and very remarkably, rare—this through causes sufficiently well understood."

He abhorred the "excessively opportune."—Of course, he says, to write of the Indians, the forests, the great natural beauty of the New World will be attractive and make a hit—so he counsels writers to AVOID it, for reasons crystal clear and well chosen. His whole insistence has been upon method, in opposition to a nameless rapture over nature. He admired Claude Lorraine. Instead of to hog-fill the copied style with a gross rural sap, he wanted a lean style, rapid as a hunter and with an aim as sure. One way, in the New World, men must go. Bust gut or acute wit. Find the ground, on your feet or on your belly. It is a fight. He counsels writers to *borrow nothing* from the scene, but to put all the weight of effort into the WRITING. Put aside the GRAND scene and get to work to express yourself. Method, punctuation, grammar—

The local condition of literature FORCED Poe's hand. It is necessary to understand this if his names are to be grasped. By avoiding, of necessity, the fat country itself for its expression; to originate a style that does spring from the local conditions, not of trees and mountains, but of the "soul"—here starved, stricken by loss of liberty, ready to die—he is *forced in certain directions for his subjects*.

But this left him in difficulties. When he had narrowed himself down to a choice of method and subject, when all the meaningless lump of the lush landscape and all that that implies had been swept away, THEN, and only then will he begin to search for a subject. A voluntary lopping off of a NATURAL landscape, forced him into a field which he must have *searched* for, a field of cold logic, of invention, to which his work must still present a natural *appearance*: into his imaginative prose.

His criticism paves the way for what *must* be his prose—
illustrating his favorite theory that the theory *includes the
practice*. . . .

It is especially in the poetry where "death looked gigan-
tically down" that the horror of the formless resistance
which opposed, maddened, destroyed him has forced its
character into the air, the wind, the blessed galleries of
paradise, above a morose, dead world, peopled by shadows
and silence, and despair— It is the compelling force of his
isolation.

The one earthly island he found where he might live in
something akin to the state he imagined, the love of his
wife, had to be single and inviolate. Failing of a more comprehensive passion, which might have possessed him had
the place been of favorable omen, only in this narrow cell
could he exist at all. Of this the poems are the full effect.
He is known as a poet, yet there are but five poems, possibly three.

When she died, there was nothing left. In his despair he
had nowhere to turn. It is the very apotheosis of the place
and the time.

He died imploring from those about him a love he could
not possess, since his own love, as his poems, had been so
mingled in character with the iron revenge which completely surrounded him that it could not be repeated once
its single object had been lost.

But here, in his poetry least of all, is there a mystery. It
is but the accumulation of all that he has expressed, in the
criticism, in the prose tales, but made as if so shaken with
desire, that it has come off as a flame, destroying the very
vial that contained it—and become, against his will almost
it would seem,—himself.

It is not by a change in character but by its quickened
motion that it has turned from mere heat into light—by its
power of penetration that it has been brought to dwell
upon love. By its acid power to break down truth that it
has been *forced* upon love—

I mean that though in this his "method" has escaped him, yet his poems remain of the single stuff of his great "theory": to grasp the meaning, to understand, to reduce all things to method, to control, lifting himself to power—

And failing, truth turning to love, as if metamorphosed in his hands as he was about to grasp it—now the full horror of his isolation comes down—

In his prose he could still keep a firm hold, he still held the "arrangement" fast and stood above it, but in the poetry he was at the edge—there was nothing—

Here in poetry, where it is said "we approach the gods," Poe was caught, instead, in his time.

Now, defenseless, the place itself attacked him. Now the thinness of his coat, the terror of his isolation took hold.

Had he lived in a world where love throve, his poems might have grown differently. But living where he did, surrounded as he was by that world of unreality, a formless "population"—drifting and feeding—a huge terror possessed him.

His passion for the refrain is like an echo from a hollow. It is his own voice returning—

His imagery is of the desperate situation of his mind, thin as a flame to mount unsupported, successful for a moment in the love of—not so much his wife—but in the escape she filled for him with her frail person, herself afflicted as by "ghouls."

Disarmed, in his poetry the place itself comes through. This is the New World. It is this that it does, as if—

It is in this wraithlike quality of his poems, of his five poems, that Poe is most of the very ground, hard to find, as if we walked upon a cushion of light pressed thin beneath our feet, that insulates, satirizes—while we lash ourselves up and down in a fury of impotence.

Poe stayed against the thin edge, driven to be heard by the battering racket about him to a distant screaming—the pure essence of his locality.

The best poem is *To One in Paradise*.

Abraham Lincoln

THE GREAT Railsplitter's, "All I am or ever hope to be I owe to my angel mother"; the walking up and down in Springfield on the narrow walk between the two houses, day after day, with a neighbor's baby, borrowed for the occasion, sleeping inside his cape upon his shoulder to give him stability while thinking and composing his coming speeches; and apart from its cowardice, the blinding stupidity of his murderer's *sic semper tyrannis*, after he had shot him in the back—in his trinity is reflected the brutalizing desolation of life in America up to that time; yet perversely flowering.

Mengelberg, a great broad hipped one, conducts an orchestra in the same vein. It is a woman. He babies them. He leans over and floods them with his insistences. It is a woman drawing to herself with insatiable passion the myriad points of sound, conferring upon each the dignity of a successful approach, relieving each of his swelling burden (but particularly, by himself), in the overtowering symphony—It is the balm of command. The violins, surrounded, yet feel that they have come alone, in silence and in secret, singly to be heard.

It is Lincoln pardoning the fellow who slept on sentry duty. It is the grace of the Bixby letter. The least private would find a woman to caress him, a woman in an old shawl—with a great bearded face and a towering black hat above it, to give unearthly reality.

Brancusi should make his statue—of wood—after the manner of his Socrates, with the big hole in the enormous mass of the head, save that this would be a woman—

The age-old torture reached a disastrous climax in Lincoln. Failing of relief or expression, the place tormented itself into a convulsion of bewilderment and pain—with a woman, born somehow, aching over it, holding all fearfully together. It was the end of THAT period.

372

A Point for American Criticism

IT IS regrettable that Rebecca West's article in *The Bookman*, New York, for September should have appeared in the United States. It puts both James Joyce and ourselves in a bad light.

It begins with relish—carefully defined to remove false implications. It is Paris, there is a pigeon bridging the rue de l'Odéon, Rebecca West has found two lines of a double quatrain in a book of Joyce's—*Pomes Penyeach*—which she has come from purchasing. "Suspicions had been confirmed. What was cloudy was now solid. In those eight lines he had ceased to belong to that vast army of our enemies, the facts we do not comprehend; he had passed over and become one of our friends, one of those who have yielded up an account of their nature, who do not keep back a secret which one day may act like a bomb on each theory of the universe that we have built for our defense.

"For really, I reflected . . . Mr. James Joyce is a great man who is entirely without taste."

She enters then upon a long account of a game of boules played upon a highway in Provence to the constant interruption of passing vehicles, its points like those scored by the sentimental artist. *Shock*. Finishing with an image of a great umbrella pine and the statement of the purpose of the nonsentimental artist, as determined and exclusive as the tree's intention of becoming a tree. Very fine. Examples: *La Princesse de Clèves, Adolphe* . . . She speaks of the bad example of Mr. Arnold Bennett's *The Pretty Lady*, of Katherine Mansfield's weaknesses, the sentimentality of Charles

Dickens, implying at the same time the nonsentimental successes of Tchekov. She compares the content of the younger American expressionist writers to that of *East Lynn*.

She states that, "Seduced by the use of a heterodox technique Joyce believes himself to be a wholly emancipated writer." Quite untrue. This is one of her characteristic pronouncements.

"But the sentimental artist (Joyce) is becoming nothing."

She criticizes the drawing of Stephen Dedalus, "He rolls his eyes, he wobbles on his base with suffering, like a Guido Reni . . . a consequence of Mr. Joyce's sentimental habit of using his writing as a means for gratifying certain compulsions under which he labors, without making the first effort towards lifting them over the threshold that divides life from art." She objects to his use of obscene words on the same grounds.

"There is working here a narcissism, a compulsion to make a self-image with an eye to the approval of others."

"This is not to say that he does not write beautiful prose." She refers to the scene of the young men bathing, in the early part of *Ulysses*, and to the evocations of Marion Bloom, "the great mother." But that does not alter the fact that James Joyce is safe only when he stays within tradition, a path prepared by Latin poetry.

Following are detailed descriptions of Joyce's short stories: "A Sad Case" and "The Dead," from *Dubliners*. "These two stories alone should explain why we rank James Joyce as a major writer." Early work.

Nevertheless, there are two colossal fingerprints left by literary incompetence on *Ulysses*. First, the reasonlessness of the close parallelism between *Ulysses* and the *Odyssey* which Rebecca West finds execrable, since the theme of *Ulysses* is essentially Manichean and opposed to everything that is Greek. She asks, in effect, what the devil is served by these analogies? But, Bloom being in Ireland a wanderer as Odysseus was a wanderer—she quite forgets that ten lines further on she herself answers herself as to the appropriateness of the parallel: "When one looks at the works of art recovered from the city of Khochu, which are our first intimations of what Manicheanism, functioning as orthodoxy, produced other than what we have gleaned from the reports of its enemies, one is amazed by the way that though the externals of Greek are faithfully borrowed and respectfully super-imposed on more Oriental forms, the admission that there is a fundamental disharmony in nature causes it to create effects totally different from anything which we could possibly experience on account of Greek art." And why not? Could anything be more illuminating than such a con-trast? Could Joyce have chosen a better way to say exactly what he means?

The other "colossal fingerprint" occurs in the scene in the Lying-In Hospital: "The imitations of Bunyan and Sterne completely disprove all that is alleged concerning the quality of Stephen's mind . . . even allowing for the increasing cloudiness of drunkenness." Possibly. But think of the "co-lossal" slip of Ibsen in the first scene, Act Four of *Peer Gynt*, the Frenchman, the Englishman, the German and the Swede on the southwest coast of Morocco, as dull a piece of bully-ragging as one could find anywhere in a work of genius. To speak of "colossal incompetence" over lapses of this sort— one need note only the word "colossal."

Now for line after line she goes on proving that sentences originate before words. It is a pretty exposition. She brings in cats, wild animals and babies. But what in God's name it has to do with any intention Joyce has had, not even after three full paragraphs totaling a page of double columns and small print, is she able to make clear; any relation, that is, beyond her own erroneous, intolerant assumption of Joyce's purpose.

In this way, she makes her points, some of them valid, some not so good. I have not attempted to sum them all. She goes at the work with a will and an enviable ability for exposition. But all she says must be thrown out of account as beside the question.

Here is the very thing most inimical to all that is forward-looking in literature, going to pieces of its own fragility, English criticism in a moment of overextension come all loose underneath. Here it is proving itself inadequate to hold a really first-rate modern moment, hanging as it must still be with gross imperfections.

I saw Rebecca West straining toward some insistence she could not quite achieve so that she appeared wholly off balance. The evidences of exaggeration and nervousness are in such things as the exhilaration at the start, the suspiciously lyric dove, the bold but unsupported pronouncements recurring through the text. But especially it appeared in the initial step of the logic, the stress upon the two lines of the little poem which would cast a searchlight of significance over all that goes before and comes after them. "The most stupendous," "colossal," etc., etc. There is the table-pounding of the "right, by Jove" attitude, the ex-cathedra "this is so." Ending finally in the summary verdict that because of his sentimental defects Joyce must be, is, in fact, debarred from the privilege of launching a technical advance in literary form; that he is great only as a conventional writer in a tradition, that of Latin poetry; the rest gibberish—nonsense.

It means just that Joyce, firing from Paris, has outranged English criticism completely and that R. W., with fair skill, is penning not so much an attack on Joyce—whom she tremendously admires—but a defense, a defense littered by a dire necessity to save all that she loves and represents, lest what he had done may "one day act like a bomb on each theory of the universe that we have built for our defense": all accountable to an inadequacy of critical resource in a respectable orthodoxy.

British criticism, like any other, is built upon the exigencies of the local literary structure and relates primarily thereto. Afterward it may turn to the appraisal of heterodox and foreign works. But if these are in nature disruptive to the first, the criticism will be found to be (first) defensive, to preserve its origins. Only when an acknowledged break has been forced upon it can any criticism mend itself in a way to go up into a more commanding position. Rebecca West is solely defensive in what she says of Joyce. Within the tradition lies "perfection," the Sacred Grove, a study of Dryden. Outside is imperfection and formative chaos.

It is quite impossible for British critical orthodoxy (R. W. its spokesman) to say that Joyce's imperfections are of inconsequence, in view of something else larger. For if it (she) does so, it invalidates its own major pretense to being an inclusive whole made up of mutually related parts. It can only say this is within, that is outside the pale.

We recognize its inviolable methods. But once having said that, we must step beyond it, to follow Joyce. It is able, it is erudite, it is ill-tempered and correct—due to its limited size and the opportunity offered thereby for measurement and thorough exploration.

Rebecca West cannot take Joyce, as a whole, into the body of English literature for fear of the destructive force of such an act. She must dodge and be clever and find fault and praise. She can only acknowledge genius and defect, she cannot acknowledge an essential relationship between the genius and the defect. She cannot say that on the basis of Joyce's effort, the defect is a consequence of the genius which, to gain way, has superseded the restrictions of the orthodox field. She cannot say that it is the break that has released the genius—and that the defects are stigmata of the break. She cannot link the two as an indissoluble whole—but she must put defect to the right, genius to the left, British criticism in the center, where it is wholly forced; a thorough imposition.

Joyce does offend in taste. Joyce is sentimental in his handling of his material. He does deform his drawing and allow defective characterizations to creep in. But this does not at all debar him from making valid technical innovations in literary form, as R. W. must say it does. Both are due to the suddenness, the leap of a new force.

It is all to an American just the English viewpoint, an old basis, without further capacity for extension and nearly ready to be discarded forever. Nearly.

Forward is the new. It will not be blamed. It will not force itself into what amounts to paralyzing restrictions. It cannot be correct. It hasn't time. It has that which is beyond measurement, which renders measurement a falsification, since the energy is showing itself as recrudescent, the measurement being the aftermath of each new outburst.

Joyce has broken through and drags his defects with him, a thing English criticism cannot tolerate.

But even so, Rebecca West does not always play the game, even within her own boundaries—it is the strain she is under. A descent to Freudian expedients of classification is in a literary discussion a mark of defeat. Here is a mixing of categories, a fault in logic—that is unimaginable in a person of orderly mind.

It has always been apparent to me that references to Freud —except as Freud—are in a literary discussion particularly out of place. But the use of Freudian arguments and classifications as critical staves is really too much. The reasons are simple. Freud like other psychologists uses the same material as literature but in another mode. To use the force of psychology in a category foreign to its devices is to betray the very essence of logic.

It must be patent that in any of the Freudian classifications a man may produce good writing. That is, it may be good or bad in any Freudian category. Comment if you like on Joyce's narcissism but what in the world has it to do with him as a writer? Of course it has, as far as prestige is concerned, but not as to writing—a division which R. W. seems anxious to make when she calls him a genius. But the expedient is convenient if we want to gain a spurious (psychologic, not literary) advantage for temporal purposes.

What Joyce is saying is a literary thing. It is a literary value he is forwarding. He is a writer. Will this never be understood? Perhaps he is fixed in his material and cannot change. It is of no consequence. The writing is, however, changing, the writing is active. It is in the writing that the power exists. Joyce is a literary man writing as he may—with as much affection from his material, his Freudian category as—Aesop from his hump or Scarron from his nerves. It is stupid, it is narrow British to think to use that against him.

The thing is, they want to stay safe, they do not want to give up something, so they enlist psychology to save them. But under it they miss the clear, actually the miraculous, benefits of literature itself. A silent flower opening out of the dung they dote on. They miss Joyce blossoming pure white above their heads. They are *literary* critics. That's what gets me.

Usually something has been disturbed, possibly outraged— so they search around, muck around in psychology for what *cause* to blame, instead of searching in the writing, in literature, for the *reason*. They shut the eyes, do nothing about the fact of the writing or cry "genius"—and avoid the issue. They forget that literature, like all other effects, by genius transcends the material, no matter what it is. That it, by itself, raises the thing that is to be observed into a rare field. I don't give a damn what Joyce happens by the chances of his life to be writing of, any more than I care about the termination of the story of Pantagruel and the Sibyl. Shock there if you wish.

And this is the opportunity of America! to see large, larger than England can.

An appearance of synchrony between American and English literature has made it seem, especially at certain times, as if English criticism could overlay the American strain as it does the English. This cannot be so. The differences are epochal. Every time American strength goes into a mold modeled after the English, it is wholly wasted. There is an American criticism that applies to American literature—all too unformed to speak of positively. This American thing it is that would better fit the Irish of Joyce.

Their duty is to conserve and explain in relation to established facts—that is all. We Americans ourselves must still rely on English models. But we must not be misled. We have to realize that an English dictum on any work is, for us, only an approximation. It exists only as an analogous appraisal, as far as we are concerned, to fill a lack on our part of actual value.

A fault-finding elucidation of Joyce's work gives Rebecca West a final satisfaction. This is what is meant by the term "insular." Surrounded, limited yet intact. It is the exact counterpart of the physical characteristic of England. They have attempted freedom but achieved only extension of insularity, for the central fear remains.

With hieratical assurance Rebecca West lays down her fiats about everything, rising to a transcendental ecstasy at last and the longing for a spiritual triumph and the life onward and upward forever. She is speaking, that is, of a life nearly at its end, just as a younger culture or one at its beginning, in full vigor, wishes for a fusion of the spirit with life as it exists here on earth in mud and slime today.

Truly her conception of the Shakespearean fool, to whom she likens Joyce's mental processes, is cloacal if anything could be so, with his japes and antics which so distress her thought, in that transcendental dream in which the spirit is triumphant—somewhere else. Whereas *here* is the only place where we know the spirit to exist at all, befouled as it is by lies. Joyce she sees as a "fool" dragging down the great and the good to his own foul level, making the high spirit "prove" its earthy baseness by lowering itself to laugh at low truth. "And that is why James Joyce is treated by this age with a respect which is more than the due of his competence: why

Pomes Penyeach had been sold to me in Sylvia Beach's book-shop as if it had been a saint's medal on the porch of West-minster Cathedral."

But the true significance of the fool is to consolidate life, to insist on its lowness, to knit it up, to correct a certain fatuousness in the round-table circle. Life is not to run off into dream but to remain one, from low to high. If you care to go so far, the fool is the premonition of the Russian Revolution, to modern revolutions in thought.

Whereas R. W.'s attitude is not noble, "an escape from the underground burrows of lust," but is bred of a terminal process of life that is ending, since in an old society, as in an old criticism, exhaustion takes place finally. Lear's fool, how-ever, is far from what R. W. paints his genus to be, but is full of compassion. Joyce, where he stoops low, has in him all the signs of a beginning. It is a new literature, a new world, that he is undertaking.

Rebecca West, on the other hand, has no idea at all what literature is about. She speaks of transcendental tosh, of Freud, of Beethoven's *Fifth Symphony*, of anything that comes into her head, but she has not yet learned—though she professes to know the difference between art and life—the sentimental and the nonsentimental—that writing is made of words. And that in just this essential Joyce is making a technical advance which she is afraid to acknowledge—that is actually cutting away all England from under her.

But Joyce *knows*—in spite of every barrier—in and out, self and world. And he is purifying his effort (in a new work) which she calls gibberish.

Joyce is breaking with a culture older than England's when he goes into his greatest work. It is the spirit liberated to run through everything, that makes him insist on un-expurgated lines and will not brook the limitations which good taste would enforce. It is to break the limitations, not to conform to the taste that his spirit runs.

Naturally they strain to drag him back.

Here it is: he is going somewhere, they are going nowhere. They are still looking back weighing (good enough); he is going on, carrying what he needs and what he can. What good is it, as far as literature is concerned, to have observed, felt the pangs of sorrow that Joyce is recognized, even by R. W., to feel if he is doing nothing about it—as literature? As *literature*. He is a writer broken-hearted over the world (stick to literature as his chosen symbol). Broken-hearted people do not bother about the place their tears are falling or the snot of their noses. As literature, Joyce is going on like French painters by painting, to find some way out of his sorrow—by *literary* means. (Stay within the figure which R. W. cannot do.) As a writer he is trying for new means. He is looking ahead to find if there be a way, a literary way (in his chosen category) to save the world—or call it (as a figure) to save the static, worn-out language.

Here Joyce has so far outstripped the criticism of Rebecca West that she seems a pervert. Here is his affinity for slang. Even if he has to lay waste the whole English structure. It is *that* the older critics smell and—they are afraid.

He is moving on relentlessly in his literary modes to find a way out. This is not an ordered advance of troops. Or it is one place only in the attack. The whole bulk of the antagonist looms above him to make him small. But the effect is tremendous.

To me Rebecca West's view seems incompatible with American appreciation, and though her observations appear mainly true, they seem narrow, inadequate, even provincial, certainly scared, protestant female—unsatisfactory. A little ill-natured, a little sliding; what might be termed typically British and should be detected as such from the American view, a criticism not quite legitimate, save for England where it may be proper due to national exigencies like the dementia of Wyndham Lewis.

Joyce maims words. Why? Because meanings have been

dulled, then lost, then perverted by their connotations (which have grown over them) until their effect on the mind is no longer what it was when they were fresh, but grows rotten as *poi*—though we may get to like *poi*.

Meanings are perverted by time and chance—but kept perverted by academic observance and intention. At worst they are inactive and get only the static value of anything, which retains its shape but is dead. All words, all sense of being gone out of them. Or trained into them by the dull of the deadly minded. Joyce is restoring them.

Reading Joyce last night when my mind was fluid from fatigue, my eyes bulging and painful but my spirit jubilant following a successful termination of a fight between my two boys I had brought to an intelligent end—subverted and used to teach them tolerance—I saw!

Joyce has not changed his words beyond recognition. They remain to a quick eye the same. But many of the stultifying associations of the brutalized mind (brutalized by modern futility) have been lost in his process.

The words are freed to be understood again in an original, a fresh, delightful sense.

Lucid they do become. Plain, as they have not been for a lifetime, we see them.

In summary: Rebecca West makes (is made by) a mold; English criticism, a product of English literature. She states her case for art. It is an excellent digest but for a world panorama inadequate. She fails to fit Joyce to it. She calls him, therefore, "strange," not realizing his compulsions which are outside of her sphere. In support of this, she builds a case against him, using Freudian and other nonliterary weapons. She is clever, universal in her informational resorts. What is now left over—Joyce's true significance—his pure literary virtue—is for her "nonsense." Of literature and its modus showing that she knows nothing. America, offering an undeveloped but wider criticism, will take this opportunity to place an appreciation of Joyce on its proper basis.

Marianne Moore

THE BEST WORK is always neglected and there is no critic among the older men who has cared to champion the newer names from outside the battle. The established critic will not read. So it is that the present writers must turn interpreters of their own work. Even those who enjoy modern work are not always intelligent, but often seem at a loss to know the white marks from the black. But modernism is distressing to many who would at least, due to the necessary appearance of disorder in all immediacy, be led to appreciation through critical study.

If one come with Miss Moore's work to some wary friend and say, "Everything is worthless but the best and this is the best," adding, "only with difficulty discerned" will he see anything, if he be at all well read, but destruction? From my experience he will be shocked and bewildered. He will perceive absolutely nothing except that his whole preconceived scheme of values has been ruined. And this is exactly what he should see, a break through all preconception of poetic form and mood and pace, a flaw, a crack in the bowl. It is this that one means when he says destruction and creation are simultaneous. But this is not easy to accept. Miss Moore, using the same material as all others before her, comes at it so effectively at a new angle as to throw out of fashion the classical conventional poetry to which one is used and puts her own and that about her in its place. The old stops are discarded. This must antagonize many. Furthermore, there is a multiplication, a quickening, a burrowing through, a blasting aside, a dynamization, a flight over—it is modern, but the critic must show that this is only to reveal an essential poetry through the mass, as always, and with superlative effect in this case.

A course in mathematics would not be wasted on a poet, or a reader of poetry, if he remember no more from it than the geometric principle of the intersection of loci: from all angles lines converging and crossing establish points. He might carry it further and say in his imagination that apprehension perforates at places, through to understanding—as white is at the intersection of blue and green and yellow and red. It is this white light that is the background of all good work. Aware of this, one may read the Greeks or the Elizabethans or Sidney Lanier even Robert Bridges, and preserve interest, poise and enjoyment. He may visit Virginia or China, and when friends, eager to please, playfully lead him about for pockets of local color—he may go. Local color is not, as the parodists, the localists believe, an object of art. It is merely a variant serving to locate acme point of white penetration. The intensification of desire toward this purity is the modern variant. It is that which interests me most and seems most solid among the qualities I witness in my contemporaries; it is a quality present in much or even all that Miss Moore does.

Poems, like painting, can be interesting because of the subject with which they deal. The baby glove of a Pharaoh can be so presented as to bring tears to the eyes. And it need not be bad work because it has to do with a favorite cat dead. Poetry, rare and never willingly recognized, only its accidental colors make it tolerable to most. If it be of a red coloration, those who like red will follow and be led restfully astray. So it is with hymns, battle songs, love ditties, elegies. Humanity sees itself in them, it is familiar, the good placed attractively and the bad thrown into a counter light. This is inevitable. But in any anthology it will be found that men have been hard put to it at all times to tell which is poetry and which the impost. This is hard. The difficult thing to realize is that the thrust must go through to the white, at least somewhere.

Good modern work, far from being the fragmentary, neurotic thing its disunderstanders think it, is nothing more than work compelled by these conditions. It is a multiplication of impulses that by their several flights, crossing at all eccentric angles, might enlighten. As a phase, in its slightest beginning, it is more a disc pierced here and there by light; it is really distressingly broken up. But so does any attack seem at the moment of engagement, multiple units crazy except when viewed as a whole.

Surely there is no poetry so active as that of today, so unbound, so dangerous to the mass of mediocrity, if one should understand it, so fleet, hard to capture, so delightful to pursue. It is clarifying in its movements as a wild animal whose walk corrects that of men. Who shall separate the good Whitman from the bad, the dreadful New England maunderers from the others, put air under and around the living and leave the dead to fall dead? Who? None but poems, such as Miss Moore's, their cleanliness, lack of cement, clarity, gentleness. It grows impossible for the eye to rest long upon the object of the drawing. Here is an escape from the old dilemma. The unessential is put rapidly aside as the eye searches between for illumination. Miss Moore undertakes in her work to separate the poetry from the subject entirely—like all the moderns. In this she has been rarely successful and this is important.

Unlike the painters the poet has not resorted to distortions or the abstract in form. Miss Moore accomplishes a like result by rapidity of movement. A poem such as "Marriage" is an anthology of transit. It is a pleasure that can be held firm only by moving rapidly from one thing to the next. It gives the impression of a passage through. There is a distaste for lingering, as in Emily Dickinson. As in Emily Dickinson there is too a fastidious precision of thought where unrhymes fill the purpose better than rhymes. There is a swiftness impaling beauty, but no impatience as in so much present-day trouble with verse. It is a rapidity too swift for touch, a seraphic quality, one might have said yesterday. There is, however, no breast that warms the bars of heaven: it is at most a swiftness that passes without repugnance from thing to thing.

The only help I ever got from Miss Moore toward the understanding of her verse was that she despised connectives. Any other assistance would have been an impoliteness, since she has always been sure of herself if not of others. The complete poem is there waiting: all the wit, the color, the constructive ability (not a particularly strong point that, however). And the quality of satisfaction gathered from reading her is that one may seek long in those exciting mazes sure of coming out at the right door in the end. There is nothing missing but the connectives.

The thought is compact, accurate and accurately planted. In fact, the garden, since it is a garden more than a statue, is found to be curiously of porcelain. It is the mythical, indestructible garden of pleasure, perhaps greatly pressed for space today, but there and intact, nevertheless.

I don't know where, except in modern poetry, this quality of the brittle, highly set-off porcelain garden exists and nowhere in modern work better than with Miss Moore. It is this chief beauty of today, this hard crest to nature, that makes the best present work with its "unnatural" appearance seem so thoroughly gratuitous, so difficult to explain, and so doubly a treasure of seclusion. It is the white of a clarity beyond the facts.

There is in the newer work a perfectly definite handling of the materials with a given intention to relate them in a certain way—a handling that is intensely, intentionally selective. There is a definite place where the matters of the day may meet if they choose or not, but if they assemble it must be there. There is no compromise. Miss Moore never falls from the place inhabited by poems. It is hard to give an illustration of this from her work because it is everywhere. One must be careful, though, not to understand this as a mystical support, a danger we are skirting safely, I hope, in our time.

Poe in his most-read first essay quotes Nathaniel Willis' poem "The Two Women," admiringly and in full, and one senses at once the reason: there is a quality to the feeling there that affected Poe tremendously. This mystical quality that endeared Poe to Father Tabb, the poet-priest, still seems to many the essence of poetry itself. It would be idle to name many who have been happily mystical and remained good poets: Poe, Blake, Francis Thompson, et cetera.

But what I wish to point is that there need be no stilled and archaic heaven, no ducking under religiosities to have poetry and to have it stand in its place beyond "nature." Poems have a separate existence uncompelled by nature or the supernatural. There is a "special" place which poems, as all works of art, must occupy, but it is quite definitely the same as that where bricks or colored threads are handled.

In painting, Ingres realized the essentiality of drawing and each perfect part seemed to float free from his work, by itself. There is much in this that applies beautifully to Miss Moore. It is perfect drawing that attains to a separate existence which might, if it please, be called mystical, but is in fact no more than the practicability of design.

To Miss Moore an apple remains an apple whether it be in Eden or the fruit bowl where it curls. But that would be hard to prove——

"dazzled by the apple."

The apple is left there, suspended. One is not made to feel that as an apple it has anything particularly to do with poetry or that as such it needs special treatment; one goes on. Because of this, the direct object does seem unaffected. It seems as free from the smears of mystery, as pliant, as "natural" as Venus on the wave. Because of this, her work is never indecorous as where nature is itself concerned. These are great virtues.

Without effort Miss Moore encounters the affairs which concern her as one would naturally in reading or upon a walk outdoors. She is not a Swinburne stumbling to music, but one always finds her moving forward ably, in thought, unimpeded by a rhythm. Her own rhythm is particularly revealing. It does not interfere with her progress; it is the movement of the animal, it does not put itself first and ask the other to follow.

Nor is "thought" the thing that she contends with. Miss Moore uses the thought most interestingly and wonderfully to my mind. I don't know but that this technical excellence is one of the greatest pleasures I get from her. She occupies the thought to its end, and goes on—without connectives. To me this is thrilling. The essence is not broken, nothing is injured. It is a kind hand to a merciless mind at home in the thought as in the cruder image. In the best modern verse, room has been made for the best of modern thought and Miss Moore thinks straight.

Only the most modern work has attempted to do without *ex machina* props of all sorts, without rhyme, assonance, the feudal master beat, the excuse of "nature," of the spirit, mysticism, religiosity, "love," "humor," "death." Work such as Miss Moore's holds its bloom today not by using slang, not by its moral abandon or puritanical steadfastness, but by the aesthetic pleasure engendered where pure craftsmanship joins hard surfaces skilfully.

Poetry has taken many disguises which by cross reading or intense penetration it is possible to go through to the core. Through intersection of loci their multiplicity may become revelatory. The significance of much reading being that this "thing" grow clearer, remain fresh, be more present to the mind. To read more thoroughly than this is idleness; a common classroom absurdity.

One may agree tentatively with Glenway Wescott, that there is a division taking place in America between a proletarian art, full of sincerities, on the one side and an aristocratic and ritualistic art on the other. One may agree, but it is necessary to scrutinize such a statement carefully.

There cannot be two arts of poetry really. There is weight and there is disencumberedness. There can be no schism, except that which has always existed between art and its approaches. There cannot be a proletarian art—even among savages. There is a proletarian taste. To have achieved an organization even of that is to have escaped it.

And to organize into a pattern is also, true enough, to "approach the conditions of a ritual." But here I would again go slow. I see only escape from the conditions of ritual in Miss Moore's work: a rush through wind if not toward some patent "end" at least away from pursuit, a pursuit perhaps by ritual. If from such a flight a ritual results it is more the care of those who follow than of the one who leads. "Ritual," too often to suit my ear, connotes a stereotyped mode of procedure from which pleasure has passed, whereas the poetry to which my attention clings, if it ever knew those conditions, is distinguished only as it leaves them behind.

It is at least amusing, in this connection, to quote from *Others*, Volume 1, Number 5, November 1915—quoted in turn from J. B. Kerfoot in *Life:* "Perhaps you are unfamiliar with this 'new poetry' that is called 'revolutionary.' It is the expression of democracy of feeling rebeling against an aristocracy of form."

> As if a death mask ever could replace
> Life's faulty excellence!

There are two elements essential to Miss Moore's scheme of composition, the hard and unaffected concept of the apple itself as an idea, then its edge-to-edge contact with the things which surround it—the coil of a snake, leaves at various depths, or as it may be; and without connectives unless it be poetry, the inevitable connective, if you will.

Marriage, through which thought does not penetrate, appeared to Miss Moore a legitimate object for art, an art that would not halt from using thought about it, however, as it might want to. Against marriage, "this institution, perhaps one should say enterprise"— Miss Moore launched her thought not to have it appear arsenaled as in a textbook on psychology, but to stay among apples and giraffes in a poem. The interstices for the light and not the interstitial web of the thought concerned her, or so it seems to me. Thus the mate-

rial is as the handling: the thought, the word, the rhythm—
all in the style. The effect is in the penetration of the light itself, how much, how little; the appearance of the luminous
background.

Of marriage there is no solution in the poem and no attempt to make marriage beautiful or otherwise by "poetic"
treatment. There is beauty and it is thoughtless, as marriage
or a cave inhabited by the sounds and colors of waves, as in
the time of prismatic color, as England with its baby rivers,
as G. B. Shaw, or chanticleer, or a fish, or an elephant with
its strictly practical appendages. All these things are inescap-
ably caught in the beauty of Miss Moore's passage through
them; they all have at least edges. This too is a quality that
greatly pleases me: definite objects which give a clear contour to her force. Is it a flight, a symphony, a ghost, a mathe-
matic? The usual evasion is to call them poems.

Miss Moore gets great pleasure from wiping soiled words
or cutting them clean out, removing the aureoles that have
been pasted about them or taking them bodily from greasy
contexts. For the compositions which Miss Moore intends,
each word should first stand crystal clear with no attachments; not even an aroma. As a cross light upon this, Miss
Moore's personal dislike for flowers that have both a satisfying appearance and an odor of perfume is worth noticing.
With Miss Moore a word is a word most when it is separated
out by science, treated with acid to remove the smudges,
washed, dried and placed right side up on a clean surface.
Now one may say that this is a word. Now it may be used,
and how?

It may be used not to smear it again with thinking (the
attachments of thought) but in such a way that it will remain
scrupulously itself, clean perfect, unnicked beside other
words in parade. There must be edges. This casts some light
I think on the simplicity of design in much of Miss Moore's
work. There must be recognizable edges against the ground
which cannot, as she might desire it, be left entirely white.
Prose would be all black, a complete black painted or etched
over, but solid.

The William Carlos Williams Reader

There is almost no overlaying at all. The effect is of every object sufficiently uncovered to be easily recognizable. This simplicity, with the light coming through from between the perfectly plain masses, is however extremely bewildering to one who has been accustomed to look upon the usual "poem," the commonplace opaque board covered with vain curlicues. They forget, those who would read Miss Moore aright, that white circular discs grouped closely edge to edge upon a dark table make black six-pointed stars.

The "useful result" is an accuracy to which this simplicity of design greatly adds. The effect is for the effect to remain "true"; nothing loses its identity because of the composition, but the parts in their assembly remain quite as "natural" as before they were gathered. There is no "sentiment"; the softening effect of word upon word is nil; everything is in the style. To make this ten times evident is Miss Moore's constant care. There seems to be almost too great a wish to be transparent and it is here if anywhere that Miss Moore's later work will show a change, I think.

The general effect is of a rise through the humanities, the sciences, without evading "thought," through anything (if not everything) of the best of modern life; taking whatever there is as it comes, using it and leaving it drained of its pleasure, but otherwise undamaged. Miss Moore does not compromise science with poetry. In this again, she is ably modern.

And from this clarity, this acid cleansing, this unblinking willingness, her poems result, a true modern crystallization, the fine essence of today which I have spoken of as the porcelain garden.

Or one will think a little of primitive masonry, the units unglued and as in the greatest early constructions unstandardized.

In such work as *Critics and Connoisseurs*, and *Poetry*, Miss Moore succeeds in having the "thing" which is her concern move freely, unencumbered by the images or the difficulties of thought. In such work there is no "suggestiveness," no tiresome "subtlety" of trend to be heavily followed, no painstaking refinement of sentiment. There is surely a choice evident in all her work, a very definite quality of choice in her material, a thinness perhaps, but a very welcome and no little surprising absence of moral tone. The choice being entirely natural and completely arbitrary is not in the least offensive, in fact it has been turned curiously to advantage throughout.

From what I have read it was in *Critics and Connoisseurs* that the successful method used later began first to appear: If a thought presents itself the force moves through it easily and completely: so the thought also has revealed the "thing" —that is all. The thought is used exactly as the apple, it is the same insoluble block. In Miss Moore's work the purely stated idea has an edge exactly like a fruit or a tree or a serpent.

To use anything: rhyme, thought, color, apple, verb—so as to illumine it, is the modern prerogative; a stintless inclusion. It is Miss Moore's success.

The diction, the phrase construction, is unaffected. To use a "poetic" inversion of language, or even such a special posture of speech, still discernible in Miss Moore's earlier work, is to confess an inability to have penetrated with poetry some crevice of understanding; that special things and special places are reserved for art, that it is unable, that it requires fostering. This is unbearable.

Poetry is not limited in that way. It need not say either

> Bound without,
> Boundless within.

It has as little to do with the soul as with ermine robes or graveyards. It is not noble, sad, funny. It is poetry. It is free. It is escapeless. It goes where it will. It is in danger; escapes if it can.

This is new! The quality is not new, but the freedom is new, the unbridled leap.

The dangers are thereby multiplied—but the clarity increased. Nothing but the perfect and the clear.

A Matisse

ON THE french grass, in that room on Fifth Ave., lay that woman who had never seen my own poor land. The dust and noise of Paris had fallen from her with the dress and underwear and shoes and stockings which she had just put aside to lie bathing in the sun. So too she lay in the sunlight of the man's easy attention. His eye and the sun had made day over her. She gave herself to them both for there was nothing to be told. Nothing is to be told to the sun at noonday. A violet clump before her belly mentioned that it was spring. A locomotive could be heard whistling beyond the hill. There was nothing to be told. Her body was neither classic nor whatever it might be supposed. There she lay and her curving torso and thighs were close upon the grass and violets.

So he painted her. The sun had entered his head in the color of sprays of flaming palm leaves. They had been walking for an hour or so after leaving the train. They were hot. She had chosen the place to rest and he had painted her resting, with interest in the place she had chosen.

It had been a lovely day in the air. —What pleasant women are these girls of ours! When they have worn clothes and take them off it is with an effect of having performed a small duty. They return to the sun with a gesture of accomplishment. —Here she lay in this spot today not like Diana or Aphrodite but with better proof than they of regard for the place she was in. She rested and he painted her.

It was the first of summer. Bare as was his mind of interest in anything save the fullness of his knowledge, into which her simple body entered as into the eye of the sun himself, so he painted her. So she came to America.

No man in my country has seen a woman naked and painted her as if he knew anything except that she was naked. No woman in my country is naked except at night.

In the french sun, on the french grass in a room on Fifth Ave., a french girl lies and smiles at the sun without seeing us.

Contact II, 1921

An Afternoon with Tchelitchew

A HOT JUNE afternoon, 1937. East 57th St., N. Y., studio apartment, 5th floor, rear. 5 P.M. The model about to leave, waiting, before going home to her husband, to pour tea for us.

Any who would know and profit by his knowledge of the great must lead a life of violent opposites. The deeper at moments of penetration is his mastery of their work, the more vigorously at other moments must he fling himself off from them to remain himself a man. But if he himself would do great works also only by this violence, this completeness of his wrenching free, will he be able to use that of which their greatness has consisted.

The failure to understand this condemns the perennial student who has, in short, by a sort of sluggishness shown himself to have succumbed to the effects of former greatness and not profited by it to establish his own mastery. This is the banality of the academic, maliciously called the cultivation of "tradition," maliciously because under it is implied an attack upon the "radical" who does not submit himself to such respectable negation.

A man must know but he will not be told how he must know nor submit to the terms of those who make knowledge no more very often than self-denial in subservience to honorific symbols by which they seek to maintain dominance over him while he is seeking the substance. But it is man who must be achieved.

These convictions had come to life in the presence of Tchelitchew's canvasses. Not a very "good" painter. He was

396

saying so himself, in deep respect for the deftness of the Spanish and French moderns among his friends. He only wished he might be able to handle his materials with their ease, their amazing facility. He referred to the new sensations, to Dali especially.

They are my good friends, he said. Dali is a jeweler in paint. And he sees everything. He has eyes that stick out, like the eyes of a crab. And he eats the world of the eyes, like a crab. Numb, numb, numb, numb! And T. brought the fingers of both hands up before his mouth rapidly wiggling them toward his moving lips as if it was a crab or a lobster jiggling his mandibles and feeding. It is very beautiful, he said. But what are they doing? Sucking it in and passing it out again, their charming compositions. What do we care? They have eaten. We are very glad. There is nothing they do not eat, there is nothing they do not see. Such eyes! They make very fine compositions. That is the French influence.

Yesterday, he said, there was a woman here in the studio. A very rich old woman. Ooo! I did not dare offend her. She had on a hat with feathers and ribbons like—I can't describe it. Many many different colors. Like a parrot. And a dress! with a piece of lace, a piece of silk, a piece of blue, green— anything you can imagine. And she talked, cha, cha, cha, cha, cha, cha! all the time. Like a parrot. She was a parrot. Perfect.

It was amazing. It was bewildering. You would not believe there could be such a person. And she was interested. She wanted to see.

So I showed her the big canvas I am working on. This here. She looked and in her voice, like a parrot, she said, Oh Mr. Tchelitchew! you paint nothing but monsters!

The painting was before us. I looked at it for a long time. Nothing but human monsters of one sort or another. It was a canvas of perhaps eight by twelve feet. It wasn't finished, though most of it had been drawn in. Figures of all sorts filled it, of all sizes, spreading out upon a background of mountain, classical ruin and Mexican adobe house, with sea and sky

going off toward the top and back. Small in the center was
the face of an old woman, a tormented, wrinkled face—as
if under a lens; above that a tennis court with naked figures
on it below a glacier prospect made of ice-heads, infants
packed in as though they were rounded ice cubes in a modern
refrigerator——

To the left, the signature, a man with one enormous foot,
the back of Diego Rivera it may be, painting the wall of a
house. Siamese twins, women with six breasts, acephalic monsters, three-legged children, double-headed monsters, sexual
freaks, dwarfs, giants, achondroplastic midgets, mongolian
idiots and the starved, bloated, misshapen by idea and social
accident—of all the walks of life.

In the foreground was a surf with a girl in a pink bathing
suit. They ask me if it is surrealist! What do you think? he
looked at me.

As a physician, no, I answered. And why not? Because
these things are drawn from life, I said. You see that, you see
that! he was delighted. Of course, you are a doctor. That is
beautiful. He was delighted.

What is surrealism? Anybody can do that. What a lot of
fooling nonsense.

As a fact every monster in the picture was authentic. It
was actually what is found in life. He has taken things which
do occur every day for his mirror. It is a mirror, he added,
for them to see themselves.

Our life is horrible, he said. We are monsters. We hate each
other and we try to destroy everything that is lovely. And we
hide it. No. We *are* beasts—I beg pardon to the beasts. Even
our language is distorted, we say we are like "beasts" who
are lovely. But we are disgusting. And when I show them
how disgusting they are they say, He only wants to paint
monsters!

I don't want to paint monsters. Pretty soon I will be tired
of monsters. I want to communicate with people. That is
painting. The ancients knew what painting was. It is to say

something. It is to communicate. It is to use beautiful colors because we love them. We enjoy what is lovely and we paint to speak of it. Because we want to tell somebody that we like this and they must see it because we like it.

That is why I want to paint everything soft. Because I love feathers and pearls and fluffy things that hold the light and split it into rainbows. I am a very poor painter. I cannot paint like those Spaniards. I work very hard but I go very slow. When I have filled these spaces—pointing to unfinished places on the picture—then I will work to get the texture I desire. I want to make it beautiful, everything the most delicate shading of the colors, light as a feather. That is why I have painted it as a double rainbow. Because the rainbow is phenomenal. It is charming to me. I like it. I will paint it that way.

Indeed all the figures in the picture, the monsters waiting to be beautified of the softness and the colors were, as they occurred in various parts of the picture, either green or red or purple or blue—but the colors quite realistically modulated. As if they had been seen toward evening here, at noon there, and at sunrise there, before a storm, as it might be.

What do they mean by composition? There are half a dozen compositions. Everybody knows them. What is that? They balance here, there. What does it mean? Cezanne! Pooh. Yes, he could paint a good composition. He knew how to paint colors. But what is it? Another tree. Another orange. Another table with flowers. What does it mean? Always the same. I am tired of that.

That is enough of that. He turned the big picture to the wall. Let me show you some portraits.

Do you like this one? I paint my portraits all after I have made the sketch, a year afterward perhaps. When I feel what I wish to see and I know how to do it. This morning I painted this face of Edith Sitwell all over. I could finish it today. What do you think?

It was a white-looking woman in a nun's habit. She was

sitting as if in a straightback, medieval chair completely self-absorbed, ascetic, severe. It was a shock to me after what I thought I had known of the woman's verse.

She is like that, he said. A very beautiful woman. She is alone. She is very positive and very emotional. She takes herself very seriously and seems to be cold as ice. She is not so. I wanted to paint her as I know her. What do you think?

I am glad to know her. I didn't know her. Never thought much of her verse.

Oh, you don't know her then, he said. This will be your introduction. You will see if I am not right. An amazing woman.

And these—this is Ford and his sister. He showed me the portraits of the two young Americans. Their faces were made to radiate the opalescent colors he loves. I looked back at the Sitwell again. Her face I saw now was not white but all the colors of the rainbow minutely blended, not *pointilliste*, but soft as feathers, as down.

You have seen enough paintings, he said, for one afternoon. Next year you shall see the big one—when I have been able to finish it. You will see the difference. Every part of it must be done as I have done the face of Edith Sitwell—this morning. Delicate and soft, with all the colors of the rainbow. You will like it then.

Lower Case Cummings

To ME, of course, e. e. cummings means my language. It isn't, of course, mine so much as it is his, which emphasizes the point. It isn't, primarily, english. It isn't at all english. Not that superb inheritance—which we both, I am sure, stand before in amazement and wonder, knowing the dazzling achievements of which it is the living monument. We speak another language; a language of which we are so jealous that we won't even acknowledge that we hold it in common.

Esoteric is the word the englishers among us would give to the languages we americans use at our best. They are private languages. That is what cummings seems to be emphasizing, a christian language—addressing to the private conscience of each of us in turn.

But if, startlingly, each should disclose itself as understandable to any great number, the effect would be in effect a veritable revolution, shall we say, of morals? Of, do we dare to say, love? Much or even all cummings' poems are the evidences of love. The french say you can't translate his poems into french: just so many words. A curious sort of love, not at all french, not at all latin. Not, above all, anything even in the faintest degree resembling the english.

I think of cummings as Robinson Crusoe at the moment when he first saw the print of a naked human foot in the sand. That, too, implied a new language—and a readjustment of conscience.

We are inclined to forget that cummings has come *from* english to another province having escaped across a well defended border; he has remained, largely, a fugitive ever since.

I don't think he should be held too closely to account for some of his doodles, his fiddling with the paraphernalia of the writing game. He has been for a good part of the last twenty years like the prisoner in solitary confinement who retained his sanity by tossing a pin over his shoulder in the dark and spending long hours searching for it again.

Without the least question cummings is a fugitive; a fugitive from the people about him whom he irritates by telling them they are human beings subject to certain beauties and distempers they will not acknowledge; a fugitive as well from the university where the bait of official recognition has brought down many of his former fellows.

cummings, who is not robust, is positively afraid of physical violence if he goes out of his rooms. For a species of americans and certain other wild animals are prone to attack a man going alone. Imagine the armed bands of the intelligentsia which roam Greenwich Village by day and night—the belligerently convinced—that a poor lone man like cummings would have to face to survive if he went so much as to the baker's for a dozen breakfast rolls. It is frightening. Important. But he hasn't run away. Just the opposite.

It would be all right if e. e. were himself more gregarious, more, what shall we say, promiscuous—at least less averse to the pack—even to very nice packs certified by the very best teachers in the very best schools here and abroad. But he isn't. He feels that among those curious things called americans there isn't one, in this inarticulate jungle, to whom he can say more than—How do you do? Was that your footprint I saw in the sand this morning?

Imagine if the startled black should turn on him and say in reply, Swing low sweet chariot! That wouldn't be it. That wouldn't be it at all. cummings would be completely defeated, and cummings cannot afford to be defeated! why he's a member of the strongest nation on earth—bar none. He's in a very tight squeeze every day of his life, Year in, year out, holding to his supplies, finding what shelter is possible to him. Writing. Isn't that the thing to do? Write.

He paints also—but I don't like his painting. I think it represents the worst of his style; an insistence that any artist will fall into when he is sick of his proper medium and of those defects which he, better than anyone else, is conscious of, and which yet he tries still to put over by a shift in direction to flout the world. But maybe he paints just because it rests him —a minor matter.

Words are his proper medium, the specific impact of words, which give them in his work such a peculiarly unhistoric, historical new world character. A toughness which scorns to avoid fragility.

When I say "new world" I do not mean american. That is just what cummings says over and over again, that's what he lives; that, too, is what makes him solitary. Not "american," sensual. I almost want to say, that that which deprives him of academic as well as popular understanding or effectiveness in argument makes him at the same time a good deal like the steeple of one of those New England churches facing the common up there, so strangely remote an effect. I avoid speaking of the clipper ships. I avoid speaking of Moby Dick.

No, it is something very much older and very modern too. Cotton Mather? Yes, he had a library. If it goes back to the King James version of the Bible, and it does, it goes there solely for what that *says* to the Christian conscience. It says, Ignore the dress in which the Word comes to you and look to the Life of which that is the passing image.

cummings is the living presence of the drive to make all our convictions evident by penetrating through their costumes to the living flesh of the matter. He avoids the cliché first by avoiding the whole accepted modus of english. He does it, not to be "popular," God knows, nor to sell anything, but to lay bare the actual experience of love, let us say, in the chance terms which his environment happens to make apparent to him. He does it to reveal, to disclose, to free a man from habit. Habit is our continual enemy as artists and as men. Practice is not a habit though it must be watched lest it become so.

The drunk, the whore, the child, are typical cummings heroes. (Is that Deacon Cummings speaking? Probably.) At the start, right out of the Greek of his college days, he threw the whole of the english department armamentarium out the window—a sort of Cambridge Tea Party.

Then he began to speak of rabbits, mice, all the sprites of the native pastures—as though he had just got sight and were afraid he was going to lose it again—with infinite tenderness, with FEELING. He wanted to feel. He wanted to see, see, see! and make the words speak of what he saw . . . and felt. For it must not be forgot that we smell, hear and see with words and words alone, and that with a new language we smell, hear and see afresh—by this we can well understand cummings' early excitement at his release. If a woman came into the picture early she vanished in favor of women: he got them badly mixed up. He didn't know what the thing meant —much. It wasn't, in effect, art. He was sure of that.

Now women, that's different. That's a subject that has some meat to it. You can love women. But how in almighty heaven can you love a woman and be free to embrace the world in new and unaccepted terms?

Then he left his entire early mountain world. Went to France and landed—*The Enormous Room.* That doesn't need explanation; but it is, for cummings, today, an annoyance. There he was and he wrote what he had to say about it, superbly. One remembers (if vaguely now) those spirits, ghosts —lost souls—victims of whom do you think? The Japs? No, by God, the French! Can you imagine the impertinence of smelling a french stink? But cummings merely smelled it.

Finally he came, with finality, to New York. The express elevators ran up and down inside him for a while—until they busted and—stopped.

To adopt the ballad forms of nursery rhymes—merely emphasizes in a primary manner . . . the continued necessity for reappraisals in the arts: and the pre-eminence of the lyric. The best of cummings' lyrics seem as if they had been taken from something else, a series of fantastic plays which he never wrote—for it would have represented an actual world which never existed save in his imagination. It is a new world—the only clue to its substantiality being the language cummings uses. It may have been Atlantis—which he knew to exist since he could tell very definitely that his father had been there also.

He lives today in a second Enormous Room, this time of the imagination—so real it is.

I don't see how you can avoid speaking of cummings in this way, dangerous as it surely is. You are likely to go off into a Never-Never Land which is so much froth. But if we lay the fact of cummings against that background we see better than in any other way how bitterly he has persisted with his revolution in the language and to what planned effect.

He has fixed it, too, that he can't be imitated. You've got to learn the *basis* for his trapeze tricks. When you have done that you'll be able to do tricks of your own—as the masters did in the past. Not before. In that he's our best schoolmaster in the language; the kind that you just don't avoid.

What fools critics are who try to make him a painter with words. With cummings every syllable has a conscience and a specific impact—attack, which, as we know now—is the best defense.

Perhaps, at some time in the future, though it is extremely unlikely, we'll be able to shed the lower case and embellish the new language with Caps. But for the moment cummings has the right idea.

On Measure—Statement for Cid Corman

Verse—we'd better not speak of poetry lest we become confused—verse has always been associated in men's minds with "measure," i.e., with mathematics. In scanning any piece of verse, you "count" the syllables. Let's not speak either of rhythm, an aimless sort of thing without precise meaning of any sort. But measure implies something that can be measured. Today verse has lost all measure.

Our lives also have lost all that in the past we had to measure them by, except outmoded standards that are meaningless to us. In the same way our verses, of which our poems are made, are left without any metrical construction of which you can speak, any recognizable, any new measure by which they can be pulled together. We get sonnets, etc., but no one alive today, or half alive, seems to see anything incongruous in that. They cannot see that poems cannot any longer be made following a Euclidian measure, "beautiful" as this may make them. The very grounds for our beliefs have altered. We do not live that way any more; nothing in our lives, at bottom, is ordered according to that measure; our social concepts, our schools, our very religious ideas, certainly our understanding of mathematics are greatly altered. Were we called upon to go back to what we believed in the past we should be lost. Only the construction of our poems—and at best the construction of a poem must engage the tips of our intellectual awareness—is left shamefully to the past.

A relative order is operative elsewhere in our lives. Even the divorce laws recognize that. Are we so stupid that we can't see that the same things apply to the construction of

406

modern verse, to an art which hopes to engage the attention of a modern world? If men do not find in the verse they are called on to read a construction that interests them or that they believe in, they will not read your verses and I, for one, do not blame them. What will they find out there that is worth bothering about? So, I understand, the young men of my generation are going back to Pope. Let them. They want to be read at least with some understanding of what they are saying and Pope is at least understandable; a good master. They have been besides scared by all the wild experimentation that preceded them so that now they want to play it safe and to conform.

They have valid reasons for what they are doing—of course not all of them are doing it, but the English, with a man such as Christopher Fry prominent among them, lead the pack. Dylan Thomas is thrashing around somewhere in the wings but he is Welsh and acknowledges no rule—he cannot be of much help to us. Return as they may to the classics for their models it will not solve anything for them. They will still, later, have to tackle the fundamental problems which concern verse of a new construction to conform with our age. Their brothers in the chemical laboratory, from among whom their most acute readers will come if they know what is good for them, must be met on a footing that will not be retrograde but equal to their own. Though they may recognize this theoretically there is no one who dares overstep the conventional mark.

It's not only a question of daring, no one has instructed them differently. Most poems I see today are concerned with what they are *saying*, how profound they have been given to be. So true is this that those who write them have forgotten to make poems at all of them. Thank God we're not musicians, with our lack of structural invention we'd be ashamed to look ourselves in the face otherwise. There is nothing interesting in the construction of our poems, nothing that can jog the ear out of its boredom. I for one can't read them.

There is nothing in their metrical construction to attract me, so I fall back on e. e. cummings and the disguised conventions that he presents which are at least amusing—as amusing as "Doctor Foster went to Gloucester, in a shower of rain." Ogden Nash is also amusing, but not amusing enough.

The thing is that "free verse" since Whitman's time has led us astray. He was taken up, as were the leaders of the French Revolution before him with the abstract idea of freedom. It slopped over into all their thinking. But it was an idea lethal to all order, particularly to that order which has to do with the poem. Whitman was right in breaking our bounds but, having no valid restraints to hold him, went wild. He didn't know any better. At the last he resorted to a loose sort of language with no discipline about it of any sort and we have copied its worst feature, just that.

The corrective to that is forgetting Whitman, for instinctively he was on the right track, to find a new discipline. Invention is the mother of art. We must invent new modes to take the place of those which are worn out. For want of this we have gone back to worn-out modes with our tongues hanging out and our mouths drooling after "beauty" which is not even in the same category under which we are seeking it. Whitman, great as he was in his instinctive drive, was also the cause of our going astray. I among the rest have much to answer for. No verse can be free, it must be governed by some measure, but not by the old measure. There Whitman was right but there, at the same time, his leadership failed him. The time was not ready for it. We have to return to some measure but a measure consonant with our time and not a mode so rotten that it stinks.

We have no measure by which to guide ourselves except a purely intuitive one which we feel but do not name. I am not speaking of verse which has long since been frozen into a rigid mold signifying its death, but of verse which shows that it has been touched with some dissatisfaction with its present state. It is all over the page at the mere whim of the man who has composed it. This will not do. Certainly an art which implies a discipline as the poem does, a rule, a measure, will not tolerate it. There is no measure to guide us, no recognizable measure.

Relativity gives us the cue. So, again, mathematics comes to the rescue of the arts. Measure, an ancient word in poetry, something we have almost forgotten in its literal significance as something measured, becomes related again with the poetic. We have today to do with the poetic, as always, but a *relatively* stable foot, not a rigid one. That is all the difference. It is that which must become the object of our search. Only by coming to that realization shall we escape the power of these magnificent verses of the past which we have always marveled over and still be able to enjoy them. We live in a new world, pregnant with tremendous possibility for enlightenment but sometimes, being old, I despair of it. For the poem which has always led the way to the other arts as to life, being explicit, the only art which is explicit, has lately been left to fall into decay.

Without measure we are lost. But we have lost even the ability to count. Actually we are not as bad as that. Instinctively we have continued to count as always but it has become not a conscious process and being unconscious has descended to a low level of the invention. There are a few exceptions but there is no one among us who is consciously aware of what he is doing. I have accordingly made a few experiments which will appear in a new book shortly. What I want to emphasize is that I do not consider anything I have put down there as final. There will be other experiments but all will be directed toward the discovery of a new measure, I repeat, a new measure by which may be ordered our poems as well as our lives.

1953

Textual Note

The dates following the titles in the Table of Contents are those of first publication in book form. For the poetry, the relevant editions are as follows:

Al Que Quiere! A Book of Poems (Boston: The Four Seas Company, 1917)

Sour Grapes (Boston: The Four Seas Company, 1921)

Spring and All (Dijon, France: Contact Publishing Company, 1923)

Collected Poems 1921-1931 (N. Y.: The Objectivist Press, 1934)

An Early Martyr and Other Poems (N. Y.: The Alcestis Press, 1935)

Adam & Eve & the City (Peru, Vt.: The Alcestis Press, 1936)

The Complete Collected Poems of William Carlos Williams (Norfolk, Conn.: New Directions, 1938)

The Wedge (Cummington, Mass.: The Cummington Press, 1944)

Paterson (Norfolk, Conn.: New Directions): Book One, 1946; Book Two, 1948; Book Three, 1949; Book Four, 1951; Book Five, 1958. The complete *Paterson*, with "fragments of a projected sixth part . . . found among Dr. Williams' papers after his death," appeared in 1963.

The Clouds (Aurora, N. Y. and Cummington, Mass.: Wells College Press and The Cummington Press, 1948)

Selected Poems, with introduction by Randall Jarrell (Norfolk, Conn.: New Directions, 1949)

The Collected Later Poems (Norfolk, Conn.: New Directions, 1950; "Revised Edition," 1963)

The Collected Earlier Poems (Norfolk, Conn.: New Directions, 1951)

The Desert Music and Other Poems (N. Y.: Random House, 1954)

Journey to Love (N. Y.: Random House, 1955)

Pictures from Brueghel and Other Poems (Norfolk, Conn.: New Directions, 1962). A collection including *The Desert Music* and *Journey to Love* together with the "Pictures from Brueghel" group.

The texts of poems in the present volume are based on those in *The Collected Earlier Poems* (1951), *The Collected Later Poems* (1963), *Pictures from Brueghel and Other Poems* (1962), and *Paterson* (1963).

It should be borne in mind that the order of publication in book form of Dr. Williams's poems is not necessarily that of composition, let alone conception. For example, "Portrait of a Lady" was composed in 1915 or earlier but not collected in a book until 1934; so also with "Impromptu: the Suckers," written apparently in 1927 but not printed in a book until 1951. However, it seemed more convenient for the interested reader to present the poems in the order here employed. Dr. Williams's original arrangements in the several collected volumes took this problem into account, but not consistently.

The prose selections are taken from *Spring and All* (noted above) and from the following books:

Kora in Hell: Improvisations (Boston: The Four Seas Company, 1920; reprinted San Francisco: City Lights Books, 1957)

The Great American Novel (Paris: Three Mountains Press, 1923)

In the American Grain (N. Y.: Albert & Charles Boni, 1925; reprinted Norfolk, Conn.: New Directions, 1939 and 1956, with introduction by Horace Gregory.)

A Voyage to Pagany (N. Y.: The Macaulay Company, 1928)

A Novelette and Other Prose (Toulon, France: TO
   Publishers, 1932)
White Mule (Norfolk, Conn.: New Directions, 1937)
Life along the Passaic River (Norfolk, Conn.: New
   Directions, 1938). Short stories.
In the Money: Part II of *White Mule* (Norfolk, Conn.:
   New Directions, 1940)
A Dream of Love (Norfolk, Conn.: New Directions,
   1948—"Direction 6")
Make Light of It (N. Y.: Random House, 1950). Short
   stories.
The Autobiography of William Carlos Williams (N. Y.:
   Random House, 1951)
Selected Essays (N. Y.: Random House, 1954)
The Farmers' Daughters: The Collected Short Stories
   (Norfolk, Conn.: New Directions, 1961)
Many Loves and Other Plays (Norfolk, Conn.: New
   Directions, 1961)

Texts for the short stories and for the scene from *A
Dream of Love* are based on the 1961 volumes just noted.
Texts for *The Great American Novel*, *A Voyage to
Pagany*, *White Mule*, *In the Money*, *The Autobiography*,
and *Spring and All* are based on their original editions. The
Kora in Hell text is from the 1957 edition and that for *In
the American Grain* from the 1956 edition. "Marianne
Moore" is based on *A Novelette and Other Prose* (1932).
The other prose selections are based on the texts in
Selected Essays (1954). I have made a few corrections in the
spelling and punctuation as well as a tiny emendation in the
Spring and All text, in which the source seemed the French
printer's error rather than the author's intention. "A Point
for American Criticism" appeared originally in Samuel
Beckett et al., *Our Exagmination Round His Factification
for Incamination of Work in Progress* (Paris: Shakespeare
and Company, 1929; Norfolk, Conn.: New Directions, 1939,
1961), by various hands.